Fergie
Confidential

Fergie
Confidential

THE REAL STORY

Chris Hutchins and
Peter Thompson

St. Martin's Press
New York

ISBN 0-312-08776-4

First published in Great Britain by Smith Gryphon Limited.

First U.S. Edition: November 1992
10 9 8 7 6 5 4 3 2 1

Contents

Prologue

'I don't think before I act.'

SARAH, DUCHESS OF YORK

Her Royal Highness, Sarah, Duchess of York repeated the words so often they were virtually a mantra: 'I am my own person,' she said. 'I want to be myself.' The problem was that Sarah, the woman beneath the top-heavy title which weighed her down like an over-jewelled tiara, did not know who she really was once she joined the Royal Family.

'You will tell me if I ever become too royal, won't you?' she begged someone who knew her well. When he later suggested she was becoming a trifle grandiose, she denied she had ever said it. She larked about with shopgirls in a designer's salon, then pulled rank with a ferocity that wiped the smiles off their faces. So often labelled headstrong and rebellious, she was misunderstood because, ultimately, she did not understand herself. 'I just trust too many people, I'm too spontaneous and I don't think before I act,' she said after four years of marriage. 'I'm less spontaneous than I was, but only because I'm more aware of my responsibilities.'

After five years, she knew what she definitely did not want and, in a very public fashion, she broke away from Prince Andrew and what she called the System. In the last interview she gave before the separation in March 1992, she told writer Georgina Howell: 'I just wanted to get away. To get away from the System and people saying "No, you can't, No, you can't, No, you can't." That's what the System is.'

'She seemed to me to be very crestfallen,' Georgina Howell told the authors. 'I got the impression that she had been trying very hard and hadn't got the credit due for her efforts. I thought she was very crushed.'

At first scrutiny, Sarah Ferguson had seemed the perfect candidate to give Prince Andrew a thoroughly merited come-uppance after his years of philandering. She was his equal in so many ways and demonstrably his better in others. Even the natural advantage Andrew enjoyed as part of his birthright was not insurmountable. Sarah was elevated to Her Royal Highness the moment the Archbishop of Canterbury had pronounced the couple man and wife in Westminster Abbey on 23 July 1986. In terms of royal precedence, she outranked Anne, the Princess Royal, and Princess Margaret, and stood fourth only to the Queen, the Queen Mother and the Princess of Wales among women in all England and Wales.

Instant royalty, though, entailed even more dangers than instant fame alone because it embodied the power and privilege of a very real prerogative that few people were skilled enough to handle. That and the drawback of having to cope with one's in-laws, which in Sarah's case meant having the Queen, the Queen's mother, the Queen's husband, the Queen's sister and all the Queen's men stand in judgment on her every action. Or so it appeared.

The Yorks seemed so compatible they could have been made for each other, the joyous celebrators of this illustrious union had mistakenly decided, noting the physical magnetism which had drawn them together. If the initial passionate embraces witnessed outside the bedchamber were to be the touchstone of a lifelong partnership, the couple were ideally suited. At twenty-six, Sarah was an intelligent, sexually experienced young woman, well-endowed, sensual, vivacious and the exponent of a decidedly uninhibited sense of humour which Andrew found immensely appealing. *Risqué*, some said. Filthy, said others. Her blue-grey eyes, however, gave a softer, more vulnerable quality to the promise of excitement that shone through her hair. Golden-red, some called it. Auburn, said others. Titian, said Prince Andrew gallantly, knowing she hated to be called a redhead.

The wedding picture was scarcely in its frame before people who had publicly admired her high spirits and beauty turned on her with a savagery that was bewildering in its intensity. She became Fergie the Frump, a walking disaster of fraught couture. Freebie Fergie signified her willingness to accept all the delights that her new status proffered. Diarists and headline writers loved to hate her.

'It used to bother me when I read criticisms of me in the newspapers,' she said. 'It was a mistake to read them. Now I have stopped.' She might have tried to shrug it off, but she could still be hurt. The Killer

Bimbos of Fleet Street saw to that. Most wounding of all, the Duchess of Pork testified to her weight problem. 'I do not diet; I do not have a problem,' she said and if she believed it nobody else did. She tried every diet from Cambridge to Crash, took courses of prescribed slimming pills, consulted unorthodox experts and worked out in the gym with manic energy because she so desperately wanted to lose weight. She was compared frequently and unfavourably with her sister-in-law, Princess Diana, whose own sylph-like figure, ironically, owed much to the cruel ravages of the eating disorder, bulimia nervosa. Even before the engagement was announced, Sarah's exploits with the outrageous Verbier Set were excavated from beneath the Swiss Alps, then passed off as growing pains common to the Sloane Ranger sisterhood of which she was a dedicated convert. One virginal royal bride was enough in the Equal Eighties.

Andrew, four months younger than his partner, was the Family's pin-up; its Robert Redford, in the words of Prince Charles. The Queen's favourite among her children, he was a war hero whose combat experience in the South Atlantic Campaign had matured him in ways that set him apart from Charles and Prince Edward. Charles was more a ceremonial warrior, and Edward had wisely side-stepped a career in the Royal Marines in favour of the theatre. They were all royals by birth, though, and Sarah was not. Like others before her, she found it incomprehensible that they were incapable of relating to ordinary people. Her Libran sun sign guaranteed that, in company at least, she would be an exciting communicator who could act as a stimulating foil to Andrew's shrewder Aquarian nature.

The couple had fallen deeply and deliriously in love with each other after Princess Diana had rekindled a childhood acquaintanceship by pushing them together during Ascot Week in June 1985. Maybe it would work, just maybe. The sceptics stifled their doubts and acquiesced to the popular notion that Sarah might well ruffle some of the stuffier shirts in the Palace. Perhaps she would survive where her predecessors, Antony Armstrong-Jones and Mark Phillips, had singularly failed. She tried, she really did; ultimately, though, she was defeated.

The wishful thinking that preceded her entry into the Royal Family had failed to appreciate the full power of the machiavellian intrigue which resided within the Queen's secretariat and Her Majesty's courtiers at Buckingham Palace. Monarchy's survival still depended largely on its mystique and distance from the masses. 'It's mystery is its life,' declared Walter Bagehot, the Victorian constitutionalist. 'We must not let in daylight upon magic.' But Bagehot did not have to contend with the insatiable appetite for royal trivia of a generation addicted to television and other outlets of a remorseless mass media. Virtually as soon as the honeymoon was over, the new Duchess of York showed that she intended to enjoy the spirit of another of Bagehot' homilies: 'The great pleasure in life is doing what people say you cannot do.' From day one, she threw open the shutters and let in daylight through curtains her mother-in-law would have wished to keep firmly shut. When the Duchess was told to obey, she reminded them that she was 'not a person to obey meekly'. Anyway, she had promised to obey only Andrew in her wedding vows. She was, in fact, temperamentally incapable of taking orders handed down from on high.

To Sarah, these initial skirmishes with Palace courtiers proved to her that an important principle was at stake: her inalienable right to 'be myself'. It was the very cornerstone of her self-esteem and she felt it was under attack. When the time came to explain some of her behaviour, she chose the unlikely venue of a drug-rehabilitation centre, where she told a small group of recovering addicts: 'The Palace and the press want me to conform to an image – but I won't.'

The superficial causes of what went wrong with her marriage were easy enough to list: Andrew's frequent and prolonged absences in the Royal Navy, Sarah's dedication to having 'a fun time' which sometimes overstepped the boundaries of good taste, the pressures of motherhood to her daughters Beatrice and Eugenie and, above all, her extraordinary friendships with Steve Wyatt, the Texas oilman, and his American jet-set buddy Johnny Bryan. It was her holiday on the French Riviera with Bryan – and publication of intimate photographs of Sarah and her self-styled financial adviser kissing beside a swimming pool – that proved the marriage was dead if not yet officially buried. Her membership of the Royal Family was instantly withdrawn. She packed her bags and fled Balmoral, the Queen's Scottish home, after the pictures were shown around the world.

The internal forces at work, however, were far more potent, partly because they were buried deep inside Sarah's psyche and tended to slip out unexpectedly. She had taken the symptoms of this inner conflict to a succession of faith healers, therapists, homeopaths, clairvoyants and astrologers. None could restore her to normality; none could save her marriage.

'She betrayed the image of a kind of iceberg of emotion, where a little is revealed and a lot concealed,' said Georgina Howell. Marriage was torture for her because she lacked confidence and, no matter how well things might have seemed to be going, she felt threatened and anxious. She was incapable of being a slave to another person or to a system. Buckingham Palace pressed all her buttons and she reacted. She was an expansive woman, but an inflated sense of her own identity did not allow her to hold anything back. She tended to become overexcited and, if the going became too rough, she took the easy way out.

Sarah knew *where* she wanted to be – at Klosters or Verbier, anywhere, in fact, in the Swiss Alps. 'For me, to go to the mountains is the way I need to be grounded,' she said. 'They talk to me and they're secure and I love them. And that's where I get my privacy and strength. I'm not allowed to go because . . . because I'm owned.'

'People say that Sarah York is rebellious, but I'm not sure that is the right word for her,' opined royal author Lady Colin Campbell. 'She just won't take too much nonsense; strong-willed, yes – but in a funny sort of way less strong than Princess Diana. Their strengths are different. Sarah is a glorious orchid in the forest and Diana is a daisy in the field. Sarah is very positive, but she will only put up with so much, then she cuts and runs. Diana will put up with an awful lot to get what she wants and to keep it. The difference is that Sarah would not sacrifice herself for anything, even to remain a member of the Royal Family. This is not about being rebellious; she just won't allow herself to be crushed, corroded or changed into someone she is not. In that sense, she is fighting for her soul.'

A few weeks before the Yorks split up, the Queen said in a television programme to mark the fortieth anniversary of her Accession: 'I think the next generation are going to have a very difficult time.' She was speaking to the former President of the United States, Ronald Reagan, and his wife Nancy during a reception on board the Royal Yacht *Britannia* at Miami, Florida.

As the year drew to a close, Her Majesty's words might have provoked an acute sense of *déjà vu* among those closest to her. Members of the 'next generation' in her own family had already had more than 'a very difficult time'; they were living proof that the Firm, as the Windsors liked to call themselves, had failed abysmally to uphold many of the basic conventions of British family life.

Before the year was half over, Princess Anne's marriage to Mark Phillips had ended in divorce; the Duke and Duchess had announced their legal separation; and the Prince and Princess of Wales had discussed divorce to end their loveless marriage. Only weeks later a tape recording of Diana's highly personal telephone conversation with her long-term close friend James Gilbey further revealed the split between her and Prince Charles. The monarchy which Britain's First Family represented, and to which Her Majesty had recently rededicated her life, was facing its gravest crisis since the Abdication in 1936. Sarah posed one of the biggest threats not so much to the crown's ultimate survival but to its immediate credibility. Without unquestioning faith, courtiers knew that the institution of monarchy would start to collapse as the United Kingdom moved inexorably towards a United Europe, where Royal Families had either been forcibly removed or integrated into more egalitarian societies as much loved but more useful members of the community.

As the Duchess of York's marriage broke down and she was planning her escape, she said despondently: 'At the end of the day, you die alone.' It sounded far too gloomy coming from someone who had so much to live for, and so it proved. Once she was freed from the royal shackles, Sarah went to a party.

ONE

Ripples on the Poisoned Pond

'Sarah is very unhappy with Andrew. She is about to do something very dramatic.'

PRINCESS DIANA

'**M**y marriage isn't the only one in disarray,' declared the Princess of Wales, defensively. 'Sarah and Andrew have also got problems.' The message Diana relayed in a telephone call to her astrologer Penny Thornton on Thursday, 2 January, 1992, was the first intimation from a member of the Royal Family to an outsider that all was not well in the marriage of the Duke and Duchess of York. When she placed the call to Branshott Court, Ms Thornton's Hampshire home, the Princess had just returned to her Kensington Palace apartment from Sandringham. There the Queen's Christmas celebrations had been marred by the obvious unhappiness of the her second son, Prince Andrew. The former Sarah Ferguson, his bride of sixty-six months, had tearfully confided in her sister-in-law that the marriage had reached breaking-point.

Fog was slow to clear on the cold winter's morning of Wednesday, 15 January. Just thirteen days had elapsed since Diana's early-warning call to her astrologer, and the Duchess's problems had multiplied beyond her wildest fears. By her own later admission, Sarah had enjoyed precious little sleep: she knew that this was not just a gloomy day. It was going to be an awful day. A call from Buckingham Palace the previous evening had warned her of the reports facing her in that morning's papers: MYSTERY OF FERGIE PHOTOGRAPHS read the *Daily Mail*'s front-page headline, adopting the nickname Major Ronald Ferguson's second daughter had been stuck with since her schooldays.

The photographs referred to in the *Mail* had been discovered by Maurice Maple, a window cleaner, who said that he had found them in dusty packets on top of a cupboard in an apartment on the second floor at No. 34 Cadogan Square, a smart stone-fronted Edwardian house no more than ten minutes brisk walk across Belgravia from the high wall which surrounded the London home of Sarah's mother-in-law, Queen Elizabeth II. Apartment F had been let for £2400 a month to Steve Wyatt, a charismatic 38-year-old Texan. Maple, who claimed that he had found the packets two months earlier, had recognized the woman in many of the 120 photographs as the Duchess of York: 'That long red hair and laughing smile are unmistakable,' he had said. But the window cleaner did not recognize her companion in many of the snaps. He had never heard of Wyatt or of his mother, the Houston socialite Lynn Wyatt, or Steve's stepfather, the immensely wealthy oil and natural-gas magnate, Oscar Wyatt Junior.

Maple later handed the photographs to police officers attached to Scotland Yard's Royal Protection Branch. 'I realized I had a huge responsibility to ensure these packets remained in safe hands,' said the cleaner. 'I felt I couldn't just walk into a police station and say, "Take these – they're pictures of the Duchess of York on holiday." I simply didn't know what to do. I thought of dumping them in a dustbin, but realized that would be irresponsible. What if someone else discovered them? In the wrong hands they might even be used for blackmail.'

Another less scrupulous might indeed have considered the photo-graphs blackmail material: in one, Wyatt's hand rested affectionately on Sarah's shoulder and her right arm was round his back. Looking as if she did not have a care in the world, Sarah was photographed wearing a white sweatshirt and blue shorts with white polka dots. Looking like a man who was in no way displeased with himself, Wyatt was clad in a red sweatshirt and shorts. Other photographs showed the Duchess lunch-ing with others by the poolside, pushing a wheelbarrow containing several children and at a candlelit dinner wearing a raised mask depicting a big-eyed green toad. Many of the pictures had been taken during a holiday the Duchess had spent at La Gazelle d'Or, a five-star hotel in Morocco's desert heartland, with Princess Beatrice, Wyatt and his actress friend Pricilla Phillips. It was the one of Wyatt clutching Beatrice which, friends said, incensed the child's father Prince Andrew, Duke of York. The first reporter to gain access to the apartment after the discovery was John Jones, a hard-driving Australian with an experienced eye for detail. 'It was a very discreet, very secure flat up two flights of plushly red-carpeted stairs at the back of the building,' he said. 'You entered through a door complete with mortice locks and a peephole. Inside, there was total silence; no noise penetrated through the drapes. It was so quiet you could have let off an atom bomb in there without anyone asking questions.

'Wyatt's drawing room was beautifully but not ostentatiously furnished; some Victorian antique furniture, two ultra-comfortable sofas, a neo-antique bookcase, sketches of old buildings on the walls and a dining-room table to seat six. It was just short of cosy, not a place you would associate with riotous living. There were two bedrooms, the main one predominantly blue with a kingsize bed. It was set into an alcove with bookcases either side and a mobile TV set at the foot.

'The pictures of Sarah and Wyatt, however, were supposed to have been found in the second bedroom on top of a mahogany fitted bookcase into which a spare bed folded. The windows stretched from floor to ceiling and anyone cleaning them would have seen the bundles from the top of a step-ladder. The bookcase was an obvious hiding-place, but it didn't make sense. There were other places in the living room or the main bedroom which would have been better. If Wyatt had hidden the pictures and moved out leaving them behind, surely he would have realized they were missing in the intervening months and tried to retrieve them.'

This begged the question: Did Wyatt stash them there in the first place or did someone else? Jones, for one, did not believe that he had. Wyatt professed to be as mystified as anyone. 'I don't know anything about them,' he said from his new home in Washington DC. A Scotland Yard source hinted that the pictures might have been planted in the flat after Wyatt's departure to embarrass the Duchess. If this were true, the Duchess was the victim of what had long been suspected: a conspiracy to tarnish her image and destroy her marriage. This line of enquiry led to Buckingham Palace where it was greeted with disdain. But, added to previous evidence of a vendetta against Sarah, the conviction grew that other forces not directly connected with Her Majesty's secretariat were at work.

'There were dirty hands all over it,' said one intimately involved in an earlier smear against Sarah's name. Someone was pouring poison into the pond. One of the culprits – codenamed Mr G – had contacted the Confidential desk of the *Today* newspaper after the diary column had broken news of Sarah's Moroccan holiday and a later trip she made with Wyatt to Cap Ferrat on the Côte d'Azur. Mr G could, he said, provide information about the couple's forthcoming movements if the news- paper were prepared to meet him. James Steen, the reporter who spoke to Mr G, was surprised by the choice of venue. 'He wanted to meet me at 11 a.m. in the car park at Streatham railway station in South London,' he said. 'It was hardly a fashionable spot but well off the beaten track so we weren't likely to be spotted. As arranged, he was seated behind the wheel of a silver Volvo. He was in his mid-fifties, bespectacled, balding and wearing a mac over his business suit. But it was his companion who caught my eye. She was a very glamorous blonde in her thirties, heavily made-up and wearing a black fur coat.

'Mr G had been asked to provide some proof of his credibility and he came up with a phone number which checked out as Prince Andrew's private line at his naval base. He also let drop that Steve Wyatt had a photograph of the Duchess of York, clutching a dagger, beside his bed at his flat in Cadogan Square. This was uncheckable but interesting just the same.

'The big story he was offering was that the Duchess and Wyatt were meeting up at a shooting-party in the country the following weekend. They were going to stay with Charles and Maggie Wyvill at their estate, Constable Burton Hall, in Yorkshire. There is no doubt he was leading me down a certain path to a particular story about the Duchess.'

No one knew much about Constable Burton then but, as the ripples spread across the poisoned pond, it was to assume the same importance as the Little White Room and the Royal Train in royal mythology.

.   .   .

Rising from her lonely bed in Sunninghill Park House – the mansion newly built on some of Berkshire's most pleasing acres with the help of a highly generous gift from the Queen – Sarah had good reason that January morning to curse the photographic record of the sunshine excursion she had enjoyed with Wyatt in Morocco.

In another part of the house, Alison Wardley, the nanny employed to look after Beatrice and her younger sister Princess Eugenie, helped to prepare the children for the day ahead. She had been told the previous evening that the Duchess would be taking Beatrice to school herself. She had not been told the reason for this surprising change in routine. The photographs, however, held little surprise for Alison; she knew all about them. She had been there when they were taken twenty months earlier in the grounds of La Gazelle d'Or. She had been aboard Steve Wyatt's hired jet when it had whisked her mistress and the other participants on that highly confidential holiday.

Sarah said little as she took Beatrice by the hand and led the child to the waiting Ford Granada which had been brought round to the front of the house by her detective – one of the men the three year old had become more accustomed to seeing than her own father who was so often away on naval duties. Sarah slipped behind the wheel and drove the four-mile journey to Upton House School not far from Windsor Castle. Waiting there was the reason Alison Wardley had been relieved of her regular morning chore – the press out in force at the school gates as Sarah knew they would be, demanding to know more about the photographs. What she was not prepared for was a question about whether it was true, as butler Anthony Fung who worked in the Belgravia mansion block was saying: that she had paid two or three evening visits to 34 Cadogan Square while Wyatt was living there. Pale and drawn, she had swept her hair untidily to the back of her head. She looked awful and she knew it, but she was determined to face the inquisitive throng like the headstrong woman she was, even if her appearance did not match up to her image as a radiant duchess.

Newsmen called out their questions but she behaved as if they did not exist, even though their presence was the sole purpose for her being there. She had reasons for wanting them to see her and photograph her, taking care of her daughter. 'Sarah knew by that time that there would be people in the Palace wanting to take her children away from her if the marriage was dissolved,' said one in whom she confided over dinner the following month. 'She determined from that day on that people would see her children with her whenever there were cameras about. She wanted to win the nation's sympathy as a mother.'

Custody was a particularly sensitive issue in Sarah's immediate family. Her father Ronald had been granted custody of Sarah and her sister Jane after her mother Susie had decamped with her Argentinian lover Hector Barrantes, and Jane had lost her children Seamus and Ayesha into the care of her husband Alex Makim in a very public divorce only a year before. Sarah marched defiantly into the school, gave Beatrice a peck on the cheek, half smiled as another mother put a consoling hand on her arm and just as defiantly marched out again. Then she went home to pack.

The following day Sarah was off to Florida, another of the all-expenses-paid trips that had earned her the label Freebie Fergie, this time as the toast of Palm Beach society at a fund-raising polo match sponsored by Cartier, the jewellers. The Duchess, who was travelling in her capacity as patron of the Motor Neurone Disease Association, one of her favourite charities, joined the packed American Airlines 767 airliner to Miami with her father, who was to play in the Sunday match, her detective John Askew and Private Secretary Jane Ambler.

Father and daughter enjoyed their first-class luxury surroundings, and during the nine-hour flight Sarah tucked into Sevruga caviare and drank four glasses of Chablis as the pair chatted happily, showing that she had not yet allowed the full gravity of the situation to flummox her. In an adjacent seat sat one of her favourite comedians, Frankie Howerd, whose easy-going, companionable repartee kept her amused. When she was offered a video film, Sarah chose *The Fourth Story*, starring Mini Rogers as a wife abandoned by her husband. As she viewed it, Major Ferguson, who had remarried another Susan after his divorce, held his daughter's hand and gave her a supportive kiss.

Ronald, the £30,000-a-year polo manager at the Royal County of Berkshire Polo Club, was travelling in his capacity as polo adviser to Cartier. Accompanying him in Palm Beach would be Lesley Player, a 33-year-old divorcee who had captured his heart. He had been bombarding Miss Player with flowers and love notes and leaving intimate messages on her answering machine. Even if she were aware of her father's dalliance with Miss Player, Sarah was oblivious to the extent of his foolishness as the plane touched down at Miami International Airport.

She had troubles enough of her own to worry about on the short hop from Miami to the airstrip at West Palm Beach. The élite residents of Palm Beach, her host and hostess Robert and Lewis Fomon included, had heard about the secret cache of compromising photographs from television reports the previous evening. Soon after Sarah swept up to their pink and white stucco home on South Ocean Boulevard in a courtesy Cadillac, she made a point of reassuring the Fomons that she was determined to enjoy her stay, come what may.

The Fomons were equally determined that she should; they showed her to a beachside guest villa connected to the main house by a thirty-yard tunnel. Nearby, a magnificent marquee had been erected in the grounds for an ostentatious cocktail party the Fomons were laying on to introduce their guest to socialites on the Palm Beach 'A List' that evening. Robert Fomon, a 66-year-old, thrice-married banker, was selected for this privilege because of the intense security he maintained around his estate. The banker's extravagant lifestyle had earned him the reputation of being one of America's most enthusiastic sugar daddies. The dapper, silver-haired Fomon kept corporate jets fuelled and ready to fly anywhere in the world in his former capacity as the head of the E. F. Hutton bank. A one-time official told *Forbes* magazine that Robert 'liked nothing better than being in a jet at 30,000 feet with talented young women – he considered it the spoils of war.'

If Buckingham Palace had vetted Fomon – and they admitted that a British Embassy official had checked security at the property with the Duchess's bodyguard the previous month – they had obviously chosen to ignore what was common gossip about the Duchess's host. He had fallen from grace when his bank admitted cheque fraud in the mid-1980s. Far from ending his career in disgrace, he walked away from the debacle with a £6-million golden handshake. Now, resplendent on his lawn, he greeted first arrivals among the 150 guests who included the television star Stefanie Powers, while Sarah, bathed and changed into a green Yves Saint Laurent suit, stood at his side. It was a humid evening and the smell of money pervaded the night air.

'I am very tired and wish I could go to bed,' Sarah told one guest, although whether it was jet lag or the growing concern about the Wyatt Affair no one could be certain. The storm she had left brewing in London was clearly on her mind as she took Swiss-born Pilar Boxford to one side and enquired: 'Have you read the newspapers? It's one thing one week and another the next. You know we were not intimate friends.' Mrs Boxford, Cartier's communications director, had no need to ask who Sarah was referring to: Steve Wyatt's name was on everybody's lips. No one had heard of Johnny Bryan yet.

After the cocktail reception on their lawn, the Fomons had arranged a dinner party in the main house for more than a dozen people Sarah knew before she became the Duchess of York. They were 'nice people but not A-List people', according to one who was privy to the Fomons' arrangements. 'Let's just say they would not have been invited to the F. Warrington Gillets' soirée at the Everglades Club the next night.' Her friends were disappointed if they had expected to be reunited with Sarah over dinner. She retired to her villa after the cocktail party and sent a message to the main house saying she was 'too tired to come over and socialize' and she would like her meal sent across to the villa where she would eat alone. Defensively, Lewis Fomon insisted: 'It was never intended that the Duchess should join us for dinner.' Sarah's friends, nevertheless, were entitled to feel a little let down.

Refreshed after a night's sleep, Sarah was in a bubbly mood the next morning when she was driven to nearby Connors Nursery to visit children diagnosed as HIV positive or addicted to cocaine at birth. This was one role in which she excelled; her protective maternal instincts and natural effusiveness came to the fore on such occasions. She was adept at memorizing names, and her open, smiling face confirmed to complete strangers that she was really pleased to meet them. She gave the children caring hugs and departed.

The children's suffering was in sharp contrast to the sheer excess she witnessed that evening at the Everglades Club. No expense was spared for the party; almost £100,000 was paid for the decorations which included life-sized papier-mâché giraffes and other animals that adorned the clubhouse. Sarah looked particularly stunning that night in a low-cut, white chiffon ballgown which showed off her new slim figure. Seated next to her was the property tycoon Warrington Gillet. 'This lady has got real class,' he said. 'People tried to get her to talk about her problem, but she was having none of that. She charmed everyone and never once showed us the pressure she must have been suffering. Her father is clearly very worried about her. He told me Fergie was deeply disturbed over the row that had broken around her. But looking at her, it was hard to believe she was under any kind of strain.'

After more than four hours at the party, she slipped out through a back entrance to avoid television camera crews hoping to ensnare her in a row over the club which, it was said, banned Jews and blacks from membership. The following morning, Sarah arrived at the Palm Beach Polo Club to watch her father play in a match. Her serenity was momentarily upset when the zip of her skirt failed as she stepped from a car, but she declined the offer of a safety-pin from Stefanie Powers and retired to the ladies room to make impromptu repairs. After the match, she received a cheque for £15,000 made out to the Motor Neurone Disease Association.

A luncheon the next day at the Palm Beach and Country Club cost £60,000, and Cartier donated £20,000 worth of prizes. To the critics, it all made the £15,000 raised for the British charity by the Duchess's four-day visit seem a meagre sum in comparison. 'When she arrived in Palm Beach, it was a really big event, as it would be if any member of the Royal Family came to a socially conscious resort like that,' commented author Dominick Dunne, doyen of American high society writers. 'She was a name that they could raise money on for charity but that wasn't the case soon after. She was celebrity then, she's notorious now. I doubt she would get invited back in that way again.'

On the final day of her stay in Florida, Sarah slipped away from the Palm Beach Polo Club with Cartier's hostess, Maggie Scherer. The two went to a private party where there were some high jinks and others pressed drinks into the Duchess's hand. Sarah told them how much she loved the Florida lifestyle, and she speculated about what it would be like to buy a house there – half-way between her present home in England and the ranch in Argentina where her mother Susie was still living after the death of her stepfather, the polo legend Hector Barrantes. Hector had played some of his best polo in Florida for the team of newsprint magnate Peter Brant, a New Yorker who spent his winters in the Florida sunshine. Sarah left the drinks party 'deliriously happy' and, after the short flight from West Palm Beach, arrived at Miami International Airport for the journey home looking as though she did not have a care in the world.

In the VIP lounge, she asked a member of staff if she could make a long-distance telephone call. British journalist Tim Miles, who was based in Florida, recalled: 'The Duchess was shown into an adjoining office where she was told she could be private. But she failed to close the door behind her and her side of the conversation could be heard by those outside the room.'

A check of the records later established that she had called Sunninghill. 'That's not fair,' she exclaimed before slamming the phone down to end the three-minute call.

'When she emerged from the office, she looked angry and upset,' said Miles, 'and then she burst into tears, brushing aside an offer of help. She wiped away the tears, smiled and shrugged as if to say everything was all right although clearly it was not.'

What followed was a nightmare journey to London during which several fellow travellers in the first-class cabin were convinced that she was either a fun-loving prankster *par excellence* or a woman on the verge of a nervous breakdown. She ripped a hole in a paper bag, pulled it over her head and poked her tongue through the hole. Obviously concerned,

Major Ferguson told her: 'Enough's enough.' But his words seemed to incite rather than quell the bizarre behaviour. Between mouthfuls of champagne Her Royal Highness the Duchess of York, wife of the Queen's favourite son and sister-in-law of England's next King, tossed sachets of sugar at her father, pulled faces at other passengers and made bird noises in the direction of the bulkhead. She bombarded her bodyguard John Askew and secretary Jane Ambler with rolled-up tissues before hurling more missiles at her father as astonished cabin staff tried to serve dinner to those around who had paid £1906 for their privileged seats. She smoked two Marlboro cigarettes – marking another return to the despised habit she had lapsed back into during a skiing holiday at Klosters earlier in the month – before falling into a deep sleep. 'It's just high spirits,' smiled the Major. 'My daughter has been working hard and I'm proud of her.'

She had displayed the same high spirits in Klosters. 'Fergie danced at the Hohwald restaurant, and she was really going for it,' recalled Mike Lawn, one of the best photographers on the royal beat. 'She was with Clare and Peter Greenall, who own a home in Klosters, and Bruno Sprecher, the ski guide she has known for years. She got up and danced with a couple of ski-lift attendants and then Arthur Edwards from the *Sun* whom she gets along with really well. We all could have danced with her if we had wanted to because she was determined to have a great time. She had arrived on a horse-drawn sledge and had obviously had a few drinks. She finished off the evening with a schnapps. She smoked several cigarettes at the table and seemed to be challenging us to put it in the paper. She was looking over her shoulder at us as if she wanted it to be in the paper. She seemed to have no cares that night despite what was going on in her life.'

In Sunninghill, safely returned from Florida, the doors closed behind Major Ferguson's high-spirited daughter and she was not seen for days.

·   ·   ·

To the Queen, Sandringham House was 'the escape place', her much loved retreat from cosmopolitan life. Her home there, originally Sand-ringham Hall, was a very large mansion rather than a castle, set in good shooting country just inland from the Wash in Norfolk. It had been bought for £220,000 in 1862 and, like Windsor Castle, remained the private property of the Royal Family.

As the best-informed person in the realm, the Queen did not rely on the media for information about the latest dramas involving her daughter-in-law. Courtiers aware of her concern and interested parties among her extended family, known as the Magic Four Hundred, kept her up to date with the latest developments. Added to that were the intelligence reports provided by her observant Royal Protection Branch officers. As the Duchess was always accompanied by one of their number whenever she set foot outside her home, her movements were under constant surveillance. It was almost impossible for her to conceal, even if she had wanted to, where she went and who she saw. 'The whole family is accompanied and protected at all times,' said royal author John Parker. 'When Princess Diana went off in a huff to the West End one night on her own, there was a huge outcry. Someone, somewhere knows what the Royals are doing every minute of the day.'

If Sarah's mother-in-law knew practically everything, it meant that Prince Andrew knew a great deal, too. From that point of view, Sarah could be forgiven if she regarded protection as just another name for intrusion into her private life. 'If she was feeling edgy or guilty, this kind of round-the-clock caretaking would tend to make her paranoid,' confirmed a therapist who treats people with disturbed emotions.

The Queen knew from her incomparable grapevine that the time had come to do something about Sarah. Prince Andrew had made it obvious to all those around him during the Christmas family holiday at Sandringham that his marriage was deteriorating rapidly. He could do nothing about his wife's mood swings and had little control over her geographicals – the frequent trips she made abroad on the flimsiest of excuses. But he had known all about her excursion to Morocco and the subsequent holiday to Cap Ferrat two months later.

Contrary to a belief that Sarah had taken the trips because she was heartbroken by his long absences on naval duties, Andrew pointed out that he had returned to Castlewood House, the couple's temporary home, on those weekends to look after one or both of his daughters while his wife was away. So much for his critics who had claimed that she was really desperate for her husband's company when she travelled with Wyatt. 'The two trips she took on the Wyatt jet were all part of a pattern that was going on all the time,' said a source with highly placed Palace connections. 'The Duke and Duchess had, in fact, been living in a state of self-imposed separation long before Wyatt's name came out into the open. Major Ron had stopped making his usual complimentary remarks about his son-in-law as long ago as the winter of 1989. He didn't criticize Andrew; it's what he didn't say that indicated the marriage was in trouble.'

The staff at Sunninghill had become accustomed to arguments between the warring Yorks, as had those who worked within earshot at Buckingham Palace. Servants could hear the rows coming from the Yorks' quarters, previously Andrew's second-floor bachelor apartment in the East Wing. 'What happened was that Sarah discovered that Andrew wasn't coming home on some of his leave,' said a royal insider. 'He was going elsewhere – and this just drove her crazy. She didn't like the fact that she was a shore widow in any event, and to discover that she was shore-widowed intentionally really set her off.'

The Queen finally gave the situation the seal of *gravitas* it deserved by instructing her Private Secretary, Sir Robert Fellowes, to convene a Family summit at Sandringham on Sunday, 26 January 1992. It was deeply ironic for Sarah that Sir Robert – married to Princess Diana's sister Jane and her own father's cousin – should be called upon to preside at what was virtually her trial by family. Sir Robert had been forced to remonstrate with the Duchess so frequently that, given to coining nicknames for people who annoyed her, she gave Fellowes the rhyming tag of 'Bellows'.

The Queen, Prince Philip, the Queen Mother, Prince Andrew, Prince Charles and Princess Diana gathered solemnly on the Sunday afternoon to hear Sir Robert spell out the situation. Her Majesty had already changed her mind about Sarah. Initially, she had been relieved that Andrew had found a woman with whom he could settle down and raise a family. The Queen had been delighted that she was an excellent rider and the two women enjoyed each other's company on horseback, sometimes on that very estate.

As a mark of their special relationship, Sarah gave her mother-in-law unusual little presents, one of which intrigued Her Majesty. Very much a specimen of the fifties, it was a mechanical ashtray with a spinning top that made the ash disappear into a cylindrical barrel. The Queen had never seen anything like it and, after admiring the curio for some time, she placed it on a table with rare and valuable *objets d'art*. Incongruously, it remained there until she worked out a better use for it. She filled the barrel with biscuit morsels which she fed to the royal Corgis.

It was Sarah who kept the Queen informed with tittle-tattle about arrivals and departures among her friends in Sloanedom. But gossip inside the same circle about Sarah's own erratic behaviour over the past thirty months, whispered at first, had become so audible that the Queen could no longer turn a deaf ear. The talk in Drones bistro, and similar stops that those on the Belgravy Train made in that select part of town, was spiced with graphic details of Sarah's alleged indiscretions. Constable Burton came up time and again as the setting for one story about the night the Duchess of York became a loose cannon at a shooting party. Just as damning, from the Queen's point of view, was that Sarah had even had the temerity to defy a royal edict issued six months earlier that she should sever her connections with Wyatt and his jet-set friends.

Long experience had taught Prince Philip to detach himself from many of the Royal Firm's less harmonious domestic moments. After forty-five years as the Queen's husband, he had learned to stand aloof from such discord; to adopt the emotional equivalent of the penguin walk for which he was famous on royal engagements. Rightly proud of his pilot son's war record in the Falklands, Philip had grown increasingly irritable about Andrew's inability to manage something as fundamental as his marriage, a prerequisite for a career officer in the navy. If Philip's renowned temper had been strained before, it was now at breaking-point.

The Royal Family's matriarch, the Queen Mother, was entitled to feel particularly let down by Sarah whom she had gone to great lengths to nurture during the difficult early months as she prepared to enter the Windsors' world of clannish privilege. The Queen had cast her own mother in the role of protector once stories about Sarah's past had surfaced even before the engagement ring was on her finger. Sarah had been a welcome guest not only at Clarence House, the Queen Mother's home in the Mall, but at her country retreats, the Royal Lodge in Windsor Great Park and Birkhall on the Balmoral Estates in Scotland. Sarah had broken the cardinal rule the Queen Mother had tried to instil in her: Above all else, the Family comes first.

Prince Charles, considered by some the most caring of the Royals, could draw no comfort from the fact that his own marriage had turned into a loveless sham. His sympathies lay with Andrew; he had never particularly liked the woman his brother had chosen for a wife after an initial infatuation with her had abruptly deserted him. A friend of the royals, confirmed: 'Diana always said that Sarah was intent on ingratiating herself all over the place, and certainly in the early stages she made a deliberate attempt to get Charles on her side. Charles did take to her and, on her first birthday as the Duchess of York, he gave her a very expensive piece of jewellery. It was only a very short-term situation.'

After that, Sarah's fun-loving, rib-digging style became anathema to the Prince. It represented the Hooray Henrietta mentality of women who cared more about possessions than the natural resources he felt bound to conserve. He had hated Sarah's early influence over his wife which had her dressing up as a policewoman and belittling herself at the bar of Annabel's discothèque on the night of Prince Andrew's stag party. He rightly blamed Sarah for encouraging Diana to mix with friends outside the royal circle.

'Sarah helped Diana to become more assertive,' said a highly placed royal source who knows both women well. 'Remember, Diana was only twenty when she entered the Royal Family and they had more or less broken her spirit. She was tremendously depressed and very tentative until Sarah motivated her. She encouraged her to have a more normal life, a life of her own, to go to lunch with her friends at San Lorenzo if she felt like it.'

As Sarah's matchmaker, mentor and erstwhile confidante, Diana might have been in a difficult position that Sunday if she had not distanced herself from the Duchess some time ago, once it became apparent that her own position was in jeopardy. 'She had welcomed Sarah as a comrade-in-arms, so to speak, because she was having a difficult time with courtiers at the Palace who had worn her down and eroded her self-confidence,' continued the highly placed royal source. 'Sarah was a chum, an ally. She is very effervescent, a very positive lady. She is a great enhancer of any situation and Diana is not. Diana is someone who turns things to her advantage, but she is not an initiator.

'Diana is very adept at distancing herself from anyone whose friendship is in any way going to reflect unfavourably on her and she started to distance herself from Sarah York at the time of Ron Ferguson's problems over his visits to a West End massage parlour. But in fairness to her, Diana is very competitive and in my opinion part of her motive was that Sarah herself had become more distant to enable herself to compete with Diana. Sarah was suddenly flavour of the month. Diana had a very patchy time because Sarah had usurped her throne.

'Diana began to resent the fact that she had been marginalized and was no longer the world's darling; that she was no longer the centre of attention. So Diana stepped back, got her act together and won a tremendous amount of acclaim, for instance, for her work with AIDS sufferers. People admire the fact that the Princess of Wales queues at the amusement park with her children or that she goes into Marks & Spencer or McDonald's. Now it has gone the full circle.' Some of the ripples on the pond led right across the Serpentine and into Diana's home in the heart of Kensington Palace.

No pheasants were shot at Sandringham on Sundays but by the time that particular Sabbath had ended, the Duchess of York had been the target of the most ferocious verbal fusillade the Royals had fired off in years. When Sir Robert, who listed shooting among his hobbies, had finished speaking, Prince Andrew had been given the Queen's permission to separate from his wife and go on to seek a divorce if he were absolutely convinced that his position was untenable, his marriage unsalvageable.

There was one condition: Andrew had to secure custody of his daughters – a condition which Sarah must have anticipated that awful morning just ten days earlier when she had continued her determined action to be photographed with Beatrice. Her campaign to keep the children had started earlier in January on the ski slopes of Klosters during her Swiss holiday. Cameramen had been given ample opportunities to photograph mother and daughter enjoying life on the piste. 'She's good, isn't she?' Sarah said proudly. 'She loves the snow. She's going to be a very good skier.'

What the newspapers did not reveal was that the whole thing was a set-up which Sarah had arranged through Brian Baston, one of her detectives. 'We met Baston at one of the mountain restaurants and, while we were discussing the picture we wanted, Sarah climbed up, sat on a slope and slid down on her bottom to crash into her other detective below,' recalled Mike Lawn. 'Then she did it again, just to see if one of us went for a camera.' No one did – and the pact lasted until the holiday ended.

It was unthinkable, Sir Robert now pointed out in his prefectorial manner, that the young princesses – fifth and sixth in line to the throne after Charles, his sons William and Harry, and their father – could be taken out of the country and raised who-knows-where: Palm Beach? Houston? Las Vegas, even. The constitutional implications were inescapable. Just four untimely deaths, an unlikely occurrence but not one that could be ruled out entirely, would place Princess Beatrice on the throne as Queen. She should, at least, speak with an English accent.

Money was another key issue. Her Majesty would ensure generous financial provisions for the departing Duchess, although the bulk of it would be paid at intervals throughout the rest of her life, as an allowance which could be severed if she were ever tempted to break the unwritten rule and sell the story of her years inside the world's most illustrious – and in so many ways tormented – family.

That night a sombre Andrew returned to Sunninghill to ponder the day's momentous events and Sarah's desire to break free of his family. A worried man, he was known to have made several telephone calls to his elder brother to go over the likely consequences. If publicly admitting that matrimony had defeated him would cause havoc, he had to remember that staying married to a reluctant Sarah might have even worse repercussions. Sarah, however, appeared to have made up her mind. No matter how many times or from whatever angle they looked at their marriage she came back to the same conclusion: it was time for her to go. She agreed with Andrew to tell the Queen herself and the couple travelled miserably to Sandringham on Wednesday, 29 January, for that purpose. The Queen's response was to advise her daughter-in-law that she wait a few more weeks before acting on her decision if she still felt it was the only course. Sarah agreed.

Andrew finished his traumatic week by driving to Buckingham Palace where he spent more than two hours with senior courtiers, including his Press Secretary, Geoffrey Crawford, an Australian-born father-of-three whom he trusted completely. Confined to Sunninghill, Sarah complained that the house was more like a prison than the home in which she had wanted to bring up a family with Andrew at her side. This was another of the ironies that was confounding the Yorks' marriage. Sarah's transatlantic tastes were most widely blamed for the creation of SouthYork, as their home was called because of its resemblance to the Ewing's ranch-style mansion, Southfork, in the television soap *Dallas*. In fact, she had deferred to Andrew's wishes – and borne the brunt of the criticism for the extravagant folly of SouthYork as silently as she could.

.   .   .

One of the big events timed to coincide with the fortieth anniversary of the Queen's Accession on 6 February 1992 was the screening on BBC television of *Elizabeth R*, an epic portrayal of a year in Her Majesty's life. One by one, members of the Royal Family shared centre stage with the Queen in various ceremonial set-pieces or in more candid moments which had rarely been filmed before. The Duchess's role in the 110-minute programme was so minimal that, had she blinked, she would have missed it. Aristocrats, ambassadors, political grandees, ladies-in-waiting, even footmen polishing the vast mahogany banqueting table at Windsor with pads on their feet, rated more TV time than the Duchess of York. Viewers among the 25 million who tuned in to relish this high point of the royal year were more likely to remember Smokey, the

Shetland pony Princess Beatrice mounted in a cobbled courtyard, than her mother.

Sarah had not, in fact, been deliberately snubbed. The vagaries of film-editing, rather than any Palace pressure, were responsible for relegating Sarah to the status of someone who seemed to have wandered into this historic milestone in the Queen's reign by chance. Yet, she had every reason, knowing how closely she was being watched, to feel mortified, embarrassed and angry, and playing an inconsequential handmaiden in the royal television tableau was not the only reason.

The day after the Sandringham summit a Buckingham Palace secretary had begun to cancel Sarah's engagements, among the more noteworthy of which was a banquet planned for 7 February at London's newest and most expensive hotel, the Lanesborough, just across Grosvenor Place from the Palace. The £100-million hotel had just been completed inside the shell of the former St George's Hospital and boasted an opulence which outshone its grand rivals. Its finest suite contained six lavish rooms, came with a personal butler and chauffeur-driven Bentley and cost £2500 a night to occupy.

Officials believed that members of the Wyatt family – probably Lynn and possibly Steve – might be among the eighty Southern socialites invited by the Queen of Dallas, Caroline Rose Hunt, whose company had opened the hotel and who had personally invited Sarah as her guest of honour. The former Prime Minister Margaret Thatcher, whose son Mark had married into Dallas society, was attending what was planned as a glittering exercise in Texan hospitality. But they had to make do without the Duchess. The Lanesborough's Wendy Strong confided: 'They've cancelled on us. The Palace insisted that the Duchess must not take up any private engagements at the moment and as this is a Texan group, she had to cancel. They were pretty honest about it. They just said she has been told officially she can't do it.'

This only reinforced Sarah's opinion of the Palace's antagonism towards her. 'It's like slow poison dripping,' said a royal insider. 'You know that you are being discouraged and denigrated. They look down their noses at you and you know it.' Sarah was fed up with being told what she could or could not do, but she was in no position to argue. Her husband had wasted little time in making her aware of all that had been said around his mother's Sandringham table and she was desperately unhappy. One engagement she did keep was a Sports Aid Foundation dinner at the Guildhall in London at which she proved that all was far from well when she stopped to speak to teenage admirers, Claire James and Paul Davidson, who had a bouquet of flowers for her.

'Oh, Claire, I haven't seen you for so long,' she exclaimed. 'Did you have your pictures pulled off the wall?' Noticing the girl's blank look, she put her hand to her forehead and apologized. 'Please excuse me, I don't know what I'm talking about.' Sarah had mistaken Miss James for Claire Grabsky, a sixteen-year-old Midlands schoolgirl she had been corresponding with on a regular basis. Miss Grabsky, who would turn up at the Duchess's engagements wearing a T-shirt emblazoned HELLO, SARAH, IT'S ME AGAIN, had written to tell her that her stepfather had ripped the Yorks' wedding pictures from her bedroom wall, and she wondered if the Duchess could have him sent to the Tower? She was overwhelmed when Sarah had responded by sending her a signed copy of the book she had recently published, *Victoria and Albert: Life at Osborne House*. A photograph was enclosed on which was written: 'Keep strong and happy – Sarah.' It was a piece of advice the obsessed fan was soon to offer back.

Sarah's days on the red-carpet, fresh-paint circuit were almost over. The Palace dropped her from all royal engagements arranged for the following eight months. Geoffrey Crawford said kindly that it was because she wanted to spend more time at home with her family. Unofficially it was made known that the Duchess, now in open rebellion, had refused to co-operate with the House of Windsor in its selection of royal duties, even if she and her husband were allowed £250,000 a year in expenses from the Civil List for that express purpose. Being told she could not go to Caroline Rose Hunt's party at the Lanesborough was beginning to have serious consequences.

The decision put more pressure on Prince Andrew who was staying in officers' quarters at the Royal Military College of Science at Swindon in Wiltshire where he was engaged on an intensive course. He had joined ninety-nine other officers to learn the applications of science and technology in defence. He was to emerge from the course as a Grade Two staff officer and take up a desk job as a planner and organizer, a career move he said he had taken to help his wife overcome the mild depression she had suffered through loneliness while he was at sea. Desperately trying to maintain a calm exterior while he decided whether his marriage could be saved, it meant he now had to turn up alone at events traditionally attended by royal couples, a dinner for families of Falklands war veterans and the Chelsea Flower Show among them.

Although he had discouraged his somewhat disturbed wife to seek professional help for whatever was ailing her and exposing her character defects to closer-than-usual public scrutiny, he was unprepared for the course she took. Taking almost no precautions to hide her identity, she turned up at a maisonette in a less fashionable part of Islington, North London, to consult Madam Vasso, a Greek medium and healer, who invited her to sit under a blue plastic pyramid in a 7-foot-square bedroom. It did not help that the treatment came heartily recommended by Steve Wyatt who, according to his erstwhile lover Denice Lewis, slept under a pyramid in his home 'to cleanse his soul' and it certainly helped his problems to go away.

Madam Vasso said that the Duchess sat under the pyramid to be cured of pains in the neck and back. The 54-year-old mystic, who learned her skill as a child in the Greek village of Nafpaktos, said in her thick native accent: 'She had a lot of pain, I think maybe it was to do with tension. I heal just by touch. I put my hands over her back, and she said she could feel the heat. She kept her clothes on and said she was happy when she left.

'There must not be any metal, nails or glue near the pyramid because it takes energy away. I talk to my clients slowly and let them be free. If you are not relaxed, it will not work. It is all down to the energy.'

Madam Vasso also ran a fortune-telling stall in nearby Chapel market, under a sign citing Diplomas in Hypnosis, Healing, Reading and Astrology. Help was promised for 'All your problems whether love, business or troubles no matter how small or big. Come and see and try.' Down in the marketplace, Madame Vasso was known less grandly as Mrs V. Awad.

That Wednesday, 19 February, was the Prince's thirty-second birthday and several friends waited all day for a summons to dine at Harry's Bar in Mayfair where he and Sarah had previously celebrated birthdays. No summons came. He remained at the college and dined alone from a tray in his study. Sarah was in no position to get to Mayfair or even the Wiltshire training establishment. She journeyed to Cornwall by train and was ensconced in a six-bedroom, pink-walled manor house in the village of Helford, the country retreat of composer Tim Rice, who was holidaying in South Africa. When she emerged, it was to take her daughters on a three-hour expedition to Land's End to see the views and to visit a seal sanctuary in the village of Gweek where other visitors were surprised to see her running down a grassy hillock clutching a princess in each hand to watch the seals being fed. She had arrived five minutes late and was worried that her daughters might miss suppertime.

Photographers waiting to snap Sarah, her children and her friend

Alison Lobel with her two daughters Emily, eight, and Sophie, six, were richly rewarded. Aware that she was providing a superb photo opportunity, the Duchess, although pale and gaunt, perched Princess Eugenie on her shoulder to point out the baby seals.

Her companion, known as Ally, was the wife of Norman Lobel, a partner in the Royal County of Berkshire Polo Club, where Sarah's father now worked. While their daughters slept soundly at the manor house after an exciting day, the two women talked late into the night and Alison pledged to help Sarah however she could in the difficult weeks ahead.

Calling from a number in Los Angeles, Steve Wyatt telephoned Sarah twice at the manor house. Later that month he was to call her a third time from Virginia on her ex-directory number at Sunninghill, a number known only to members of the Royal Family and their closest friends. It was changed soon afterwards. Wyatt also chatted with a Chelsea-based friend called Johnny Bryan, whose name meant nothing outside his own circle at the time, but who was to play a major role when the events now taking place had reached a very public climax.

For her part, Diana made her second phone call about the state of the Yorks' marriage from Kensington Palace to Penny Thornton on Monday, 9 March, only hours after a private meeting had taken place at Sunninghill. The situation had deteriorated even further. 'Sarah is very unhappy with Andrew,' the Princess said. 'She is going to do something very dramatic.'

TWO

Escape from Sunninghill

'My wife was crashing round the room at four o'clock this morning.'

PRINCE ANDREW

When the Queen arrived at Sunninghill Park House for a highly confidential tête-à-tête with the Duke and Duchess of York at four o'clock on the afternoon of Sunday, 8 March 1992, no visible evidence remained of an enjoyably informal party which had taken place only a few hours earlier. The little Princesses Beatrice and Eugenie greeted the grandmother they so clearly adored with hugs, kisses and gales of laughter. As they showed her in, there were no tell-tale signs of recent festivities in the spacious drawing room where Her Majesty liked to sit. The dining-room table had been cleared and the dirty dishes – just a few of the 600 dinner plates that the Yorks had received as wedding presents – were silently going through the dish-washer elsewhere.

Andrew and Sarah, putting their personal difficulties on hold, had invited a group of friends, the American businessman Johnny Bryan among them, to spend Saturday night at the ranch-style home which had been only one of the Queen's gifts to the newly-weds. The overnight guests had also been asked to stay on for lunch the following day.

Of all the friends the Yorks had gathered into their most intimate circle, Johnny Bryan was easily the most intriguing. Balding and bull-necked, the 36-year-old financial adviser mixed comfortably with those more likely to be found in this five-acre enclave in the Royal County of Berkshire by virtue of their birth or social rank. Not that Bryan was a nonentity. *Habitués* of such nightspots as Annabel's in London's Mayfair knew him as a man who was making enough impact in Sloanedom to qualify as one of the more visible social astronauts on the London skyline. His most immediate claim to fame was that he had been a friend of Steve Wyatt's since high-school days in Houston, Texas, and that he was related through marriage to Lynn Wyatt.

None of that in itself explained his presence at Sunninghill. The truth was that Bryan was now the Yorks' particular friend in his own right, a position Steve Wyatt had occupied until his handsome profile became so high that it had started to annoy the Queen. Johnny Bryan, however, had been excluded from the royal veto. One reason for that was the help he was giving the Yorks with their financial affairs. In the convoluted worlds of money, power and position, he had already made his mark as a boyfriend of Geraldine Ogilvy, daughter of Lord and Lady Rothermere. Geraldine's estranged husband, Lord David Ogilvy, was nephew of Angus Ogilvy and Princess Alexandra, and his father was the Earl of Airlie who, as the Lord Chamberlain, had despatched the invitations to Andrew and Sarah's wedding. Not everyone in *Debrett's* had gone to the wedding, of course, but the current list of somebodies now figuring in the disintegration of the marriage was growing longer by the minute.

Among the twelve who sat down for lunch was Princess Margaret's son David Armstrong-Jones, Viscount Linley, who had travelled up from London on his black Harley-Davidson motorbike with his girlfriend, Stephanie Struthers, riding pillion. Linley was one member of the Royal Family who had remained in close contact with Sarah despite the Sandringham summit on her marital problems. A special bond between them was that Linley was also Beatrice's godfather. 'Sarah often calls him to share her joy and woes,' said a friend. Another present was Sir Robert Fellowes, the bespectacled head prefect of the young royals. His studious demeanour gave no indication that his thoughts might be on anything more serious than the food platter in front of him. It turned out to be a 'carefree and relaxed' occasion, the atmosphere giving no hint of the tension beneath the surface which had erupted into anger recently when someone carelessly mentioned Steve Wyatt's name. Prince Andrew had stood up and flung his plate down on the table, sending china and glass flying everywhere, said one of the guests, who added: 'Andrew was so angry he looked like he was going to explode. He walked out of the room swearing and shouting.'

That storm had soon passed. 'Everyone was roaring with laughter,' said one friend. 'It didn't seem possible that Andrew and Sarah were a couple on the brink of separation. It just didn't seem possible.'

From all accounts, the night before lunch had been memorable as well. 'My wife was crashing round the room at four o'clock this morning,' Andrew teased the assembly. 'Can't think what she was up to.' In fact, Sarah had stayed up late drinking and chatting with house guest Johnny Bryan.

Stephanie Struthers, a newcomer to royal circles, had grown very fond of Sarah in the nine months that she had been going out with Linley. She had met the Queen's nephew when they were both invited to stay at Windsor Castle during Royal Ascot the previous June. Sarah had shown kindness to Stephanie by giving up her place in the royal carriage so that the young brunette could enjoy the thrill of riding past the packed stands in the company of the Royal Family. The privilege had been made even more special for Stephanie, then twenty-two, because her shipowning father, Alastair Struthers, was deputy senior steward of the Jockey Club and a mainstay of the Ascot racing fraternity.

After lunch, as the staff started clearing away, the Yorks apologized and asked their guests if they would mind departing before 4 p.m. as, they explained, the Queen was driving over from Windsor Castle for afternoon tea. Linley and Stephanie took off on his motorbike and the others drifted away. Johnny Bryan drove back to London in his hired Vauxhall. Screened from prying eyes by six-foot-high walls and protected at vast public expense by armed officers of the Thames Valley Police Force, Sunninghill Park that Sunday afternoon had all the outward signs of a desirable totem of wealth and prestige. Inside, though, the sounds of revelry now muted, a once loving relationship was entering the throes of its final days, and even the Queen was powerless to prevent it. Before the afternoon had ended, Sarah had expressed her unswerving wish to separate from Andrew, the husband she had told the world time and again she loved, cherished and admired. At her request, the lawyers were called in.

The Queen did not leave Sunninghill without letting her daughter-in-law know that she was bitterly disappointed by her obstinacy. Her Majesty's attitude had hardened considerably since their last meeting at Sandringham. Little else had been discussed when the senior royals had gathered in the intervening weeks and although Princess Margaret, sometimes waspish, had been sympathetic towards Sarah, both the

Queen Mother and Prince Philip expressed the view that the Duchess was being ungrateful and selfish. Coming towards the end of a heady weekend, Sarah was taken aback by her mother-in-law's forthright approach and surprised that her guest Sir Robert, who had been asked to stay behind, slipped immediately into his role as Her Majesty's senior courtier.

The glee of the young princesses over their grandmother's visit added to the atmosphere of confusion and, as a glum Sarah saw the Queen to her car, her dispiritedness was reflected in her gait – a characteristic which had caused one member of the Royal Family to dub her the Milkmaid from Dummer Down Farm, and another to remark uncharitably: 'She's a bolter just like her mother.'

Sir Matthew Farrer, a kind and gracious man, had been Private Solicitor to the Queen since 1965. He kept an understandably low profile under his head of greying hair. As the legal brain at the Royal Household, he needed not only his professional ability but the additional skills of a courtier to cope with Her Majesty's sensitive and complex legal affairs. 'I've only handled one divorce,' he once told a young lawyer seeking guidance on a point of matrimonial law. With admirable modesty, Sir Matthew refrained from mentioning that it was the divorce of Princess Margaret and Lord Snowdon. In more recent times, he had prepared the papers for the divorce of Princess Anne and Mark Phillips.

The Sunday following the Queen's afternoon visit to Sunninghill Park House, Sir Matthew's legal team from Farrer & Co. of Lincoln's Inn Fields travelled there to discuss the terms of an imminent separation with the Yorks. Looking mournful and close to tears, Sarah left the meeting to attend her last engagement. It was a thanksgiving service in the Chapel Royal of St Peter's Church at the Tower of London – the very prison in which Claire Grabsky had jokingly asked Sarah to have her stepfather incarcerated for tearing pictures of the royal wedding off her bedroom wall. Claire was there wearing her IT'S ME AGAIN sweatshirt. 'I had brought Fergie a toy for Eugenie,' she said. 'But there was no way I could get to her. She looked sad, but as the car pulled away she caught sight of me and craned her neck to wave and give me a little smile. And then she was gone.'

'Sarah York is not as tough as Diana,' explained the royal insider. 'Her action was that of a desperate woman trying to save herself. She wanted to be free. It would never have occurred to her that she would be condemned far more viciously than the Princess of Wales.'

. . .

The Sheraton Park Tower hotel stood out like one of Prince Charles's architectural carbuncles among its Edwardian and Georgian neighbours along London's most salubrious boulevard. Restaurant 101 faced directly on to Knightsbridge and despite the tinted glass windows, diners were on full view to passers-by on the main road to Harvey Nichols and Harrods.

The attraction behind the glass at 3.30 on the afternoon of Tuesday, 17 March, was the Duchess of York, who was gaily drinking champagne with Johnny Bryan. 'The Duchess and her companion sat there laughing and chattering,' said a guest staying at the Sheraton. 'Then someone from the hotel management came over to greet her and she said something like: "We're here celebrating – my friend has just become the father of twins." They seemed to find it terrifically funny. They sat there drinking and talking for ages. In the end they must have been there four hours.'

As she left the restaurant, the Duchess saw an eye-catching advertisement which flanked the hotel's casino right on Knightsbridge. FLY THAI DAILY, said the Oriental script on the display panels in letters 18 inches high. An illuminated map showed Thai Airways' flight paths to Bangkok and Bali. The Duchess made a mental note for future reference. Only hours later, first editions of the *Daily Mail* – proprietor: Lord Rothermere – breaking news of the Sunninghill legal meeting and foreshadowing the collapse of the marriage, were arriving at the newspaper's offices off Kensington High Street, a mile up the road from the Sheraton.

As quickly as the morning mist over Sunninghill Park, interest faded in the General Election which Prime Minister John Major had just called for 9 April. Immediately, there was only one talking point among an electorate which had already become bored with the lack-lustre performance of the political vote-catchers. For the next seven days, just one topic intrigued and infuriated the constituencies as the mystery surrounding the break-up began to unfold. Somehow, the economic issues on which the election was being fought rated a poor second to the problems of the troubled royals. The Labour Leader Neil Kinnock, for one, was left to ponder whether this sudden distraction would cost Labour the election.

At this stage, the Yorks carried on as though nothing untoward was happening. In truth, the *Mail's* editor, Sir David English, had forced

31

the Queen's hand. Prince Andrew left Sunninghill on time at 8 a.m. at the wheel of his blue H-registration Daimler, his detective in the passenger seat, to motor to the Army Staff College at Camberley in Surrey where he was in his third week of an intensive Command Training Course. Carefully made up for the performance she knew lay ahead and wearing black patterned leggings and a long, loose-fitting white jumper, Sarah strode from the house thirty-five minutes later escorting Princess Beatrice to a waiting Ford Granada.

Looking confident, Sarah chatted to Beatrice as they were driven to Upton House School, the Duchess once again carrying out the duty that nanny Alison had performed in more normal times. For Beatrice's sake, it was crucial for Sarah to put on a brave face in front of the other mothers whose natural curiosity had, understandably, reached a fever pitch of genteel excitement. Such was her determination that this day should proceed as normal that she even went ahead with an appointment with her visiting physical fitness instructor, Josh Salzmann. He arrived at Sunninghill soon after the school trip, and she worked out for forty-five minutes at the exercise routine which, along with other slimming aids, had kept her figure trim since the birth of Eugenie. Salzmann, thirty-five, a Windsor-based American, had been taking Sarah through his Bodyfit regime three times a week for the past two years. 'It has made me feel more positive,' the Duchess testified.

Inevitably, Salzmann was asked about the Yorks' marital troubles. 'I feel sorry for them both, having to sort out their problems in the public eye,' he said. 'They are being watched all the time. Not many marriages can stand that – I'd hate to see any reports about the rows that my wife Laura and I have.' The Duchess, he added, was 'one of the strongest people I know – always mentally strong, and also one of the strongest women physically.'

At 1 p.m. Prince Andrew returned home to join his wife for lunch. It was all going according to their plan to keep everything outwardly normal. Sarah collected Beatrice from school after Andrew had returned to Camberley and she took both her children for a walk in the grounds of Windsor Castle. Normal enough, but to all intents and purposes, it was Sarah's last day as a member of the Royal Family. Even while she was walking, a Washington public-relations company was issuing a statement on behalf of Steve Wyatt. The company's Robert Schneider read: 'If the rumour is true, I am deeply saddened by the news, and I wish the Duke and Duchess of York the very best of luck in these trying times.' Schneider said his client had no more information about the royal couple's troubles than had appeared in newspapers in the United States and on British television.

If ever Sarah had projected the way fate might intervene in her marriage, she could hardly have conjured up a more miserable scenario. There could have been few worse ways to celebrate an anniversary. Six years ago to the day, Sarah had proudly shown off her engagement ring which Andrew had helped to design – a large oval ruby set in ten drop diamonds. As she told the world: 'We are good friends, a good team.' Now, on Thursday, 19 March 1992, the engagement ring and her wedding band of Welsh gold were the only tangible evidence of that once loving friendship. As Sarah dashed from the schoolyard with Princess Beatrice after morning classes, only a few inches of bare arm separated those rings from the symbol of another friendship – Steve Wyatt's black-strapped wristwatch, which was clearly visible beneath the sleeve of her rose-patterned black jumper.

At 11.30 a.m., the six correspondents accredited to the Court of St James passed through the Privy Purse Gate and crossed the fore-court to Buckingham Palace. A red-liveried doorman ushered them into the ground floor office of Charles Anson, the Queen's £50,000-a-year Press Secretary. Each of the reporters was handed a brief press release. It read:

In view of the media speculation which the Queen finds especially undesirable during the Election Campaign, Her Majesty is issuing the following statement: Last week lawyers acting for the Duchess of York initiated discussions about a formal separation for the Duke and Duchess. These discussions are not yet completed and nothing will be said until they are. The Queen hopes that the media will spare the Duke and Duchess and their children any intrusion.

Anson, who had given up a more highly paid job as head of public relations with the merchant bankers Kleinwort Benson, parried the reporters' excited questions for a few minutes with the usual non-committal replies before seeing them out of his office. At 12.15 p.m., Paul Reynolds of BBC Radio had filed his news story from a radio car parked at Canada Gate and went back inside the Palace 'for another chat' with Anson, with whom he had a good working relationship. What Anson told him in a non-attributable briefing in the next few minutes resulted in Reynolds's frantic report during the *World At One* programme that lunchtime. He began:

'The knives are out for Fergie in the Palace. They [the Palace] are claiming that she has been employing a public-relations firm to brief

the Daily Mail, *which is the source of the story. They even name the firm and the gentleman concerned and they are getting their briefing in now in retaliation.*

When he got a chance to reply, Sir Tim Bell, head of Lowe Bell Communications, acknowledged that he was the man referred to, but strongly denied he had played any role in the break-up. A member of his firm, David McDonough, however, had been consulting the Duchess in an unofficial capacity. Sir David English made it clear that his newspaper did not need to rely on PR consultants for exclusive royal stories. Reynolds's report continued, however:

I have rarely heard Palace officials speak in such terms about someone. They are talking about her unsuitability for public life, royal life – her behaviour in being photographed in Hello! *magazine, fooling around, putting paper bags on her head on the aircraft while she was being watched by reporters.*

Hello!, the Spanish-owned weekly which shunned scandal in its columns, had featured a pictorial essay on the Duke and Duchess at home with their children eighteen months earlier. The Palace had not been asked to vet the project, much to its chagrin. Now Sarah was getting the blame. From Reynolds there was more.

I think the thing that has stunned them most of all is the fact revealed in the Daily Mail – *and they say she can only have been the original source of this – that she had a private lunch with the Queen. One official said: 'It is unusual for this kind of private lunch to pitch up in the papers.' The Queen is said to be very sad at the whole thing and if one added that the Queen was pretty angry one would not be far wrong. But I can tell you the Palace officials have been stung by what has happened. They didn't expect all of this to appear in the papers. They were rather hoping that this could be handled rather quietly and in a civilized manner, and now it is all out in the open.*

As the nation tried to digest this catalogue of Sarah's supposed wrongdoings, one thing was immediately clear: Reynolds's report was proof of what she had long been telling her husband and friends that, in her opinion, the Palace was out to crucify her. The impact of the BBC report was immediate and explosive. Although Reynolds had respected Anson's anonymity, it was soon revealed that the tirade had come from his lips. The aplomb he had exercised in front of the assembled journalists seemed to desert him once he started talking to a lone reporter he knew well. It was also implicit in the words Reynolds chose that the Queen had in some way sanctioned Anson's comments about

Sarah's suitability for public and royal life. Sarah was rightly furious. She demanded an apology and got one. This was like applying a tourniquet to someone's neck after they had been guillotined. The damage had been done, and it was irreparable. 'Despite the apology,' noted *The Times* Diary, 'she has clearly been declared a non-person by the Palace.'

Whatever their private feelings, Andrew and Sarah now made a conspicuous effort to be seen together despite the turmoil surrounding them. This strategy had been carefully worked out. Only hours after the couple were supposed to be at daggers drawn, they surprised staff at the Capital Hotel in Basil Street just a few yards away from Harrods by arriving to have lunch with four friends in the hotel's French restaurant. One who occupied another table said: 'They were there when I arrived at 12.45 and they were still there at three o'clock when I left. You wouldn't have guessed there was anything wrong from their behaviour.'

A member of the Capital's management said: 'The Duchess has been coming here for some years, but I don't expect we will be seeing much more of her.' Forecasting what the unpredictable Duchess might, or might not do was to become a fascinating pastime for *aficionados* of royal scandal. They would have known, for instance, that it was to this very dining room that Sarah Ferguson had invited her lover of three years, the Grand Prix millionaire Paddy McNally, to tell him of her growing love for Prince Andrew. 'Paddy had been widowed for five years and, although Sarah had asked him about their future, he wasn't prepared to settle down,' said one who skied with them at Verbier. 'She did the decent thing by telling him what was happening between her and Andrew.'

Keeping up the face-saving charade, the Yorks were out and about again that night for a candlelit dinner at chef Michel Roux's Waterside Inn by the River Thames at Bray. Even though back at Sunninghill they were sleeping in separate bedrooms, the Yorks were anxious to conform to one of the axioms of upper class manners: when in public, keep it civilized. This was precisely the way they continued the next night when they went to a party at Elton John's mansion, Woodside, at Old Windsor. They arrived in Andrew's Daimler at 8.45 p.m. He was at the wheel and Sarah was at his side, although that had not been the case when they left Sunninghill just a few miles away. To fool waiting reporters and TV cameras, they had made their exits separately and teamed up along the road, a detective taking back the spare car.

Some of the guests, who included Billy Connolly, rock star Sting and his wife Trudie Styler, Dame Edna Everage's creator Barry

Humphries and the husband and wife acting duo Kenneth Branagh and Emma Thompson, were surprised to see the Yorks there so soon after the declaration that they were unlikely to continue living together. When Elton greeted them at his front door, his newly spawned hairstyle gave them something to smile about. In common with most of the guests assembled at Woodside to admire its three-year renovation, they were seeing Elton with a full head of hair for the first time. For years, he had worn headgear – usually decorative baseball hats – to conceal his thinning locks. He stood grinning before them with a full head of reddish-brown hair which had been woven into his own in Paris at a cost of £15,000. The secrets Elton kept under his thatch easily outnumbered his many hit records. He was a loyal friend to the Yorks, one person they could safely turn to in their crisis. The Rocket Man was not only a long-standing friend of Andrew's, having played piano at the Prince's twenty-first birthday party at Windsor Castle; he was one of the very select few who had survived Sarah's entry into Andrew's bachelor life.

It had been Elton who had arranged for the couple to show their affection for each other in public for the first time when he invited them to attend his Christmas concert at Wembley three months before their engagement. They kissed and cuddled during the show, hoping – as Elton had forecast – that people would see them and realize they were sweethearts. Someone would tip off the press. Sarah was astonished when she read every newspaper the next morning to find that they had completely missed the story. Later, Elton and his wife Renate had been guests at the royal wedding, and Andrew and Sarah had done their best to play Cupid when the piano-player's own marriage was running into trouble. When the Yorks finally moved into Sunninghill, Elton had entertained guests with his rock classics at a house-warming party.

Elton was a royal favourite who, according to rock star Phil Collins, had the distinction of jiving with the Queen at Buckingham Palace. Not many people could claim that privilege. Both the Queen Mother and Princess Margaret had been guests at Woodside. On one notable occasion after Margaret had called for tea, she told her mother back at Windsor Castle that Elton was so patriotic he was flying the Union Jack over his house. 'Let me see,' said the Queen Mother, picking up a pair of binoculars to direct at the house she had come to know quite well. Alas, following Margaret's departure, Elton had taken down the national flag and replaced it with his Watford Football Club's ensign in preparation for his next visitor, one of the club's directors. The Queen Mother was too tactful to comment on her next visit that she was aware Elton had replaced the Union Jack with more commercial colours.

Dining at the Queen Mother's home once presented her neighbour with an awkward moment. Sugar and salt were laid out in separate bowls amid a confusing array of sparkling silver cutlery. 'I poured sugar all over my food instead of salt, but I had to eat the whole thing,' said Elton. There were no such problems of etiquette at Elton's own party that night. It carried on until the early hours, but the Yorks left at 1 a.m. They had to keep up appearances the next day to face the Queen over tea with Beatrice and Eugenie at Windsor Castle. This went off smoothly enough for Sarah to drive the family back to Sunninghill while Andrew chatted pleasantly at her side. A party at Sunninghill to celebrate Eugenie's second birthday was equally successful. The strategy was working exactly as they had hoped it would. Separated they might be, enemies they were not.

. . .

Whatever her critics at the Palace might have wished, the exclusion zone around the Duchess of York did not include Claridge's, nor did it extend to King Constantine. The exiled Greek monarch, however, was growing steadily impatient as he surveyed others enjoying the buffet in the Causerie, the hotel's green pastel-shaded restaurant which he often patronized. He was not accustomed to being kept waiting, even by a guest with HRH as a prefix to her name. Royalty, in fact, were invariably punctual for each other out of respect. Twenty minutes late, Sarah, wearing a tartan skirt and a black-and-white woollen top, arrived full of apologies delivered in her unmistakable public schoolgirl accent. She had, she explained, been obliged to drop into Buckingham Palace to talk to Prince Andrew after they had driven down from Sunninghill in separate cars.

'She was quite sloppily dressed and bounded in looking more like a terrorist than a duchess,' said the author Dominick Dunne, who was staying at the hotel to write on the royal break-up for *Vanity Fair*. 'I left the hotel to keep an appointment but I'm told that after she had said goodbye to the King she joined a balding, athletic-looking American who was carrying a squash racket. They talked animatedly at a table under the staircase for thirty minutes. After she left, he asked staff if he could use the hotel's back entrance to reach the Bath & Racquets Club a couple of doors away in Brook's Mews. He wanted to avoid going out the front door where he had seen photographers waiting on his way in.'

Dunne knew the description fitted his friend Johnny Bryan, and the next time he spoke to Bryan he raised the matter. Bryan, still an unknown quantity in the York equation, denied point-blank that it was him. Dunne did not give up that easily. Pressed, he conceded finally that he had indeed had a rendezvous with Sarah beneath the stairs at Claridge's.

By this time, Sarah had already told Bryan that she wanted to get away for a break to avoid the harassment she was receiving every time she set foot outside Sunninghill if she were unable to shake off the posse of relentless pressmen who were camped on her doorstep. Now there was a new urgency. The real reason she was late for the lunch date with the King was that Andrew had discovered that morning about the two phone calls Steve Wyatt had made to her during her stay at Tim Rice's Cornish home.

Bryan, whose business interests included a health-care company based in Frankfurt, had a reputation as a man who could keep a confidence. He may have been pleasantly surprised to find himself described as a millionaire, although he was well-off and well-connected. The Bath & Racquets Club, for instance, charged members over thirty £3000 a year for the privilege of using its squash courts, gym and steam room. Prospective members needed a proposer, seconder and written references. 'Johnny is not wealthy by Texan tycoon standards,' said a friend. 'His office is in his rented flat in Chelsea, with his fax and telephones in his bedroom. He has a little rented car and a rented cottage in the country.'

Nor was he a Texan at all, a misunderstanding he would politely rectify for anyone who cared to ask him. Steve Wyatt was the Texan; he was born Anthony John Adrian Bryan at Wilmington, population 70,000, on the Delaware River, and his father Tony was of British descent, a former Spitfire pilot with the Canadian Air Force in World War II. Bryan's rented cottage was on the estate of Detmar Blow at Painswick in Gloucestershire, where he had taken up fox-hunting. He had ridden with the Berkeley Hunt. His riding activities brought him into the company of Bryan Morrison, Major Ferguson's boss at the Royal County of Berkshire Polo Club. 'He was charming and friendly – what we in England regard as a typical Yale type,' said Morrison. 'He was certainly a normal geezer, the kind you could trust with your daughter.'

The Duchess had given Bryan the task of masterminding her escape from Britain, a job which appealed hugely to his sense of adventure. It put Bryan on familiar terrain and the phone calls he made in the next few days were to contacts he had met on business trips in the Far East. Sarah, carrying a shopping bag and a briefcase as she left Claridge's, headed straight to the Knightsbridge clinic of aromatherapist Micheline Arcier. The £45-a-time sessions on Ms Arcier's table had been helping Sarah to combat stress twice a week. She was also seeking a treatment for the withdrawal symptoms she had been suffering since she stopped taking a course of controversial pills. This involved massaging essential oils from flowers and plants like petunia and rosemary through the skin to rid the body of toxins. A senior Palace source admitted he believed that the Duchess's mood swings had been caused by a slimming pill prescribed initially for her by a doctor in Paris and subsequently by a Harley Street specialist. 'They are supposed to be very good in helping people to shed excess weight but these pills apparently have an unhealthy mind-altering side-effect and should certainly not be taken for sustained periods,' he added. The tablets contained a mixture of a 'speed' drug combined with Valium and acted on the thyroid gland, suppressing appetite and stimulating unnatural levels of energy. Patients were cautioned about the dangers of combining them with alcohol. Failure to heed the warning, they were told, could result in uncharacteristic behaviour.

Nor was Andrew able to cope with the stress of the break-up without some help from alternative therapy. 'Andrew's external activities mask an inner discord and recklessness,' said one who made a detailed study of his birth chart. 'He's more hidden, but he's needy.' And so he was visiting the No.1 Synergy Centre in Cadogan Gardens for sessions with Jenny Shannon, who specialized in holistic stress management.

'Most of the work is treating physical symptoms although the cause may well be mental,' said Jenny Shannon's assistant. 'That's what synergy means. When the two parts work in harmony, you get a much greater life-force and you work more efficiently.'

Seven days after their meeting at Claridge's, Sarah reconvened Johnny Bryan's escape committee at Scalini's, an Italian restaurant in the middle of Chelsea's trendy Cosa Nosheries' belt, hardly the most anonymous of venues. Toto's, where she had dined with Steve Wyatt and held wine-and-pasta bashes with Sloaney friends, was practically next door, and Diana's favoured San Lorenzo was around the corner. Sarah's choice confirmed that she no longer cared who saw her or what they might think. She was a free woman, almost.

'The Duchess was wearing no jewellery except her wedding ring and a gold Rolex watch. She had obviously abandoned the Wyatt watch she had been sporting for almost a year,' commented a witness to the proceedings. 'Johnny Bryan was wearing a light blue shirt without a jacket and he sat on Fergie's left at one of the tables in the conservatory area. The other three were all Americans, a larger-than-life balding man in spectacles and a loud black design-print shirt, and two women, one in her early twenties with long fair hair, no make-up, very plain-looking and wearing a pale cream jumper. The other woman was also very plain and wore a dark brown dog-tooth jacket which she took off to reveal the top of a leotard. I thought, "My goodness, how casual." Fergie was wearing what can best be described as a man's outsize shirt, pale green with pink stripes. She wasn't wearing a scrap of make-up.

'The group laughed and joked so loudly they could be heard from three tables away. Fergie ate a melon starter and had the Trota di Montagna – fresh trout cooked in butter, pine nuts and fresh grapes, which at £8.10 was one of the less expensive dishes on the menu. She was obviously watching her weight, she didn't touch a pudding and she drank only one glass of white wine and a little mineral water.

'When she got up to leave, it could be seen that she had a large double-buckled belt holding up an incongruous blue skirt. Although she looked slightly ridiculous she was very relaxed and certainly not fazed.'

The Duchess was not even fazed when she spotted Ricci Burns at a nearby table. She obviously mentioned this chance encounter to Bryan, who intermittently turned around to observe the woman who had introduced Prince Andrew to Sarah's predecessor in his affections, the actress-turned-photographer Koo Stark.

Ricci Burns, who was divorced from the Mayfair hairdresser Leonard Lewis, ran her own public-relations business and possessed one of the most impressive contacts books in Belgravia. She had enjoyed a long-term relationship with Charlie Young, who was Andrew's best friend at Gordonstoun. Indeed Young was charged with the royal pupil's welfare and helped to keep at bay the bullies who took exception to Andrew's regard for himself as The Great I Am. Soon after the Yorks' engagement, Young had invited them to Harry's Bar for dinner with himself and Ricci. Andrew and Sarah were heedlessly late for the meal but the foursome enjoyed a lively evening. The next morning a huge bunch of flowers arrived at Ricci's home with a note signed, 'Kisses and hugs from Sarah'. Ricci's relationship with Young had since ended although they remained on the friendliest terms. At Scalini's, the two women gave no indication that they even recognized each other.

Sarah's mind was already drifting to faraway places with exotic-sounding names. In the April issue of *Tatler,* she had read a feature in the travel pages about the Thai island of Phuket, pronounced Foo-kay, a tropical paradise that, according to the magazine, offered refuge from prying eyes. The writer described staying

> *in a friend's villa on a private beach next to the Amanpuri, the ultimate resort in Phuket and the last word in understated comfort. The forty suites and pavilions are hidden away in a coconut planta-tion which ends abruptly on the edge of the Andaman Ocean [sic]. This is as far removed from a resort hotel as you could ever want, with not even a single television to disrupt your thought.*

Just the place for a disappearing duchess. As she drove away from Scalini's, a detective at the wheel, she spotted a chauffeur who was waiting patiently outside. 'She smiled broadly and gave me a big wave,' he said. 'She looked very happy with life.' Certainly not like a woman who was preparing to leave her husband.

The countdown to Sarah's getaway proceeded to go extremely well. Bryan gave her a ninety-minute update over supper near his Chelsea flat. Andrew was kept informed. The evening before her departure, however, while she supervised the packing, he left Sun-ninghill and drove himself to Mayfair. Andrew had known the ubiquitous Johnny Bryan for two years. The personable American had impressed the Prince with his grasp of financial matters. He trusted him to take care of his estranged wife and daughters while Sir Matthew Farrer, for himself, and Charles Doughty, of the London firm of Withers, for Sarah, sorted out details of their legal separation. Bryan, he hoped, would also fulfil an important role as honest broker in a delicate line of action he was being urged to take. Aware that sympathy had swung in the Duchess's favour after Charles Anson's bungled character assassination, the Queen was anxious to float the idea of a reconciliation. If Sarah turned it down, no one could say that the offer had not been made.

Andrew parked his car in South Audley Street and made for the canopied white door of Harry's Bar, which, unlike establishments of the same name in Paris and Venice had the words 'a private club' minutely appended to its shining gold plate. He was to dine as a guest of the club's millionaire owner Mark Birley with a party which included his aunt Princess Margaret, Prince Michael of Kent and Birley's ex-wife Annabel Goldsmith, after whom the royals' discothèque in Berkeley Square was named. They had been patronizing an art exhibition Birley had hosted earlier at a gallery in Bond Street. Andrew was in no mood to celebrate, but he had wisely decided to attend to spare himself the misery of witnessing preparations for a holiday from which he was excluded. The prospect of losing Beatrice and Eugenie for a month at this crucial time was painful enough without seeing the little girls' nervous excitement for himself. 'Prince Andrew looked very relaxed and perfectly normal,' noticed Jarvis Astaire, the boxing promoter, who was dining at another table. 'I've met him several times at Variety Club functions or at the homes of friends like David Frost, and he's a very nice fellow. He came to the Variety Club première of *Never Say Never Again* not long after the Falklands and although he chatted to Sean Connery, he was charming to my grandson as well.'

· · ·

As Thursday, 9 April dawned bright and clear to signal polling day in the General Election, Sarah made her move. Knowing that the nation's attention would be focused on the biggest political cliffhanger of the century, she kept the rendezvous with Johnny Bryan that would take her out of the country without detection. Travelling with her, the children and nanny Alison Wardley was Inspector Brian Baston, who had often guarded Sarah since she became engaged to Prince Andrew, and another detective. Their getaway was so smooth that, for almost two weeks, they managed to keep a low profile. Sarah kept in touch with Andrew by phone from the Amanpuri Hotel which, she discovered, was everything the *Tatler* had promised, except that the possibility of spiders or even a snake crawling into her £510-a-night villa from the lush tropical foliage surrounding it terrified her. 'Are there any poisonous ones here?' she asked a houseboy. 'Can they get into the house?' She was assured that, among its job descriptions, the hotel included a resident snake-catcher. When a spider did creep in, she chased it away. 'I can't stand spiders,' she said. 'They make me shiver.'

Apart from that, the Amanpuri was living up to its name, which means 'region of tranquillity'. The three-bedroomed villa was air-conditioned and had a sunken jacuzzi should the heat around its private pool become unpleasant. Sarah worked up some colour on her fair skin lounging on the private sundeck. She passed the days reading Jilly Cooper's ribald novel, *Rivals,* drank the rum-based cocktail Planter's Punch and listened to Prokofiev's *Romeo and Juliet.* A pummelling massage from the hotel's resident expert See Wan helped her to unwind. The excitable princesses described their holiday adventures to Andrew at the end of a phone 8000 miles away; a boat ride to a nearby island, a water fight Mummy had started in the pool and building sand-castles with 'Uncle Johnny' on the beach. Andrew had spent Easter with his family at Windsor, the Queen and the other royals carrying out their traditional devotions in church as though nothing were amiss.

It was at the beach that Sarah finally surfaced as far as the rest of the world was concerned when, inevitably, someone who wasn't privy to her desire for seclusion recognized her. She and her party had lugged enough water wings, buckets and spades to keep the children amused for several hours, but they remained only six minutes after she realized she had been spotted. Inspector Baston intervened when a tourist tried to photograph the royal party by holding up a rubber dinghy to shield them from the camera.

'Two Volvos came down to the edge of the beach in a cloud of dust,' said George Baker, a company director on holiday from the Midlands. 'My wife said, "Good God, it's Fergie." I tried to take a picture but the bodyguards prevented me.' Back at the Amanpuri, the Duchess was, however, photographed while walking in a courtyard with Johnny Bryan, incognito in shorts and T-shirt. His bald pate, nevertheless, was unmistakable. The secret was out.

Bryan, who was not registered on the guest list, had been occupying a room close to Sarah's villa. Although a friend of the hotel's owner, Adrian Zecha, a Hong-Kong-based property tycoon, he was puzzled when hotel staff bowed low to him each time they encountered him. The workers had been told that he was Sarah's brother-in-law, Prince Edward. 'We were all very excited because we were told that the son of the Queen of England was coming to stay,' said Aree, a housekeeper. When she was shown a picture of Bryan, Aree said: 'This is Prince Edward. He smiled a lot and we liked him very much.' The hotel's receptionist Chaweeaan confirmed the harmless deception which Bryan, a dedicated anglophile, would have enjoyed. 'We were told in advance that the Queen's son would accompany the Duchess of York and all staff were told to keep it a secret for security reasons,' she said. 'I was even told not to tell my family. We received instructions on what to do if we met him or the Duchess of York. We were told to call them Your Highness.' Bryan, however, became known to the chambermaids as Mr Hua Lan, or Mr Smooth-head. 'He behaved like a gentleman and always went back to his own room,' said one. The hotel bill of £13,000 for the Duchess's stay was paid by American Express Gold Card. It was widely believed that Zecha who, as a friend of George Harrison, the publicity-shy Beatle, and the fiercely private Yoko Ono and Madonna, was subsidising Sarah's expensive disappearing act.

Once they had been spotted, Sarah and Bryan held a hurried conference and decided to undertake Plan B of a complex operation she and the American had worked out for just such an exigency. It was time to move on anyway. Sarah was bored. Bryan made some long-distance phone calls to Indonesia and, probably with Zecha's help, chartered two private jets to fly the seven-strong party in separate hops to Banda in the remote Moluccas Islands. They were booked into the three-storey Maulana Inn, an idyllic pink-and-yellow Dutch colonial residence with arched colonnades built on the shores of a blue lagoon. Overlooking the island was the 2200-foot cone of the still active Banda volcano.

Tillman Jens, a German film-maker, was shooting a travel documentary about the island and its volcano for the German airline Lufthansa when the Duchess of York, carrying Princess Eugenie on her shoulders, walked barefoot into camera range. Johnny Bryan, in the surrogate-uncle mode that was to become so familiar, was carrying Princess Beatrice. When he had recovered from his surprise, Jens followed the party back to the Maulana Inn. Sitting on the hotel verandah, Sarah chuckled as she recalled her rapid retreat from Phuket. 'She talked happily about how the Indonesian Government took pity on them and deliberately leaked false reports that the Duchess was headed to Australia for a reunion with her sister Jane Makim,' said Jens.

The Duchess was enjoying her new-found freedom to go where she liked, when she liked, without hindrance from her enemies at the Palace or harassment from pursuing newsmen who had no idea where she might turn up next. The false trail had sent reporters scrambling frantically towards the island of Bedarra, a tree-covered speck in the Great Barrier Reef five miles off the coast of Queensland. Sarah had spent a wonderfully relaxing holiday on Bedarra with the princesses, her sister Jane and Jane's boyfriend Reiner Leudeke eighteen months earlier. When things had become too quiet for her liking, she dressed up as Wonderwoman, complete with blonde wig, green jump suit and flowing red cape, for some memorable high jinks with other guests. 'She wasn't there this time,' said a newsdesk executive back in London. 'We didn't know where she was. I felt at one point that we might as well stick a pin in the map and hope for the best. It was costing us a fortune and we still couldn't catch up with her.'

Vanuatu, an island further south in the Pacific, Richard Branson's island of Necker over in the Caribbean, Susie Barrantes's ranch in Argentina, even Verbier, were all listed as possible destinations. The chaos Sarah created among her media tormentors tasted as sweet to her as the succulent jumbo prawns and tropical fruits she was devouring on Banda. Revenge, she found, was a dish best eaten cold. Kelvin Mac-Kenzie, editor of the *Sun*, captured a universal feeling of frustration in an aptly phonetic headline: WHERE THE PHUKET IS FERGIE?

Parting company with Bryan, Sarah flew to Bali and checked her party into the Amankila Hotel, also owned by Adrian Zecha. As she settled down in a private thatched pavilion with its own 100-foot terrace and three bedrooms, each containing a kingsize bed beneath a hand-carved wooden canopy, Bryan returned to London to complete the next part of his confidential mission. He spent most of the afternoon of Sunday, 26 April at Sunninghill with Prince Andrew. After the meeting, Bryan phoned a lifelong friend, Whitney Tower, in New York. 'Johnny said they discussed the divorce – divorce was the word he used,' said Tower.

Bryan had conveyed a set of extraordinary terms the Duchess had laid down for a reconciliation. She wanted Charles Anson removed from any position which might affect her in the future. She also wanted something done about Sir Robert Fellowes, her erstwhile luncheon guest, whom she did not feel had her best interests at heart. Such unreasonable conditions fell on deaf ears when they were conveyed by Andrew to the Queen. Anson had made a grovelling apology within hours of his howler and had already offered his resignation, which the Queen had refused to accept. Sarah's vague insistence that Palace policy be altered to prevent her suffering at the hands of its officers was another non-starter. The reconciliation which few believed either Sarah or Andrew really wanted, but which protocol decreed should at least be offered, was as distant as the enchanted sunsets Sarah was enjoying on Bali.

By making a list of demands, however impossible, she was playing the House of Windsor at its own game and on her own terms. The Queen, for one, must have recognized at this point what was becoming apparent to people who really understood Sarah that while her son was growing older, it was his wife who was growing up.

Prince Andrew was not the only one Bryan acquainted with Sarah's demands. Sarah had provided him with a short list of journalists who could be trusted to take her side. Calling at the south London home of one of them, the *Daily Mirror*'s James Whitaker, he reported that he had telephoned several newspapers from Sunninghill while Prince Andrew was out of the room: 'Johnny described Buckingham Palace people as "arrogant assholes" – unpleasant, nasty people who had been vicious to Fergie. He stressed that he was just as friendly with Prince Andrew as he was with Fergie and referred to her as the Duchess,' said Whitaker. 'He said the Queen was insisting that he take part in all negotiations and trusted him.'

Bali was famous as the setting of the Rodgers and Hammerstein musical *South Pacific*. One of its best-known songs was 'I'm Gonna Wash That Man Right Out-a My Hair'. If anything summed up her attitude towards the overtures she had received, the lyrics of that song said it all. With her sense of mischief fully satisfied and feeling that she was at last 'being herself', Sarah emerged from Bali with a suntan and a smile and caught a scheduled Boeing 747 flight from Jakarta back to London. It did not matter that she and her party had to be bundled unceremoniously on to the plane as reporters and photographers moved in. She had made the point to Andrew, his mother and anyone else who wanted to buy into the argument that she could survive in the alien world outside cloistered Chelsea and secure Sunninghill, albeit with the help of rich friends. 'She's a strong person, strong-willed,' said Bryan Morrison, Norman Lobel's partner in the Royal County of Berkshire Polo Club, whom she phoned soon after her return to sort out a little misunderstanding. 'She is probably misguided at times, as we all are, but she is growing in strength.' Morrison spoke with some authority; unlike most of the 'friends' commenting unfavourably about the Duchess's South Pacific odyssey, he had known her since she was thirteen. 'She has always loved life.'

Even while the Duchess was still airborne, more ripples were racing across the poisoned pond. 'Everybody connected with the Royal Family is absolutely horrified about her holiday,' said a tennis-playing friend of Princess Diana. 'There is no sympathy left for her. Andrew is everyone's hero and he is doing everything he can to retain support for when it comes to the issue of the children. Charlie Young is very close to him and giving him good advice. One or both of the children is really quite poorly with a bug picked up on the trip. That hasn't helped Sarah because obviously everyone blames her for dragging them around the Far East the way she did.'

Nor was Johnny Bryan faring much better among the self-appointed defenders of 'the Fam', as they liked to call the Royal Family. The mood towards him among Chelsea royalists was said to be hostile. 'He is disliked for his part in helping her to belittle the Royal Family,' said Diana's friend from the Vanderbilt Racquet Club in West London. This seemed extremely disingenuous because any one of Bryan's critics would gladly have given a Barbour-clad right arm to have changed places with him.

At Heathrow, Sarah swept through the air terminal in a navy jacket and polka-dot culottes, a princess on either arm. She looked great even after the seventeen-hour flight, and she knew it. Revitalized, she headed back to the place she no longer considered home to confront her husband, among other things, about her new address and the new life she would be leading as a single mother.

THREE

The Sloane from St Trinian's

'Only a moral imperative can persuade husbands and wives to be faithful to each other.'

PRINCE PHILIP

The door of the smart Knightsbridge office burst open unceremoniously and, to Christina Dumond's surprise, in stumbled a young woman who looked 'not like something out of Benenden or Roedean – more like St Trinian's'. This was Sarah Ferguson, nineteen and anxious to make a good impression, turning up for one of her first job interviews. Things had gone more than slightly wrong on the way to Durden-Smith Communications, located in an office complex attached to the Basil Street Hotel. 'The heel of one shoe had snapped off, she had ladders in her stockings, her umbrella was broken and she was soaking wet,' said Christina, who worked for the public-relations company. 'She really was St Trinian's. She had obviously been out late the night before, and her first words were, "Oh, my God, have I ballsed it up?" I said, "No." We tidied her up and she got the job as a secretary. She was a lovely girl, a great girl with a great sense of humour. I couldn't help noticing her hands, they were so beautiful and immaculate.'

One thing Sarah never quite learned during her blissfully naïve though splendidly liberating years as a trainee Sloane Ranger was how to make a gracious entrance. 'She would sort of gawk through the door,' said Christina. 'Other people would open the door but, with her, it would be Bang! and it would be lifted off its hinges. And those big strides down the hallway.' The Dummer Down Milkmaid had arrived in town.

Sarah might have been more St Trinian's than Benenden, but if genealogy were the art of tracing your roots back to people better than yourself, she was uncommonly well-placed. Her family tree included clusters of blue-blooded lords, barons, viscounts, earls and even grander dukes. What's more, she was related to Prince Andrew and Princess Diana. Her father Ronald was the son of Colonel Andrew Ferguson, who was commanding officer of the Sovereign's Escort of the Household Cavalry for King George V's Silver Jubilee parade. When Ronald Ferguson followed in his father's footsteps in the Life Guards and led the Queen's Escort, she had occasion to chide him gently when his mount overshot the mark during a parade. 'Back a bit, Ronald,' said Her Majesty, 'they have come to see me, not you.'

His mother, Marian Montagu Douglas Scott, was the daughter of Lt.-Col. Lord Herbert Montagu Douglas Scott, son of the sixth Duke of Buccleuch. Sarah's connection with Andrew ran back through this bloodline to James, Duke of Monmouth, who was the illegitimate son of Charles II and his mistress Lucy Walters. Sarah and Andrew, sixth cousins, were both descended from the Royal House of Stuart. Her kinship with Diana came through Ronald's aunt Jane and her husband Sir William Fellowes, the parents of the redoubtable Sir Robert who had married Diana's elder sister, Lady Jane Spencer.

More important than heredity in Sarah and Andrew's love story, however, was polo, the tough body-contact sport for strong men, which their fathers played with equal vigour and which aroused even stronger passion in the women who watched it. It was in the pony lines at Smith's Lawn in Windsor Great Park that Sarah first met her husband and although they were childhood playmates, neither makes much of that early encounter. 'Sarah met him on the polo field, but then doesn't everybody?' said her mother, Susie Barrantes, a remark that sounded more snobbish than she intended. It was all the more unfortunate because it was true; polo was famous as a meeting place for upper-class singles. It was also notorious as a setting for upper-class dalliance. Susie met the man she left her husband for, Hector Barrantes, in precisely these surroundings. Nor was Ronald immune; his roving eye had sometimes made Susie feel that she was being taken for granted.

It was through polo at Smith's Lawn and Cowdray Park, the home of British polo in Sussex, that Sarah the distant cousin became very close to Princess Diana. It was the manipulative Diana who decided that Sarah would make an ideal partner for Andrew, the prince she had considered marrying herself before Charles became an even better prospect. Sarah was a willing conspirator, and the way the two women set about persuading not only Prince Andrew but his family that Sarah was the One would have had their forebears chuckling with glee. 'The match was Diana's doing,' said Diana's tennis friend. 'She wrote the script and Sarah played her role perfectly.'

'Her family background is landed gentry rather than aristocracy, with generations of distinguished service in the Cavalry,' *The Times* noted when it became time for the Fergusons to stand up for inspection after Sarah's engagement. 'Her great-great-grandfather died on active service with the Royal Horse Guards in 1896, taming the Ashanti on the Gold Coast and every generation since, down to her father, has held a commission in the Life Guards. It is a family of old money, but not much.'

Susie more than compensated for what Ronald lacked in the silver-spoon department. She was born Susan Mary Wright into a distinguished Derbyshire dynasty, the daughter of Doreen and Fitzherbert Wright. Her father, after a career with the 15th/19th Hussars, worked as a director for a firm of agricultural engineers. He and his wife raised their son Bryan and three daughters, Davina, Brigid and Susie, the youngest, in imposing Bridgewater House at Grantham in Lincolnshire.

Susie, a beautiful, lively young woman, cared little for formal education and left school early with no O levels. She enrolled at a secretarial school in London, more for the access it gave her to the Season and its supply of eligible suitors than any ambition to learn shorthand and typing. She was following a traditional path which led to a good marriage and a fulfilling life among her own class as a Lady of the Shires. When Susie was seventeen, she made her début in front of the Queen at a Coming Out ball at Buckingham Palace.

'She was always full of jokes, and she loved organizing everybody and everything,' said her mother, Doreen Wright. 'She was frightfully bossy and all the others teased her about it. But she was brave and full of life.'

An accomplished rider, Susie's sparkling personality made her an eye-catching addition to the hunting set of which Ronald Ferguson, a lieutenant in the Life Guards and six years older than Susie, was an enthusiastic member. He fell madly in love with her. Both the Fergusons and the Wrights were of Irish descent, and when Ronald set his heart upon Susie he lived up to his Gaelic surname, which translates as 'forceful and vigorous man'. But he was romantic as well or he would never have got anywhere with the very particular Susie. Ronald proposed, Susie accepted.

'I knew Major Ferguson's mother Marian very well,' said Doreen Wright. 'We were all pleased and very happy.' After a six-month engagement, the couple were married in January 1956, while the bride was still a teenager. The wedding was an elegant society affair at St Margaret's Church, only a few steps across a strip of lawn from Westminster Abbey. Debonair in a morning suit and 6 ft 2 in tall, Ronald cut a striking figure as he posed with his bride on the lawn, his shiny red hair slicked back in the manner of the matinée idol of the period. The reception was at Claridge's, a hotel the Ferguson family got to know extremely well through birthday treats and not a few traumas.

Comfortably off but not exactly rich, the newly-weds moved into Lowood House, a grand Edwardian residence set in spacious wooded grounds three miles from Sunninghill Park in Berkshire. Like their gentrified neighbours, the Fergusons lived in enviable style. Servants helped with the domestic duties, and a groom tended the horses which were more essential to their status than any mere motor vehicle. There were invitations, through hunting and polo, to Sandringham to join the Queen and Prince Philip at riding and shooting parties. This was the era of Harold 'Supermac' Macmillan, whose election slogan 'You've never had it so good,' inspired the forerunners of the ultimate upwardly mobile credo, Thatcherism. The Iron Lady herself, like Susie a Grantham girl, was elected to Parliament as MP for Finchley for the first time in the same month Susie gave birth to Sarah.

Sarah Margaret Ferguson arrived without much fuss at the Welbeck Nursing Home in Marylebone, London, at 9.03 a.m. on 15 October 1959. Susie had brought home her first daughter Jane from the same private clinic two years earlier, and the first-born regarded the new arrival with sisterly curiosity. They were best friends from the start, a bond which survived the turmoil of the next thirty years. 'They always got on very well,' said one of the sisters' first au pairs. 'Sometimes they would quarrel over toys and Sarah would cry – but she usually got her own way.'

One of Sarah's favourite pictures from her childhood album showed her as a precocious six year old posing in front of a rocking horse she and

Jane loved to ride even after they were old enough to saddle up their real ponies. Sarah was wearing a white trimmed dressing-gown, her eyes raised appealingly, a mischievous smile playing on her lips. The famous golden-red curls she inherited from Ronald had been cropped short in an unsuccessful attempt to make them more manageable. Friends noted an obvious physical similarity between the child Sarah and Little Orphan Annie, but there was a touch of Shirley Temple as well: the unmistake-able aura of a little actress playing to a make-believe audience, too young to fear the camera that was to make her so miserable in later life and yet confident enough to express her already outgoing personality.

'I called her My Little Redhair,' said the au pair, Ritva Risu. 'I still think of her as a little girl full of smiles and red hair. She was so energetic and had a great sense of humour.' Sarah's natural ebullience came from her mother, as did the restless, questing side of her character that would cause her – and others – so much emotional pain. She showed a mind of her own even when it came to the serious business of coming to terms with her Maker at an early age. 'Her parents could never get her to say, "Thank you, God" after dinner,' continued the au pair. 'Instead she would always say "Thank you, God, for my good strawberries," ' Sarah liked to do things her own way from the start.

When he wasn't serving abroad with the Life Guards or mixing with Susie on the cocktail circuit, Ronald shone as a player at the Guards Polo Club whose home base was Smith's Lawn. Prince Philip was in his prime as a player, and the Queen and her children often came down from Windsor Castle to watch him compete. As a chubby child with a determination to hold her own, Sarah joined the other children, Prince Andrew included, between chukkas to stamp down divots the flying hooves had dug up on the playing field. His early assessment, it was said, was that she was a tomboy worthy of the name.

Horse-riding was bred into Sarah's bones. She could ride almost before she could walk, and as soon as she was eligible she trotted off to the Garth and South Berkshire Pony Club on a Shetland called Peanuts. She was highly competitive, a born achiever in a sport that required a high degree of risk-taking. She took plenty of tumbles but, unlike Andrew who disliked riding for precisely that reason, she never gave up. If she fell off or if her pony refused at one of the fences at a gymkhana, she rarely cried. When they came, her tears were of frustration and not self-pity. Harvey Smith, the abrasive Yorkshireman, was her equestrian hero.

Her devil-may-care attitude worked equally well with skiing; she simply did not know the meaning of fear. When her parents took her to the slopes as a four year old, she braved the falls without complaint and quickly mastered the skills which made her an intrepid downhill racer at Klosters and Verbier in Switzerland. 'She is a great technical skier,' said Bruno Sprechner, a long-time ski-guide at Klosters, who knew both Sarah and Princess Diana.

It was Diana's family, the Spencers, who provided dinner tables far from their native Norfolk with the juiciest aristocratic scandal for years during April 1969, when her father Viscount Johnny Althorp divorced her mother Viscountess Frances Althorp over her admitted adultery with Peter Shand Kydd at Queen's Gate in South Kensington two years earlier. Frances lost custody of her four children, including seven-year-old Diana. That year, the Ferguson family moved from Berkshire to more rural Hampshire when Sarah was ten after her grandfather, Colonel Ferguson, died of leukaemia and bequeathed Dummer Down Farm to Ronald, his only surviving son. It was an event which would bring the unspoiled village a pre-eminence its three hundred souls would never have thought possible.

The farm grazed Friesian cattle and a flock of sheep on its 876 acres of prime land and stabled horses in its yard. In a very practical sense, Sarah became a country girl who invariably preferred a pair of jeans to the more ladylike clothes her father wanted her to wear. Ronald resigned from the Life Guards as an honorary major, accepted a captain's pension from the army and began the demanding and often unrewarding life of owning a farm while still competing with the 'big boys' on polo pitches around the country. His mother Marian, a spirited woman whom Sarah adored, became Lady Elmhirst after she married Air Marshal Sir Thomas Elmhirst and moved into a bungalow on the farm.

Sarah, who first experienced school life at Mrs Laytham's kindergarten 'for children of the gentry', now went to Daneshill in the town of Old Basing, not far from Dummer, and there, as well as developing her sporting skills, she acquired the inevitable nickname, Fergie. It had belonged to Grandfather Andrew Ferguson before her, and he had started using it. Her close friends at Daneshill, Louise 'Lulu' Blacker, now Mrs Edward Hutley, and Clare Steel, later Clare Wentworth-Stanley, called her Ginge.

A cheekily freckle-faced young girl, Sarah was surrounded by people who loved her – and people she loved in return. She had her own horse and her own pet labrador which Susie had given her as a puppy.

Her mother seemed to be everywhere, driving her to gymkhanas, chatting to her friends and mixing easily with their parents, tending the garden, supervising the housework, organizing birthday parties and Christmas celebrations. She was more like a warm and precious friend who had grown more beautiful with time than a figure of maternal respect; always reliable, always the centre of Sarah's world. The most commonplace of domestic mishaps, however, was about to tear Sarah's life apart. Her parents' marriage was, like that of Diana's parents, failing irretrievably, and, also like Diana, Sarah would carry the scars of the next three painful years well into adulthood.

Whatever the initial causes, the break-up started after Susie met the Argentinian polo player Hector Barrantes, who was recovering from a personal tragedy. They met initially on the polo circuit, but it was during a summer holiday in 1972, to which Barrantes had also been invited, at the Villa Petra on the Greek island of Corfu that it became a serious affair. Barrantes, a ruggedly handsome man with a Kirk Douglas dimple in his chin, had lost his pregnant wife Luisa in a car crash near Buenos Aires. The death of his wife and unborn child had devastated the big man, El Gordo as he was called, 'a great bear of a man who used polo sticks like telegraph poles', according to his patron Lord Vestey, the beef baron who brought him to England to play polo at Stowell Park in 1967.

Nor was the crash the only tragedy in his life. To make the death of his wife even more heart rending, Luisa had previously given birth to a son who died soon afterwards. Hector found a willing and sympathetic soulmate in Susie, who had become critically ill after miscarrying her third child some years earlier. Her husband desperately longed for a son which she could no longer conceive after a hysterectomy. Susie and Hector fell in love as they talked, walked on the beach and eventually laughed that summer. From the moment Susie committed herself, she never seriously considered a life without Hector, no matter what price society might make her pay. He made her a complete woman; gave her life a meaning and a passion it had lacked. 'With Hector, I knew real love,' she said simply. Her greatest worry in the early stages was that her lover might change his mind.

'I couldn't help wishing it hadn't happened,' said her mother, Doreen Wright. 'But I have to say that Susie found her *métier* in life.' The neighbours were scandalized. Hector was nothing more than a paid polo player and a foreign one at that. It was the social equivalent of losing one's wife to the gamekeeper. Nor was it an isolated instance. Lord

Vestey's wife Kate ran off with Eduardo Moore, Argentina's best polo player who, like Barrantes, played for his lordship. The Vesteys were reunited, but later divorced. Susie, however, was unshakable despite the pressure put on her over the next few months. If she had fallen out of love with Ronald, Sarah and Jane were still of great importance to her but, stricken though she was with guilt, she had surrendered to a force more powerful than anything she had experienced before. She packed her bags and left home. 'It was a frightful scandal,' said Doreen. 'No one could understand how she could have left the children.'

To minimize the damage, Sarah joined Jane at Hurst Lodge Girls School in Sunningdale as a weekly boarder when she was thirteen. The school had been chosen because it had a reputation as a progressive establishment which made it fulfilling in other than academic ways; ballet and modern dance were among its specialities. Sarah settled in and made friends easily, but she had reached that vulnerable age when she had looked in a mirror and hated what she saw.

'She had such a massive insecurity problem that I used to despair for her sometimes,' said Jilly Adams, a former Hurst Lodge pupil. 'She was a real stunner even then, but she was convinced she was hideous. Fergie was always wailing, "Oh, just look at the state of me. I'm so fat and my bottom's so huge. And I'm so spotty." ' It was no consolation that some of the other pupils came from glamorous families in showbusiness such as Sarah and Emma Forbes, daughters of the film director Bryan Forbes and his actress wife Nanette Newman, and Florence Belmondo, daughter of the French film star Jean-Paul Belmondo. 'The other girls would chatter away about the boys they had met and the ones they fancied,' continued Jilly. 'But Sarah didn't have a boyfriend, and she used to get really down about it. She always used to ask, "What boy would look at me? I'm so ugly." '

Her low self-worth meant that she placed some of the blame for her mother's sudden and traumatic departure firmly and unfairly on herself. Much as the other girls tried to reassure her, Jilly concluded that 'deep down she was really sad and often had a quiet weep at bedtime.'

To compound her sense of isolation, Sarah knew that Jane had fallen in love the previous summer with Alex Makim, a 21-year-old Australian who had been working with the horses at Dummer Down Farm while he improved his polo. Jane was able to unburden her heartache about her parents' marriage and her fears about the future in letters to Alex who, although flattered by her confidences, felt uneasy. Jane, at fifteen, was too young for him. For her part Sarah came to regard Alex Makim as someone she, as well as Jane, could trust and although she infuriated him by humming Donny Osmond's hit song 'Puppy Love' whenever she was at home, she had started to call him 'my Big Bruvva'. As the love affair would later run into the difficulties Alex had anticipated, he could take comfort from the fact that Sarah already regarded him as one of the family.

.   .   .

Sarah, in the words of her former headmistress, Celia Merrick, 'was not a superficial girl and she had a stubborn streak.' This motivated her to make an effort, and she became a team player until her self-confidence had time to grow. 'She was a child who always made the best of everything,' said grandmother Doreen, whom Sarah called Grummy. 'She didn't delve into the separation too much and we tried not to talk about it. Sarah had a very happy life and we tried to make sure it continued in much the same way as before. Between the lot of us, she always had someone there.'

At school, things were looking up. Sarah was made captain of the netball team, and she excelled at tennis and swimming. When the girls watched television, she was not afraid to stand up for her choice of viewing. If *Horse of the Year* was on, she would tune to that channel no matter what arguments it might cause. 'She wasn't top of the class but she was fairly bright,' said Elizabeth Pipe, who shared a dormitory with Sarah. 'She was enthusiastic and everyone treated her like a leader because she was so confident.'

Her friendly attitude, particularly towards younger girls who adored her, saw her elevated to prefect and given responsibility for the first time. She did so well that in her final year, she shared the honour of being appointed head girl with Fenella, daughter of television comedian Ted Rodgers. 'I was so uncontrollable they had to make me head girl so I would start behaving,' joshed Sarah, savouring the kudos of being the naughtiest girl in school. In truth, the job severely tested her sense of loyalty towards her friends.

'She so desperately wanted people to like her and being head girl created problems,' explained Jilly Adams. 'It was a responsible position and she was often called on to bring other girls into line if they misbehaved. But as soon as she had done it, she would rush round and apologize for pulling rank. She was constantly frightened of doing anything that might upset anyone. For example, the school had a swimming pool which was strictly out of bounds after lights-out. There

56

was always a bunch of us who would break the rules. Fergie would go frantic because she really should have reported us. But rather than get in our bad books by telling on us, she would end up diving in too.'

'If there was any fun, Sarah would be in the midst of it,' said Celia Merrick. 'She had a very sunny disposition; enormously cheerful, bubbly and fun-loving.' The head might have modified her opinion had she witnessed one escapade which 'fun-loving' Sarah became involved in with other girls. Just before one harvest festival, fruit and vegetables had been piled high on a big table in the assembly hall as a seasonal reminder of nature's bounty. 'I don't know who started it,' said one culprit, 'but all hell broke loose. Suddenly, there were squashy tomatoes, melons and pears flying all over the place. We all joined in pelting each other with whatever came to hand. At one point, Fergie and I were booting a prize marrow which belonged to a very strict teacher. Luckily, we all came to our senses and cleaned up before we got caught.'

Sarah could also be a considerate friend even if the consequences might be personally harmful. 'I particularly remember her taking a risk once just to help me because I was depressed,' said Jilly Adams, 'I was homesick and wanted to ring my parents. But the phone was out of bounds. Fergie sneaked out when no one was looking, called my folks herself and asked them to phone me. She could have been in serious trouble if she had been caught.'

Back at Dummer Down Farm her father, angry and distraught over his wife's departure, had applied the discipline twenty years of Army life had drilled into him to cope as best he could. He was not only surviving, he did everything in his power to keep the home together for the sake of his daughters. He even learned to cook, and he hired a young nanny, Rosalind Runnell, to help look after his daughters during school holidays and on their weekends at home. 'I went to stay at Dummer one weekend and I remember being woken up at 8 a.m. on the Saturday morning by having the window thrown open,' said Elizabeth Pipe. 'Sarah was a very good rider and we all went to Newbury to watch the horses.'

But it was never the same for Sarah without her mother. Slowly, she learned to cope on her own; fathers simply did not understand necessities in life such as clothes and boyfriends. 'I wish Mummy was here,' she would say. Mothers understood.

Sarah knew that her mother, who had moved into the family's flat in First Street, Chelsea, as a prelude to divorce, no longer loved her father and, that being the case, she reluctantly became resigned to her absence. This acceptance strengthened an already important bond between father and daughter which was to become unbreakable. When- ever she could, she tagged along with him and, to the polo fraternity, she became Ronnie's little girl Sarah. No matter how far Ronald later strayed in his extra-marital adventures, no matter how juicy the scandal, the one person who could not bring herself to judge him was Sarah. He would always remain her beloved 'Dads', the one man who had been there for her as best he could in her hours of greatest emotional need.

The divorce finally went through in the spring of 1974 when Sarah was fifteen and Jane seventeen. 'Sarah was fifteen when I left, fifteen not thirteen,' said Susie, all too aware of the criticisms levelled at her. 'We were very close, and she was totally supportive of what I had decided to do.' Susie and Hector set up the first of their English homes together near Midhurst in Sussex as a stepping stone to their ultimate goal, a ranch high on the pampas where Hector dreamed of breeding his own polo ponies. They were married in the summer of 1975 at Chichester Register Office. If Sarah ever saw Hector as a home- wrecker, she hid it well. It was a measure of her forgiving nature that she could accept the man who was not only her father's arch rival on the polo pitch but the one who had stolen his wife. She grew to trust El Gordo and, as the years passed, to love him for the exceptional human being he was. 'He advised her on many aspects of her life,' said Susie.

To boost his income, Ronald had taken a part-time job as a director of Neilson McCarthy, a public-relations firm based in Mayfair, to advise on polo. Nigel Neilson, one of the partners, was a distinguished World War II veteran who, among other accomplishments, had taken part in the last cavalry charge in warfare when he was serving with the Trans- Jordanian Frontier Force in Palestine. 'The most unpleasant thing about it was seeing the horses shot and dying,' he said. A shared love of horses gave Sarah an easy point of reference when she met Neilson and visited his office in Grosvenor Hill with her father. It was her first experience of the bold, entrepreneurial world in which things rarely happened by chance. When Ronald's exploits at a massage parlour were exposed years later, Neilson gravely doubted that even that was by chance. 'There's no doubt about it – he was set up,' he said.

Sarah also met Bryan Morrison, a rough diamond who brought a touch of East End panache to polo when he joined the Guards Polo Club in the early seventies. 'Sarah was then thirteen and I saw her quite often until she was sixteen or seventeen.' Morrison remarked how 'she stood out because of her hair, obviously, but she was always smiling and always very happy. She was a nice young girl'.

Jane's troubled romance with Alex Makim had given Sarah a chance to prove just that. Major Ron had been furious to discover that the young Australian with the whipcord physique and unreconstituted accent had taken his daughter's virginity. He had just been appointed manager of Prince Charles's polo team, and there was talk that Jane might even marry the heir to the throne. Ronald exiled her to Kenya to stay with Susie's brother Bryan Wright where he hoped she would meet more acceptable young men from her own class. Jane was strictly forbidden to contact Alex, who had returned to his father's sheep and wheat farm near North Star on the remote border of Queensland and New South Wales. Sarah kept the lovers in touch by writing to each of them with news about the other and, in that way, showing that she believed her father's decision was wrong. Her own search for a boy-friend was not bringing the results she wanted. She was a dumpy nine and a half stone, and spots were still a problem. But she was learning to be unselfish.

After much soul-searching, Ronald relented. Finally, he allowed Jane to visit Alex at his homestead, Wilga Warrina, to taste Outback life for herself. Ronald was in the process of falling in love himself with Susan Deptford, a beautiful blonde of twenty-eight he had met through mutual friends during one of his rare social sorties into Chelsea. She was, Sarah and Jane found to their relief, having a smoothing effect on some of their father's rougher edges. If Jane didn't like Australia, Sue reasoned sweetly, she would return home cured of her infatuation. Major Ron grunted and agreed.

Far from unnerving the slim young Jane, the Outback's proud, beer-swilling chauvinism and anti-British sentiment, to say nothing of the heat, flies and snakes, only made her more determined. This was God's Own Country, Godzone in the Strine argot she soon picked up, and a woman's place was definitely in the wrong. Pommy sheilas like Jane Ferguson, with public-school accents and snooty social connections, stood out like sore thumbs. Jane saw the challenge and, with admirable if foolhardy pluck, she accepted it. She lived in Alex's tin-roofed wooden house set among gum trees on the 8000 acres Alex farmed on the dusty red plains. It was, literally, a world away from tiny Dummer Down Farm nestling snugly among willow and oak in green pastures. But Dummer had made a farm girl out of Jane and, when she showed that even the castration of young rams held no fears for her, the locals were impressed. Their engagement was announced in *The Times* on 9 March 1976: Mr William Alexander Makim, son of Mr and Mrs W.

A. Makim of Wilga Warrina, North Star, New South Wales, had become engaged to Jane, daughter of Major Ronald Ferguson of Dummer Down House, Hampshire, and of Senora Wright de Barrantes of Trenque Lauquen, Argentina.

Delighted for her sister, Sarah was a bridesmaid when Jane and Alex were married in All Saints parish church in Dummer on 26 July 1976. Alex was twenty-four and Jane still eighteen, the same age as her mother had been when she married Ronald. By previous arrangement, Sarah caught the bride's bouquet.

Ronald, now engaged to Sue Deptford, organized the wedding breakfast in a marquee on the farmhouse lawn. With Susie and Hector in attendance, the extraordinary Fergusons were, in the wedding pictures at least, united again as one big happy family. Ronald and Hector had sorted out their differences in the most appropriate place, the polo pitch. Hector – handicap seven – had turned out for Lord Vestey's team at Smith's Lawn and, opposing him in the No. 4 position, was Major Ron – handicap five. The game ended in an honourable draw.

It was slightly different for the two Susans. No matter how hard she tried, Sue felt she was being compared with her predecessor, the glamorous Susie. As she and Ronald had delayed their own wedding, she felt slightly uneasy about her position. To her credit, though, she never thought of coming between Ronald and his daughters and she never tried to turn them against their mother. For that, Susie was deeply grateful. Sarah was pleased with just about everything. 'I'm so happy for you, Big Bruvva,' she told Alex. 'I know you and Jane are going to be really happy.'

.   .   .

Sarah had left Hurst Lodge with more than happy memories of swimming nude in the pool at midnight and examining the list of eligible males of her own age, Prince Andrew among them. She passed six O levels in art, English language, English literature, geography, maths and biology. She still, however, did not have a boyfriend, and it played on her mind. Compared with the slim, beautiful Jane, Sarah at sixteen was still plump, but she was learning that personality counted as much as looks. Well, nearly as much.

As the newly-weds headed back to Australia, Sarah made plans of her own to visit her mother in Argentina for the first time. Trenque Lauquen, 300 miles south-west of Buenos Aires, was the location Hector had chosen to start breeding his polo-pony herd in preparation for the ranch he planned to build 60 miles away on the pampas. He and Susie already had 4 stallions, 24 mares and foals and 34 ponies. Hector was buying parcels of richly fertile land for what would become El Pucara, Indian for Fortress, the home he had promised Susie at the end of the earth.

Susie, her hair bleached blonde by the Argentinian sun, was thriving, and any misgivings Sarah might have had about her mother's happiness soon disappeared. She spent six months with the couple and managed to ride off some of the puppy fat that had made her adolescence so miserable. She and Hector talked for hours. 'They confided in each other a lot,' said Susie. 'Hector was a well-rounded person; he was well read, had great common sense and an optimistic view of reality. He knew how to communicate with people.'

Like Jane in the Outback, Sarah showed a willingness to help out with the chores. The gaucho wolf whistles that greeted her ample figure as she galloped across the prairie or bumped into town in Hector's truck did a lot to boost her self-confidence. She was in a mood to celebrate when news reached the ranch that Ronald had married Sue at Chelsea Register Office. Not without testing his new bride's patience to the limit, Ronald had mended the broken home Susie had left behind. It was now a place Sarah could return to confident of finding a loving welcome. She would no longer need to say: 'I wish Mummy was here.' Sue, now secure in her marriage, took great satisfaction in presenting her husband with his first son, Andrew, born on 7 September 1978.

Sarah had moved to London the year before to study shorthand, typing and bookkeeping at The Queen's Secretarial College, South Kensington, for nine months. It was the same route her mother had taken and her priorities were exactly the same. The social whirl of the Queen's Silver Jubilee year, which culminated in Her Majesty and the Duke of Edinburgh riding in a carriage down the Mall to a Thanksgiving service at St Paul's, provided far more appeal than the intricacies of secretarial know-how.

'We were both dunces at shorthand and typing,' said Charlotte Eden, daughter of former Tory MP Lord Eden of Winton, a contemporary who became a good friend. 'We used to sit at the back of the class and giggle.' There was, though, a serious side to the girls' friendship. Like Sarah, Charlotte's mother and father were divorced in 1974 and, coincidentally, her father was also embarking on a second marriage. 'Fergie is very intelligent but, like me, she was never cut out to be a secretary,' said Charlotte. 'We were at the college because we knew it was important to get some sort of training, and we both managed to scrape through the course. So much is talked about Sloane Rangers, but we were practical and knew we had to become working girls. Money was very tight. Fergie was much more likely to be rushing to a corner café for a takeaway hamburger than sipping champagne.'

Her assessment card did not harp on her lowly position at the bottom of the class with Charlotte:

Bright, bouncy redhead. A bit slapdash, but she has initiative and personality which she will well use to her advantage when she gets older. Accepts responsibility happily.

Yet, Sarah still confided her deepest thoughts to Jane, 12,000 miles away in the Outback, and in one letter even asked: 'What's the point of going on?' But she was not a depressive and her mood picked up enormously once she started going out with her first serious boyfriend, Kim Smith-Bingham, six-foot tall and, at two years older, more worldly wise.

They had met briefly when Sarah visited Argentina, where Kim was working on a ranch before starting a job in the City, but it was Kim's sister Laura who brought them together back in London. They hit it off and soon became an item among their Chelsea friends. Sarah invited him home to Dummer Down Farm to meet Ronald, Sue and half-brother Andrew. Towards Kim, Sarah started a loyalty in relationships which followed her into married life. 'She was a one-man woman from the start,' says the well-placed royal source. 'When she fell in love, she fell very deeply and wasn't unfaithful.'

Kim saw things differently. 'We were too young for people to have thought of us as a long-term couple,' he said when it was time to rewind the video. Ronald must have picked up on this hesitance from the beginning because he was soon urging Sarah to accompany him on a visit to see Jane and Alex in Australia. It was an experience Sarah would remember for years, and not all that fondly when the time came to cut off her Big Bruvva.

If Sarah had found her mother's new lifestyle among the Spanish-speaking Argentinians a trifle disconcerting, Jane's chosen home, Wilga Warrina, was positively primitive. Like all bushmen, Alex had loved to yarn to Sarah about his rough and ready life in the back-of-beyond and, in the childhood safety of rural Hampshire, it had sounded quaintly romantic. But even Jane's descriptive letters had not fully prepared her for what she was now seeing for herself. The reality was difficult to take in. 'It was a rundown, L-shaped house, just a wooden shack with a patio, and nets to keep out the flies,' said Poppi Smith, who later worked there. 'There were four bedrooms and the house was furnished with plain wood cupboards, tables and chairs. There were just a few family pictures on the walls and a cabinet full of polo trophies. The only carpet was in the living room and that was threadbare.'

There was no air-conditioning to take the sting out of the heat, just enough hot water to draw two baths and the toilet was an outdoors dunny which attracted the snakes Sarah dreaded. There was a hole in the wall of the house where Alex had blasted an intruding black snake with a shotgun. Ronald was thankful to find that the few luxuries included a television set and video recorder. He found reruns of *The Two Ronnies*, even in black and white, a welcome diversion from the monotony of farm life. 'I would break my neck to get into town just to post a letter,' said Sarah.

In typical Outback style, every day began at 6 a.m. with bacon, sausage and eggs, lunch of cold lamb followed at noon and dinner of roast lamb, roast pumpkin and roast potatoes was finished by 9 p.m. Sarah wondered how Jane could bear such a lonely existence. The sisters sometimes rode out through fields of green young wheat to meet Alex for 'smoko', the traditional bushman's break from work, when someone boils a blackened billy if the bushfire risk isn't too high, and cake and scones are not considered too fancy for blokes to eat. Kangaroos crashed out of the scrub, and flocks of pink and white cockatoos screamed overhead. Jane, it seemed to the visitors, was happy. She had settled down to married life and was looking forward to raising a family.

The big event during Sarah's stay was Jane's twenty-first birthday party, which the family celebrated with an open-house party. Three hundred people turned up, some from homesteads hundreds of miles away, 'to crack a few tinnies with Jane's posh rellies from England'. The nearest town, North Star, was twenty miles distant, and Goondiwindi, the nearest big town, even further across the border in Queensland, but it was worth the effort to meet a genuine, dinky-di English officer who knew the Queen. Ronald did not disappoint them. He played some bone-crunching games of polo with the locals at the embryonic North Star Polo Club on their rock-hard pitch. When Sarah eventually left Wilga Warrina for Sydney on her way home, she was asked to write something in the visitor's book. She scribbled: 'Pretty fair dinkum', which translates as 'room for improvement'.

Back in London, Sarah looked for work and spent three months in the office of Flatmates Unlimited, an accommodation-sharing agency in, appropriately, Kangaroo Valley, as Earls Court was known. Then, despite her St Trinian's style introduction, she landed her first steady job with Durden-Smith Communications. 'She was a complete contrast to the other well-groomed applicants, but she was so keen we took her on,' said Neil Durden-Smith. 'We drew the line at her doing blouses up with a safety pin.'

This up-market public relations outfit was situated at the very epicentre of the Sloane Ranger kingdom. Harrods was one way and Harvey Nick's the other. Her salary was £4000, and she could afford to buy the clothes and accessories she really wanted. Out went country denim and in came skirts and jackets, although she sometimes looked completely unco-ordinated as she sailed along Sloane Street on her bicycle.

'She didn't really care what she looked like, and yet when she did get it together she was stunning,' said Christina Dumond, who became Sarah's friend, although she was several years older. 'Even though she was a big-built girl, she would look striking when she dressed up for a party.' One of Sarah's personal trademarks made its first appearance. 'She would put her hair in a big black bow,' said Christina. 'She looked really super.' Their boss, Neil Durden-Smith, was the urbane husband of Judith Chalmers, the television presenter, and his accounts included BMW, Trusthouse Forte and Garrard, the royal jewellers. She rose from a secretary to assistant to Peter Cunard, one of the senior account executives.

She adored the work, which involved carrying the corporate message of her clients to as many people as she could at receptions and presentations. She made friends with television celebrities Sue Lawley, Angela Rippon, Cliff Michelmore and David Jacobs. It was a lively office and the staff liked to enjoy themselves in the less formal setting of local wine bars and bistros. 'We used to go to the Basil Street Wine Bar next door – that was our drinking haunt,' recalled Christina. Sarah liked to drink wine, 'by the bucket; I can't remember if it was white or red. I don't think she cared as long as it was wine. For food, we used the Stockpot, and we lived in Harvey Nichols and sometimes shopped at H.A. Rods. We were all members of the Parrot Club in the Basil Street Hotel. It was for ladies only, and you could leave your shopping there. It got its name because one of the waiters or doormen had a pet parrot and, every time one of these frightfully grand old ladies walked past, it would say, "Go on, give us a bit." We used to pop in there.'

The office was expanding and it was typical of Sarah that she recommended Charlotte Eden, her fellow dunce from secretarial college, for a job. Clare Johnston, daughter of the BBC Radio cricket commentator Brian Johnston, was also one of the bright young things on the staff – as Christina put it: 'Anyone who was anyone was there, my dear. It was a fantastic atmosphere. Once a month, we would have Buck's Fizz and croissants in Neil's office and go through who was doing what and discuss any ideas we could come up with. I used to make sure all the girls were in on time. Some of them would come in late after being on the toot the night before. Sarah was very good – she would come in on time. She didn't gossip and she would never really complain. Occasionally, she would come in to me and say, "God, I need a fag. I'm bloody fed up." But she rarely let anything get her down.'

One thing that annoyed some of the other girls in the office was the number of personal calls Sarah received from friends eager to arrange a roisterous night out or a skiing trip. She was politely ticked off and the calls stopped. Some had been from Lady Diana Spencer, whom Sarah had been bumping into regularly when she motored down to polo in her blue VW at weekends.

They first met at Susie and Hector's home near Cowdray Park after a polo match. Charles and Diana dropped in, Sarah was visiting, and the two young women started talking. The friendship had developed from there. Diana, who was nineteen and worked at a kindergarten in Pimlico, wanted to talk about her none-too-smooth relationship with Prince Charles. In Sarah, she found a confidante who would listen patiently to her problems, then give her the benefit of her advice. The young women would meet for shopping expeditions in Harvey Nicks and discuss tactics for landing the biggest catch in the realm over coffee in the cafeteria. Their girl talk in Knightsbridge as the decade came to a close confirmed Diana as the most influential friend Sarah ever made. Her intervention in Sarah's life had only just begun.

Sarah thrived on her experiences at Durden-Smith Communications, but PR was a cut-throat business beneath its transparent geniality, and she learned some important lessons. Kim Smith-Bingham had moved to Verbier to work in a ski-store and, when Durden-Smith told her he was selling his company, Sarah decided it was time to move on. She was already planning to spend Christmas with her mother in South America and when Sarah asked her, Charlotte jumped at the chance to join the back-packing grand tour. The two friends spent hours poring over maps to plot the most interesting – and cheapest – route and they set off in the autumn of 1980 after Ronald and Sue hosted a cocktail party at the Berkeley Hotel to celebrate Sarah's twenty-first birthday.

Champagne glasses clinked as guests drank a toast to Sarah and wished her Happy Birthday and *bon voyage*. She cried tears of sadness at leaving her workmates behind, but the exciting prospects ahead filled her with a joy she did not bother to contain. Travel and distance meant freedom. Her philosophy of taking life as it came and making the most of it was already firmly ingrained.

.   .   .

El Pucara now existed in more than name alone. Susie and Hector had cleared some of the land and planted saplings which were growing fast in the rich soil. 'We worked like mules,' Susie recalled. 'It was a real fight.' For living quarters, a pre-fabricated wooden chalet had been built as a forerunner to the grand ranch house that would one day stand there. Sarah and Cha, as Sarah called her friend, enjoyed a traditional English Christmas dinner there with all the trimmings, despite the vast distance from home. In fact, the only link with the outside world and a high point of the festive season was a radio phone call from Dummer Down Farm to say that Sue had given birth to her first daughter, Alice. She asked Sarah to be godmother.

As the New Year got under way, the girls shouldered their rucksacks and headed north by bus, sleeping rough and living on burgers or free *tapas* in roadside cantinas on a long journey to the top of the Argentinian spur that juts into Paraguay and Brazil. Here they marvelled at the Iguazu Falls, one of the most spectacular sights in South America. Next stop: Rio de Janeiro. 'The roads were bumpy and the buses were old,' said Charlotte. 'We shared our journey with farmers and chickens, roughing it with very little money. We stayed for days on end on those buses, travelling thousands of miles without even being able to change our clothes.'

Outside Rio, the girls' luck almost deserted them. 'We ran out of money in the middle of nowhere,' Charlotte recalled. 'We simply sat there on our bags, sleeping and waiting for the next bus to come along. I wouldn't do it today – it's far too dangerous.' Safely in Rio, the girls welcomed hot baths, clean clothes and comfortable beds at the home of friends of the Ferguson family. Copacabana, the golden beach of *bosa nova* fame, lost some of its allure when they saw the city's crippling poverty. Homeless urchins who had turned to drugs and crime roamed the streets, one step ahead of the death squads who hunted them for a bounty.

They were glad to fly out of Rio for the United States, where they took a Greyhound bus ride to the ski resort of Squaw Valley overlooking Lake Tahoe in the Rockies. After working as childminders and cleaners in the family chalets until the season ended, Sarah and Charlotte flew to Florida to meet up again with Susie and Hector, who was in great demand as a player at the Palm Beach Polo Club. Sarah was in considerable pain from a skiing accident which had damaged an ankle, and she needed a rest.

As a finale, the girls journeyed to New Orleans to hear the jazz along Bourbon Street in the French Quarter. Hobbling along, Sarah knew it was time to go home. She had been away six months; not only was she missing her father, who listened with some consternation when she regaled him with her adventures, but she was also missing out on the biggest royal event for absolutely yonks. On 5 February 1981, Prince Charles had formally proposed to Lady Diana Spencer in his blue sitting-room at Buckingham Palace. Nineteen days later, their engagement was announced. Diana, her pal from polo, was to be the Princess of Wales.

FOUR

Verbier Bon Vivants

'What do you do about your wives?'

PRINCE CHARLES

Diana had been so sure she was destined to marry Prince Andrew that she kept his photograph beside her bed when she attended the Institut Alpin Videmanette near Gstaad in Switzerland in 1978. 'I'm saving myself for Prince Andrew,' she told more than one person who enquired about her romantic interest in the dashing young man with the open-topped Steinway smile. Sarah, in complete contrast, became a star pupil at what *Tatler* called 'McNally's exclusive Swiss finishing school', a large chalet at Verbier in the shadow of Mont-Gelé. If Switzerland were 'an inferior sort of Scotland', as one nineteenth-century traveller put it, Verbier in the 1980s was a poor relation to the more glamorous ski resorts of Gstaad or St Moritz. Diana's one term at finishing school did little more than improve her intermediate French and skiing. Sarah learned much, much more. Same country, different curriculum.

It was at the holiday home of Grand Prix millionaire Paddy McNally in what was called Chelsea-on-Skis that Sarah completed a very necessary phase of her education: an obstacle course in relationships. McNally had few peers in his knowledge of the subject and, by the time Sarah left three years later, she had graduated with honours.

Sarah had contacted Diana in May 1981, soon after her return from her grand tour of the Americas. Charles's bride had moved into the nursery section at Buckingham Palace to be near him after a brief stay with the Queen Mother in Clarence House. Diana was delighted to have someone who understood the Royal Family to confide in. Buckingham Palace, she admitted, overawed her, not so much because of its size but more the atmosphere which testified to what it really was: the Queen's seat of sovereign power. When Charles was away, she felt cut off. When he was at home, he often dined alone with the Queen. When she ventured out, her companion was her police bodyguard, Paul Officer, whose constant presence annoyed her. Officer had accompanied Prince Charles on many of his foreign trips and had Diana been less resentful and more receptive, he might have told her the Old Wives' Tale.

During an Australian tour, Charles was being driven along a pot-holed Outback road way beyond even the most modest outpost of civilization. Through the shimmering haze, he spotted a group of roadmenders toiling in the century plus heat up ahead on the long, unwinding road. 'Stop here,' Charles ordered the driver. 'I must speak to those men.' Astonished, the chauffeur pulled to a halt and Charles alighted. The roadmenders, in Jackie Howe singlets, cotton shorts and dusty boots, leaned on their picks and shovels as the heir to the throne approached. 'It must be very lonely out here,' Charles said to them. 'What about your wives? What do you do with your wives?'

Waives? The men looked at each other, puzzled by his pronuncia-tion. Then one of them, recognizing Charles, whispered to the others: 'It's the Prince of Wales, ya mugs. He want us to wave to him.' So as a flustered Charles climbed back into his car, the road gang waved their sweaty straw hats and knotted handkerchiefs as he sped off into the distance. Even at this early stage, Diana felt a similar isolation from her husband-to-be. She was needy; she craved affection from him. Charles had learned little from his failed experiments with other women. He could not comfort Diana because he simply did not know how.

A vital page headed How to Relate to Other People had been misread in the instruction manual which Palace courtiers and, later, his beloved Uncle Dickie – the manipulative Lord Louis Mountbatten – referred to in raising the young Charles. Three years before Andrew was born, Charles was enrolled at Hill House International School in Hans Place, Knightsbridge. The infants school had a distinctive uniform of knee breeches and matching jackets but, on his very first day, Charles, 'timid and quiet', was the only child to arrive in a grey overcoat with a black velvet collar.

'My father was the chauffeur who drove him to school in the morning and picked him up in the afternoon,' said one who was raised in the Royal Mews section of Buckingham Palace. 'An equerry or a lady-in-waiting and a detective were always in the car. One day, Charles, who was eight years old, had made a little friend, and he asked if the boy could be given a lift home. He lived not far away in the living quarters at Westminster Abbey. The equerry said no; no one else was allowed into the car under any circumstances. Those were the rules.

'Charles had to drive off, leaving his friend behind on the pavement. My father kept a diary and he recorded the incident because it showed how Charles was being brought up. He felt that the Palace were putting the royal children into two worlds. In one sense, they were letting Charles go out into the real world but he didn't have an equal chance. If anything went slightly wrong, he was grabbed back into the old world. Charles didn't understand what was happening, and my father feared it would lead to difficulties in his life because he was neither one thing nor the other.'

Anne was the first girl Charles had to contend with and she 'bullied him terribly'. 'She used to put sticks between his legs to trip him up,' continued the former Mews resident. 'My father went up to Balmoral to drive the Royal Family and he said that Anne used to lay traps for Charles in the grounds. She was very much the tomboy, a real little goer, very energetic and fearless. Charles was very much the passive one.'

Under the tutelage of the Germanic Lord Mountbatten, Charles learned to bite before he was bitten. His nickname for Diana was Plumpkin, an affectionate albeit unkind reference to her plump cheeks and puppy fat. It hurt Diana more than she let on. She yearned for some quick-witted 'girl talk' to relieve the stress. The sudden and dramatic change in her life had put her nerves even more on edge as the wedding day approached. Sarah was happy to oblige.

The two young women got on so well that Diana asked Sarah if she would be willing to act as one of her ladies-in-waiting once she was carrying out her duties as Princess of Wales. Sarah eagerly agreed. Major Ron, although Charles's polo manager, was surprised. 'You've only known her for a year,' he said to his daughter. But Diana was serious. She short-listed Sarah in the recommendations she put forward to the Queen. Her choice was vetoed on the grounds that Sarah, at twenty-one, was too young and, therefore, presumed to be unsuitable for royal life. Even then, the Windsors had a stand-offish attitude towards Sarah. She was let down gently, though, and greeted Charles with her usual cheerful smile when she went to Smith's Lawn to watch him play in his last polo match as a bachelor, a five-chukka contest between England II and Spain. Later, she and her father were guests at the wedding on 29 July 1981, in St Paul's Cathedral, and when Diana moved into Kensington Palace, one of the first people to whom she gave her private telephone number was Sarah. Diana was clearly determined to keep in touch.

Sarah's own domestic arrangements were more suited to her lowly station. She had moved in with Carolyn Beckwith-Smith at 40 Lavender Gardens, Clapham, just across the river from Chelsea, but south of the border that divides Sloanedom from its less fashionable neighbours. Carolyn was well-connected; her cousin Anne, a solidly reliable woman, had become one of Diana's ladies-in-waiting in Sarah's stead. The two young women got on famously from the start. Carolyn encouraged Sarah to stick to her diet without resorting to any of the unkind digs that usually accompanied such suggestions. She also advised her on the kind of clothes that would most flatter her voluptuous figure. Fashion still was not Sarah's strongest point and, because of her fair skin, she preferred a natural, unmade-up look. She became a much sought-after newcomer on the party scene. The Edwardian house, which Carolyn had bought, provided a perfect sanctuary whenever their social lives became too hectic.

One of her favourite restaurants was the Pasta Express, a friendly trattoria popular with yuppies in Battersea Rise. 'At birthday parties, the waiters dash around banging on saucepans to a tape recording of "Happy Birthday to You",' said one of them. 'One night, the wooden dining chair Sarah was sitting on broke during some riotous celebration or other. The minute she became famous, the restaurant's owner, Mr Bastillo, took it upstairs to his flat, and it now remains there, a cherished possession.'

Money, however, was always in short supply. Sarah went job-hunting and her quest for work led her to *The Times*, whose new proprietor was Rupert Murdoch. Through its columns, she found William Drummond, an art dealer based in Covent Garden who had advertised for a secretarial assistant. Sarah, her office skills more or less intact, provided the organizational back-up Drummond needed for his lone forays into the savagely competitive world of buying and selling paintings. Drummond's one criticism of her was that she spent a lot of time on the telephone. 'It eventually came out that she was a friend of the Princess of Wales and I suddenly realised that many of the phone calls she had were from her,' he said. Diana, who was expecting Prince William, was weak from morning sickness and close proximity to courtiers 'had worn her down and eroded her self-confidence', according to a highly placed royal source. Sarah would drive over to Kensington Palace in her blue Volkswagen to cheer her up. When Diana was well enough, they shopped in Harvey Nick's and took coffee in the cafeteria as before. Sometimes, Diana visited the house in Lavender Gardens.

During that time, to help Diana out Sarah agreed to let Prince Charles escort her to a dinner at the Savoy and to see a performance of *An Evening's Intercourse*, in which Barry Humphries played the Moonee Ponds megastar, Dame Edna Everage, and the drunken cultural attaché, Sir Les Patterson. 'Sarah wasn't allowed to sit next to Charles,' said Christina Dumond. 'She had to sit next to his aide in the front row. "Oh God, Barry spits all over the place and we were showered the whole time," Sarah told me later.'

Sarah left Drummond and started taking part-time jobs because she wanted to spend as much time as possible skiing in Verbier. One of the jobs she took was with Christina, who had moved on from Durden-Smith Communications and entered the new world of video-cassette promotions. 'I formed a company called RSVP – Red Star Video Promotions – and Sarah came and joined us,' said Christina.

In faraway Wilga Warrina, Jane kept in touch with Sarah's exciting new life by letter and phone. She now had a toddler of her own for company, a son called Seamus who was born at Goondiwindi Hospital in December 1980. She understood the role Sarah was fulfilling as Diana's soulmate. 'We had the opportunity when we were growing up to see how members of the Royal Family lived,' she said.

Loyalty to her own family, the cornerstone of Sarah's life, was severely tested when the Falklands War broke out in April 1982, and she learned from her mother that Hector Barrantes had enlisted in the Argentinian forces. It wasn't so much that Prince Andrew, a family friend, was taking part in the combat that made it so difficult for her. The hard bit was that the scandal surrounding her mother's desertion came back with renewed spite at a time when it was impossible for Sarah to defend her without seeming to endorse the military junta. Even the fact that Hector never bore arms did not help. Major Ron still had friends serving in the armed forces and, as news of the casualties came in, all the old venom came to the surface.

Sarah's own needs now took precedence. She started spending less time working in London and more time improving her skiing in Verbier, which she had first visited on family holidays. The little resort, perched 5000 ft above sea level on a rocky plateau above Châble in the Val de Bagnes, had developed into a modern skiing centre. 'I went skiing almost every weekend because I worked very hard during the week,' she said. 'Whether I got the ferry and the train to get there, I still did it. Skiing is my dream because I love the mountains. Give me the mountains and I'm happy.'

Her affair with Kim Smith-Bingham was still alive, but if she hoped for a permanent relationship with the curly-haired Old Etonian she was to be disappointed. She stayed in Smith-Bingham's apartment during these trips, but their love of skiing had to compensate for the intimacy that was missing in other, more personal, areas. Smith-Bingham was a near Olympic-class skier and he pushed her to the limit. 'Kim would slide over a precipice and disappear into space, leaving Sarah at the top wailing that she couldn't do it,' recalled a Verbier regular. 'When he got down, he would yell at her to get a move on or she would miss lunch. Fergie would dry her eyes and somehow ski down.'

'I met her on the slopes when she was going out with Kim, who was a friend of mine,' said Nigel Pollitzer, an art-dealing member of the Verbier Set. 'She was a brilliant skier who could go down a mountain with virgin snow on it without faltering. She was a lot of fun and I loved her joke-telling. Sarah was the kindest-hearted person I'd ever met. If anyone was ill, she was the one who looked after them.'

As her father had predicted, her relationship was gradually dissolving into nothing. The denouement came when Sarah arrived to find that Smith-Bingham had been spending time with a new partner, Sarah Worsley, the Duchess of Kent's niece. So, Sarah moved on too. It was Kim who had introduced her to Paddy McNally, the undisputed king of the mountain and, after getting to know him better, Sarah moved into Les Gais Lutins, the Gay Gnomes, the chalet McNally owned jointly with property developer David Elias.

'Fergie pushed herself on to Paddy,' said Diana's tennis-friend, who skied in Verbier for several seasons. 'He wasn't interested in her at first other than for her gaiety and laughter, and the fact that she got people organized. She was licking her wounds after several short-lived friendships with men had gone wrong.'

The Verbier Set were a hard-living bunch whose regulars included Jamie Blandford, heir to the Duke of Marlborough, the Hon. Michael Pearson, heir to Lord Cowdray, the financier John Bentley and Nigel Pollitzer. They made McNally's chalet their base during the winter months of nocturnal frivolity. 'The furniture was functional to cope with people coming and going skiing rather than luxurious,' continued Diana's tennis friend. 'When you sat on a settee, you weren't worried that you might be sitting on something 150 years old. So you could relax, which was in keeping with the mood of Verbier then.'

As Sarah grew more attached to McNally, who did not respond with the same enthusiasm although he was immensely fond of her, she shared her romantic problems with Lulu Blacker, her childhood friend from Daneshill. Lulu, who ran a crèche called the Dawmouse in Fulham, knew plenty about troublesome men. She had the dubious distinction of moving from Blandford, a self-confessed heroin addict, to Bentley, who was estranged from his wife Kitty, daughter of the Marchioness of Bute.

Dai Llewellyn, the playboy brother of Princess Margaret's erst-while paramour Roddy Llewellyn, was another who enjoyed Verbier's uninhibited high life. 'Fergie was quite an ordinary girl then, not terribly attractive,' he remembered. 'She rather suited Paddy, who looks like a little accountant.' Llewellyn introduced Sarah to his then wife Vanessa, a niece of the Duke of Norfolk, at the chalet in 1982. 'I took Vanessa there for a skiing holiday and Fergie, whom I knew, was staying with Paddy,' he said. 'I had to go back to London four days ahead of Vanessa and when she came back she and Fergie were good friends.'

McNally might have looked like an accountant in his spectacles but he had few equals in the art of making money. After stints as a journalist and as a racing manager to Niki Lauda, the Austrian world motor-racing champion, McNally started to exploit an obvious source of revenue. Allsport, his Geneva-based company, sold advertising space on hoard-ings at Grand Prix tracks around the world. The global televising of motor racing meant that corporate sponsors had to pay big money for pole position. McNally had long since abandoned his ambition to drive Formula One cars in favour of watching them increase his fortune with every lap of the circuit they completed.

Paddy McNally had been married to Anne 'Twist' Downing, daughter of a wealthy Monte Carlo racing driver. Her nickname, McNally joked, derived from her ability to get her knickers in a twist. She had style, though. 'Jackie Stewart always gave a party prior to the Geneva Motor Show and I met her at his home in Begnins,' said Diana's tennis friend. 'We were chatting and I asked her what she did. "I mostly go shopping," she replied. As it was a motor-racing party, I asked her what car she drove. "A Miura," she replied. That was quite sensational, a woman who went shopping in one of the most expensive Lamborghinis!'

The couple had two sons, Sean and Rollo, before the marriage ran into trouble and they separated. Anne died of cancer in 1980, leaving McNally a widower with two young boys to raise on his own. He was rarely alone, however. McNally's conquests were legendary but 'his children always came before the girlfriend . . . before anything,' according to Becky Few-Brown, who was in a position to know. He had squired Becky around Verbier before she married Jamie Blandford and became a Marchioness. McNally, to show there were no hard feelings, was best man at their wedding. He was like that.

McNally's success with young women raised questions about the secret of his undoubted sex appeal, apart from the obvious explanation that money was one of the most potent aphrodisiacs known to mankind. Becky was nineteen when she met the mature bon vivant with the thinning hair at a dinner-party in his chalet. 'I didn't notice him as especially attractive or remarkable but then I didn't think like that because Fergie was there', the exquisite young blonde said. 'Everyone says this OLD man Paddy McNally but he's not an old sort of person. I'm not going to say he's wonderfully sexy or anything because he's not.' Like others before her, she found his sense of fun and open-handed generosity just as enchanting. 'You only have to look at the way Paddy has brought those boys up to see how nice he is. I admire the way he's done it.'

McNally was forty-five when he started his affair with Sarah, twenty-two years her senior and old enough to be her father. When he met McNally, Ronald Ferguson decided it was best not to interfere; the relationship would run its course if Sarah were left alone to make her own decisions. There were frequent separations. McNally's business interests took him around the world, so much so that Sarah was often packing and unpacking her bags on the same day to keep up with him. Longed-for hellos were rapidly followed by abrupt goodbyes.

Sarah had learned from the efforts her stepmother Sue had made to get close to her and Jane, and she doted on McNally's sons without trying to monopolize them. She tried to cook their favourite meals, steak and kidney pie for McNally, sausage and mash for the boys. McNally's protestations that he had no intention of remarrying did nothing to deter her. 'She was totally besotted and in love with Paddy McNally,' said the highly placed royal source. 'She was never free with her favours.'

McNally teased her good-naturedly about her weight, but he also coached her on the slopes until, the tail of her home-made Davy Crockett hat flying behind, she was more than a match for many of the men on the most demanding black runs. 'She was a very competent skier, fast and furious,' commented Diana's tennis friend. 'In those days, she tended to ski outside her limit, which is when the adrenalin starts running. It gives you a high which some people might find orgasmic.'

Sarah called McNally 'Toad', after Mr Toad in Kenneth Grahame's classic *The Wind in the Willows*, and gave him a sweater with a toad motif on the front as a present. Unlike his namesake, McNally had no need to boast about his accomplishments. 'He bought the chalet in the seventies when he was climbing up in the world of motor racing,' continued Diana's tennis friend. 'He had people like Jackie Stewart, a good friend, to stay. He spent his money discreetly – he wasn't at all flamboyant. But some of the people in Verbier then belonged to a very louche, pseudo world.'

'Paddy is a great talker,' an admiring friend told *Tatler* when the magazine decided to investigate the McNally phenomenon. 'He really, *really* can charm the hind legs off a donkey.'

Dai Llewellyn begged to differ. 'His language is very limited,' he said. 'He calls everybody wanker.' This was probably justified, considering some of the people who tried to hang on to McNally's coat-tails. His favourite watering hole was the Farm Club, an expensive though not very up-market disco, where King Toad held court in a reserved alcove at a wooden table laden with bottles of Russian vodka. Acceptance into the inner circle was by invitation only. The social cachet it carried in this alpine enclave of Sloanedom was enormous. Well-endowed young chalet girls gravitated towards McNally's table, eager for some of the magic to rub off on them. Some of the prettiest, most personable girls were invited back to the Castle, as McNally's place was called, for a meal or a party. Gatecrashers and drug pushers were told bluntly to get lost. 'McNally was quite a big spender so he had a helluva lot of hangers-on to contend with,' recalled one who partied at the Castle.

Inevitably, drugs both hard and soft had made their appearance on the Verbier scene. *Habitués* retailed the story of an unsuspecting newcomer who carried a frozen chicken through customs at Geneva Airport which, when it was broken open at the chalet she was staying in, contained a large quantity of cocaine. Unknown to its owners, drug addicts played pharmacy at the Farm Club with a variety of narcotics and stimulants. McNally was aware of the danger, but it was difficult to avoid. 'I have a strict house rule that no one who has anything to do with drugs is allowed to stay with me,' he said after a newspaper alleged that 'high society swingers took part in one long party of sex, drugs and blue movies' at his chalet. The discredited informant, a convicted drug addict, had worked briefly for McNally in 1981 before he sacked her 'for obvious reasons'. He sued for libel and won. Snow bunnies of one kind or another were one of the hazards of the slopes.

'It was all quite innocent in the seventies,' said Diana's tennis friend. 'The odd marijuana ciggie might be handed around in the chalets, but it wasn't regarded as naughty or bad. It was an accepted way of life. Then, in the eighties, the Americans started coming over to work for a few months, and they brought in hard drugs.'

It was on a visit to the United States after her life had been changed forever that Sarah spoke openly about her personal contact with the drug menace. 'A lot of my friends have been alcoholics and drug addicts', she said. 'It is important that we all stand together. I think this is the way to open our eyes to this problem.' Jamie Blandford was jailed and twice appeared in court on drug charges. Lulu Blacker confessed that she had taken 'all kinds of drugs' when she dated Blandford.

Whenever McNally flirted with attractive newcomers, Sarah, at first, would storm out in a rage and burst into tears. She once unceremoniously dumped a bucket of iced water over his head to cool his ardour. Gradually, she became adept at shutting out aspiring rivals. 'I'm Sarah,' she would tell them, drawing herself up to her full 5 ft 8 in, 'I'm Paddy's girlfriend.' Looking more vampish than sophisticated in skin-tight black leather trousers and high heels, she made sure the interloper got the message. She drank vodka, smoked Marlboro cigarettes and joined in the often waspish conversation until it was dawn. Verbier could be vicious.

'Sarah became used to a bit of heavy, sharp banter across the table,' said one who took part. 'It was fast teasing, and she was no slouch at it.' Her exploits added to her popular image as a 'carefree fun-lover' who liked nothing better than to indulge in cream-bun fights. A picture taken at that time showed her riding a go-kart in a mini skirt so short it exposed her underwear. Someone had written across the print: 'Smile if you're wearing clean knickers.' Sarah smiled broadly.

Contact with some of the more cosmopolitan Americans, though, had given her a new philosophy to enjoy her freedom while she could, to become more laid-back about things. It was an important influence in her life and one that would return when her liberties became more restricted. When things got too much for her, she would sit for hours, taking in the sheer majestic beauty of the mountainous panorama around her. The size and solidity of the Alps gave her a spiritual strength; people might come and go, but mountains were for ever. They could not let you down.

'She could have gone on like this for years – hanging around the chalets and skiing all day,' said Diana's tennis friend. 'Some of the slopes are even skiable in summer. She could still be doing it. That's one reason she couldn't cope with the Royal Family – she had experienced so much freedom; much more so than anybody else.'

McNally, however, was not only her emotional mentor: he introduced her to Richard Burton, a former racing driver, who gave her the chance of a fulfilling career. Burton, who had quit the sport after being badly burned in a pile-up, ran a fine-art publishing house, BCK Graphic Arts, out of Geneva. He was on the look-out for an intelligent self-starter who would set up an office in London and bring in prestigious coffee-table books under his imprint. Sarah jumped at the chance to be her own boss. She could still regard herself as Paddy's girlfriend, but she would be able to exploit her freedom on her own terms. Excitedly, she found premises on the fourth floor of a building next to Sotheby's in St George Street, Mayfair, and started work in April 1984. She had kept Lavender Gardens as her London address during her time in Verbier and now she had reclaimed her independence.

Her salary of £20,000 a year meant she could afford shopping expeditions to Fenwicks, Russell & Bromley, Benetton, Laura Ashley and Ralph Lauren. For work, she favoured the Sloane uniform of cardigan, pleated skirt and boots, a shawl tossed around her shoulders in cold weather. She drove a second-hand blue BMW, a gift from her father, and joined Bodys Health Club in the King's Road to work out. Helen Hughes, later Helen Spooner and a friend from her time at Durden-Smith Communications, was running Halcyon Days, a gift shop in Brook Street around the corner from her office. The two met for lunch and played tennis together. Sarah worked hard setting up deals as an acquisitions editor. Like the Sotheby's girls next door, she bought her morning coffee – black, no sugar – from Queen's, an Italian eaterie opposite her office.

'The Sloane Clones used to arrive in ones and twos to get coffee, croissants or Danish pastries,' said a journalist who frequented the place before it became famous and changed its name to the Royal. 'They were great girls; all headscarves, bicycle baskets and shapely ankles, very chatty and fresh as daisies.'

If things were full of promise for Sarah, her sister Jane's life in Australia had reached a tragic turning point. She had become pregnant in 1984 in the hope of providing a sister for Seamus but, after twelve weeks, she suffered a miscarriage. It had always been one of the Jane's deepest fears that she might have inherited her mother's childbearing problem. When she and Alex flew to Florida on a polo trip, she conceived again, much to her joy and relief. But she began to have contractions after seven months and, desperately concerned, Alex flew his wife to the best hospital he could find in Sydney. A little girl they named Florida was delivered by Caesarean section, alive but barely able to breathe. The baby's lungs were too unformed to sustain life. Alex had no choice but to tell the hospital staff to take the baby out of the respirator. Jane was pleading for her in the recovery room. A nurse brought her in and Jane cuddled the little girl until she died two hours later.

Carving a living out of the drought-plagued Outback and raising a family in its hostile environment had brought Jane and Alex closer together. Sarah sympathized deeply with her sister's grief, but she wondered how much more pain she could reasonably be expected to bear. Her own relationship with McNally had taught her to deal with her emotions even if the outcome were painful. She raised the question of marriage. McNally held the position he had taken from the start. He loved her, but marriage – to her or anyone else – was not on his agenda. 'Sarah used to say she would love to marry and have children,' recalled Christina Dumond. 'She actually said she would hate to go through a divorce, having been a child in the middle of one. That was her big worry.'

'Basically, Fergie tried to force Paddy down the aisle and he didn't want to know,' said his friend Richard Jefferies. 'Paddy wasn't keen on remarrying and, to put it bluntly, Fergie's demands scared him.'

About this time, Sarah visited one of her favourite art galleries, Lefevre, in Burton Street, Mayfair. 'I've broken off with my boyfriend,' she told a friend who worked there. 'I can't stand my job – can you introduce me to someone?' Had Sarah glanced across the road, she would have seen a plaque commemorating a very special event in British history. She would have been looking directly at her future mother-in-law's birthplace.

McNally's influence had prepared Sarah for what lay ahead. *Tatler*'s conclusion that 'McNally virtually prepared Fergie for marriage' was about to come true in the most spectacular way.

In the spring of 1985, Princess Diana had put Sarah's name forward to the Queen as a guest at Windsor Castle during Royal Ascot, Britain's most fashionable race meeting held at the Queen's own racecourse in the third week of June. Prince Andrew would be on leave from his duties as a lieutenant with HMS *Brazen*'s Lynx helicopter flight at Portland. The omens were encouraging for the delicate manoeuvre Diana had planned so carefully: the aptly named Slip Anchor had won the Derby at Epsom on 5 June.

The coveted invitation duly arrived at Lavender Gardens on the Queen's behalf from Old Etonian Lt.-Col. Blair Stewart-Wilson. When Sarah told McNally, he did not read any particular significance into it. He knew that Diana, now the mother of two young princes, enjoyed Sarah's company and, if she had any designs on Andrew, she had kept them secret from him during their affair. He even volunteered to drive her. McNally was like that. Sarah accepted the offer, packed her bags, and he whisked her the twenty miles along the M4 to Windsor Castle.

Among her little idiosyncrasies, Queen Elizabeth II was known to be uncommonly superstitious about the number thirteen. If there were thirteen guests for dinner, she either tried to even the number up or, if that was impossible, two tables were laid in the royal dining room, one for ten and one for three. Thirteen never sat down at the same table. As McNally's car crunched on to the castle's gravel forecourt, neither Sarah sitting beside him, and certainly not the Queen in her parlour, suspected that in precisely thirteen months' time Sarah would walk down the sceptre'd aisle of Westminster Abbey on the arm of her son Prince Andrew.

FIVE

Peccadilloes of the Playboy Prince

'My life will change drastically now.'

PRINCE ANDREW

G ene Nocon, photographic guru to the stars, never forgot the evening his friendship with Prince Andrew was sealed. It was long before the arrival of Sarah, and it happened the first time Prince Andrew went to his home at Beaconsfield in Buckinghamshire for dinner. The Filipino American was fast establishing his reputation in London's highly competitive photographic world as a particularly fine printer. A detective had brought the Prince to his Photographer's Workshop studio in Covent Garden to meet him and, once the formal introductions had been completed, Andrew produced a camera from the bag he was clutching and disarmingly asked the expert: 'Can you show me how to use this?'

Nocon devoted several weeks to showing the Prince how to operate his expensive equipment to the best advantage and, as a mark of gratitude, he was invited to dinner at Buckingham Palace. 'When I got home that night, my wife Liz was jumping with beans,' said Nocon. She wanted to know what it had been like and I said, "Oh, it was fine, big house, lots of rooms, great dinner." Then we went on holiday and Liz was telling her aunt about my evening at the Palace. She got quite carried away and I heard her saying, "We plan to have him over next week." I thought, Oh really?

'When we got back, I called Prince Andrew up and asked him if he would like to come over for a meal and he said, "Sure, be delighted." Liz got in quite a state. She got the gardeners in and made sure everything was just right. I called him Sir, but it was an informal occasion and I realized what a wonderful person he was. He was so easy to entertain. I just can't say enough about how nice he is.'

The Nocons' home provided the Prince with a bolthole to which he could take his new girlfriends, safe in the knowledge that they would respect his confidence and, equally important, give him an honest opinion on whether or not they might be suitable princess material.

'We had some very interesting people to dine at that house during our friendship with Prince Andrew,' Nocon revealed. 'We were holding a birthday party for him there and, at the last moment, it was switched to the home of one of our other guests, Katie Rabett. Her place happened to be close to Peter Jay's [the former British Ambassador to the United States], which the newspapers had staked out for some reason. When the reporters saw the royal car go past, they followed it to Kate's, and suddenly she was romantically linked with the Prince. If it hadn't been for that fluke, Kate would never have been a name to be reckoned with in any shape or form. It amused the Prince, but he knew it wasn't his job to deny it – or even the Palace Press Office's, for that matter.'

On another occasion, the photographic printer invited the Prince back to Beaconsfield only to discover that a host of mutual friends had gathered in honour of his own birthday, a surprise event which Andrew had helped Liz to set up. 'I had organized a photographic session in London for that particular day and, when it was finished, I called Liz and she said, "Well, why don't you invite him over?" He played along with the game and said, "All right, I'll follow you home." When I got there, this whole mob were shouting, "Happy Birthday" and Andrew had been a party to the whole bloody thing.'

As a young man, Andrew's smile had the ability to light up any room he entered, even some of the gloomier inner sanctums of Buckingham Palace. Those closest to the Queen often noted that if Her Majesty were miserable or unhappy about something, Andrew had only to appear and she would cheer up. Even the mention of his name could make her eyes sparkle and her face soften.

The Queen's reaction proved what had long been suspected: that if the monarch were allowed to show favouritism as a mother, Andrew was certainly the pet among her four children. When the pilot prince had sailed for the South Atlantic in HMS *Invincible* on 5 April, 1982 – three days after General Leopoldo Galtieri's Argentinian forces invaded the Falkland Islands – Her Majesty found herself confronted by the very real prospect that he might be among the casualties of war.

'Prince Andrew is in the navy and I am sure he will fulfil whatever duty he is given,' she said with outward calm. Inside, she was as fearful as any mother with a son in the forty-ship convoy steaming to an uncertain future. *Invincible* was crammed with Harrier jump jets and Sea King helicopters, one of which was Prince Andrew's. Then just twenty-two, he was setting off on a mission that his brother Charles, twelve years his senior, would never have to experience. During his absence, his sister-in-law the Princess of Wales would give birth to her first child, Prince William, and the Queen herself would receive the Pope at Buckingham Palace and entertain President Reagan at Windsor Castle.

For Andrew, those weeks were filled with a heady mixture of excitement and terror. There was no more dangerous job in the entire conflict than that which Andrew was instructed to perform – and it torpedoed suggestions that he might be given preferential treatment. His helicopter was one of the Sea Kings used as a decoy to attract enemy fire. Death in the shape of French-made Exocet missiles came skimming over the horizon at supersonic speeds and headed straight for the Sea Kings.

'The idea is that the Exocet comes in low over the waves and is not supposed to go above a height of 27 feet,' he recalled. 'When the missile is coming at you, you rise quickly above 27 feet and it flies harmlessly underneath . . . in theory. I was frightened, absolutely. Everyone was frightened, I'm almost certain. I think to a large degree if you're not frightened then you make a mistake. It is never more lonely than during the moments when you are lying down on the deck with missiles flying around you and you are on your own.'

He witnessed the damage an Exocet could inflict when he saw

from his helicopter the sinking of the supply ship *Atlantic Conveyor* – a calamity made even more terrible because he knew that the missile was intended for his own ship. 'It was horrific. At the time I saw a 4.5 shell come quite close to us, I saw my ship *Invincible* firing her missiles.'

The Prince's Sea King rescued three of the survivors, but many were killed in the awful ensuing moments. In all 255 Britons died in the conflict and 777 were wounded, so when someone said to the prince following the surrender of the Argentinian forces: 'Bet you wouldn't have missed the experience for the world?' he fixed the questioner with a steely eye and responded:

'I would have avoided it if I could. So would any sane man.' Then he expanded: 'I think when I first came out, people were asking, you know, would I actually stay here until the end. I'm jolly glad I stayed here. I'm jolly glad I came here. I've learned things about myself that I never would have learned anywhere else. There were no favours for me on board because I was a prince. My life will change drastically now.'

If it had been his parents' desire that one of the changes in Prince Andrew would be an end to his obsession for the actress Koo Stark, then they were to be disappointed. No sooner had he returned from the Falklands as a national hero – clutching a rose between his teeth in a gesture of understandable bravado as he strode from his ship – than he whisked Koo off to Les Jolies Eaux, the holiday home of his aunt Princess Margaret on the Caribbean island of Mustique. The Prince and the actress travelled as Mr and Mrs Cambridge and looked, according to a fellow passenger, for all the world like a couple on their honeymoon. For Andrew, however, the holiday did not turn out to be a happy one. Islanders used to entertaining the royals – even the Queen and Prince Philip had visited Les Jolies Eaux – said that he seemed irritable and ill at ease throughout.

'I went up to the house to cook one day when Miss Plough, who always prepared the meals, was unwell,' reported a helpful Mustiquan. 'I told my husband later that I was worried for the Prince. He looked as though he had been crying. His eyes were all puffy and red, and he said sorry to me later for not finishing his meal. He explained that he had not been eating or sleeping very well. I was not surprised. He looked like a man who was wrestling with a great problem rather than a hero who was enjoying the victory we had all heard about.'

Grappling with a problem he certainly was. At night, Andrew sat alone for hours in Princess Margaret's gazebo, looking out across the waters of Gellicaux Bay. As part of the maturing process which had begun in far colder waters with Exocets whistling past his aircraft, the Prince realized that he had to end what his father had bluntly told him was a hopelessly ill-suited relationship. The secret which Andrew had taken to the Falklands was the depth of his total obsession with the diminutive actress two years his senior whom he had then known for just a few months. Their meeting had been arranged by Ricci Burns after Andrew had been told that another girl he wanted to date was unavailable on a particular evening. At sixteen, that girl's mother thought she was too young to go out and paint the town red – even with a prince. Andrew's disappointment was conveyed to Ricci by her live-in lover Charlie Young, Andrew's Gordonstoun comrade-in-arms. Ricci remembered 'a rather nice girl who lived around the corner and who doesn't seem to go out much.'

Koo Stark, however, was free that evening and accompanied the party on their trip to Tramp, the discothèque favoured by film and rock stars in a St James's basement, in sharp contrast to Annabel's, where royals more comfortably rubbed shoulders with high society. From that very first evening together, Andrew was besotted with Koo. His friends said he bombarded her with telephone calls and love notes, even during the Falklands conflict using his precious private moments to write long love letters to her.

Blinded by love for the first time, he would not listen to early warnings that her career ruled her out as a possible wife. She became a frequent guest in his rooms at Buckingham Palace, and at one stage Andrew even planned to take a cottage in the Little Boltons in South Kensington with Koo for what he, much to the concern of his parents and their courtiers, was keen to regard as a trial marriage.

Andrew had always had greater freedom than his elder brother to woo his women at Buckingham Palace. Even as a small boy the Queen had allowed him to play in her private office as she worked on her red boxes. Born ten years after his sister Princess Anne and twelve years after Charles, he was an isolated child until the arrival of Prince Edward four years later.

The Queen had completed more than 4800 engagements in the first ten years of marriage. Following her Coronation in 1953, she could not allow herself to become pregnant. In addition to inheriting all her father's responsibilities at home, she travelled abroad as no monarch before her had, visiting twenty-eight countries. It had been no family into which to introduce new babies; even her son and daughter regarded her as an absentee parent and when she returned from one extensive tour, Prince Charles greeted his mother by shaking her hand – a gesture which would have given any psychiatrist a field day.

The royal duties had taken their toll on the marriage of the Queen and Prince Philip. The Duke of Edinburgh became more and more prickly and travelled extensively without his wife. Even when he was at home, he preferred dining out in Mayfair and Soho to intimate dinners in the private suites at Buckingham Palace. In 1956 he travelled abroad to open the Olympic Games in Melbourne and stayed away for five months during which he toured America, the Falklands and Antarctica. Back home Her Majesty even had to suffer the slings and arrows of an outrageous American columnist who claimed that their marriage had run into particular difficulties as a result of the Duke's friendship with a woman he had met at a party. Matters were not helped when the Duke's friend and companion, his Australian private secretary Michael Parker, found himself obliged to resign when it was discovered that his wife was suing her absent husband for divorce on the grounds of his adultery.

By the end of the fifties, it was clear that the best way to cement this family was to extend it. The Queen and her Prince duly obliged and on 7 August, 1959, Buckingham Palace announced that the Sovereign was pregnant. A line of several hundred cars crawled past the gates of Balmoral Castle where the Queen had just begun her annual Scottish holiday with Prince Philip. Thousands more tourists thronged the streets of Ballater village ten miles away hoping for a glimpse of the royal mother-to-be. Dr George Proctor Middleton, doctor to the Royal Household at Balmoral, paid a routine call on his illustrious patient and pronounced that all was well.

At 2.30 p.m. on Friday, 19 February, 1960, the Queen gave birth to Andrew Albert Christian Edward, the first child born to a reigning British monarch since Victoria had Princess Beatrice in 1857. The delivery took place in the Belgian Suite on the ground floor of Buckingham Palace overlooking the gardens. The brown-haired, blue-eyed baby weighed 7 lb. 3 oz. First news of the safe delivery was telephoned to the Prime Minister, Sir Harold Macmillan, at 10 Downing Street, and he relayed it to the House of Commons which was about to rise for the weekend recess, so a motion for a loyal address of congratulations was deferred until the Monday.

An early caller at Buckingham Palace was the Westminster Registrar Mr William Prince who took with him the red cloth-covered register of births for Westminster South. Prince Philip approved the entry and Mr Prince signed it before issuing the proud father with two forms: an

EC58 enabled the parents to put their baby on the list of a National Health Service doctor for free medical attention, and the RG54B which ensured that the new arrival got the welfare foods – cheap milk and vitamins – to which he was as entitled as any other infant in the land. Prince Andrew's number in the register was 194 and followed that of one Laurence Farrell, whose father was a builder's labourer.

Londoners were notified of the birth in the traditional loud manner – a forty-one gun salute was fired in Hyde Park by the King's Troop, Royal Horse Artillery and another at the Tower of London by the Honourable Artillery Company in the presence of the Beefeaters.

The Prince who was to play such a large part in Sarah's life was subsequently baptized in a thirty-minute ceremony at the Palace by the Archbishop of Canterbury, Dr Fisher. When he asked: 'Who names this child?' it was Princess Alexandra, one of his five sponsors, who supplied his names. The first two of his Christian names came from his grandfathers, Prince Andrew of Greece and Prince Albert, later King George VI. The third and fourth were derived from his great-great-great grandfather, King Christian IX of Denmark – an ancestor the Queen and Prince Philip had in common – and his great-great-grandfather, King Edward VII. After the ceremony during which he was baptized with water from the River Jordan, the seven-week-old Prince, wearing a robe of Honiton lace ordered by Queen Victoria for her children, was passed back to Princess Alexandra, who duly handed him to his nurse, Miss Mabel Anderson.

To the surprise of many, no official photographs were taken and the Prince was not seen in public for the first sixteen months of his life, precipitating a rumour that there might be something wrong with the Queen's new baby. In a bid to counter the gossip, a second nurse, Sister Helen Rowe, gave regular progress reports describing the infant no one was allowed to see as 'simply wonderful in every respect'. The Queen stayed firm in her resolve to shield her new son from public glare, allowing her subjects just a glimpse of him on the balcony of Buckingham Palace after the Trooping the Colour ceremony in June 1961. Even when he had reached the age of six, he was being smuggled to and from a private gymnasium for physical exercise and to an army sports ground where he learned the rules of cricket and football in conditions of great secrecy.

The arrival of Prince Andrew and the Swinging Sixties signalled the promise of new happiness not only for the Queen but also for her sister; on 26 February, the Queen Mother announced the betrothal of

Princess Margaret to the photographer Antony Armstrong-Jones. News of the Princess's love came as a pleasant surprise to a nation which had virtually resigned itself to accepting that she would never marry following the termination forced upon her of her amazing romance with the divorced Group Captain Peter Townsend.

.   .   .

The Queen doted on her new son. She looked forward to days which Mabel 'Mamba' Anderson took off, spending hours with her infant in his nursery. Andrew said that it was his mother not his nanny who taught him to read and how to add up. His early education was officially in the hands of Miss Catherine Peebles, known as Mipsy to the royal children, and he shared a palace schoolroom with several other young pupils. He became the class monitor as his learning progress accelerated rapidly. His parents decided to send him not to Cheam, where Prince Charles had been, but to Heatherdown, a prep school conveniently close to Windsor. The Queen and Prince Philip learned from the mistakes they had made with Charles and Anne. Andrew did not have to endure being put on show for thousands of pairs of eyes to gaze upon. Instead he enjoyed a relative freedom during his first few years.

Being in the spotlight had meant that Charles and Anne had been house-trained virtually from birth. But the same could never be said of Andrew who showed all the hallmarks of being spoiled from a very early age. Just as he was the apple of his mother's eye, he was easily the least popular royal child the servants at Buckingham palace had ever seen. They grew tired of his tantrums and talked of him below stairs as 'the one with the paddy'. He showed respect for no one, enjoyed being addressed as 'Sir' and learned to adopt a condescending tone with those whose livelihood he knew depended on his parents' good grace. He tied together the shoelaces of powerless guardsmen, drove his pedal car at his mother's pet corgis and poured bubble bath into the swimming pool at Windsor Castle.

He frequently pushed the staff too far and when one footman snapped and delivered a blow which sent the young Prince across a room, the Queen accepted that he got no more than he deserved and, to Andrew's chagrin, no punishment was meted out to his assailant. Even the crew of the Royal Yacht *Britannia* were not exempt from his bad behaviour. On one occasion when he was permitted to light the rockets which the vessel traditionally fired as it carried the Royal Family past the Queen Mother's Scottish home, the Castle of Mey, he set them off in rapid succession. Instead of starting a gentle firework display he made it appear as if *Britannia* were a battleship under attack and no one – least of all the Queen Mother – was amused.

From an early age, therefore, Prince Andrew enjoyed all the privileges and pleasures of being a member of Britain's First Family without having to experience any of the drawbacks. He was not required to suffer the early discipline which had been imposed on his elder brother, and the result was to show in his later behaviour when even his doting mother acknowledged that Andrew's angry moods were a problem. During Christmas holidays at Sandringham, he was often out of control to the point of recklessness and other members of the Royal Family, who initially regarded him as high spirited, got around to concluding that he was something of a pain. Prince Charles had always been taught never to sulk for such behaviour would always bring instant rebuke from his father. Not so Andrew who knew perfectly well that tearful eyes and pouted lips usually got him his own way. His truculent manner did, however, earn him a few admirers, not least from some of the girls who moved in royal circles.

During their stays at Sandringham over the New Year period, Andrew and Edward would go to Park House to swim in the pool that Earl Spencer had built there. One of Andrew's poolside admirers was Lady Diana Spencer with whom he also played hide and seek in the corridors at Sandringham. The late Lord Spencer saw that she was much smitten by the chunkiest of the Windsor boys. At that stage she showed no interest in his elder brother, Prince Charles, who was so much older and more interested in her sister, Sarah. Diana's grand-mother Ruth, Lady Fermoy, encouraged Diana to get to know Andrew better. Even at that early stage, Her Ladyship harboured the ambition that when Andrew became the Duke of York, Diana would be his Duchess. In anticipation of such a great day, Diana became known to her young friends, who knew that she kept his photograph in her locket, as 'Duchess'. One New Year's Eve, Andrew plucked up the courage and kissed her under the mistletoe.

A problem arose when it came time for eight-year-old Andrew to mix with ordinary boys of his own age. There just weren't many of them around. So, a chauffeur was despatched to round up three small boys from the Royal Mews to form a Cub Scout pack at Buckingham Palace. When it became obvious from their boredom that their numbers were insufficient and outside interests too limited, the 1st Marylebone Pack, whose members had previously met in Bryanston Square, were obliged to merge with them. The boys of 1st Marylebone were bussed to Buckingham Palace for regular meetings in the gardens in fine weather and the private cinema when it rained. Like the other parents, the Queen and Prince Philip had to provide their son with a uniform costing £3 and from his own pocket money Andrew paid a small weekly subscription. Three years later, a Scout group was conveniently formed at Heatherdown with His Royal Highness among its first members. He wore the regulation uniform of mushroom-coloured trousers, bottle green shirt and a green beret.

From Heatherdown he was dispatched in the footsteps of his elder brother to the somewhat spartan Scottish public school of Gordonstoun – by now co-educational – which had a reputation for turning out well-balanced pupils, although not necessarily brilliant ones. Again, not the most popular pupil with the other boys, he nevertheless reversed that situation with the female pupils. Despite earning a reputation as the Sniggerer because of his never-ending repertoire of blue jokes, Andrew did quite well scholastically and by the end of 1977 passed the last of his six O-level examinations, prompting his headmaster to declare: 'Our philosophy is to give a broad education, but we don't overemphasize the academic at the expense of other activities. Prince Andrew, for instance, enjoys all sports.'

Earlier that year, the school's most celebrated pupil had joined an exchange scheme which took him to Lakewood, an exclusive college in Ontario. Having travelled there as Andrew Cambridge, he learned to camp out in Arctic conditions in snow-bound forests, canoe down a polar river, ice skate and earn from the Canadian media the tag 'six feet of royal sex appeal'.

It was in Canada – at the 1976 Olympics – that Andrew was first romantically smitten. Also sixteen at the time was Sandi Jones, his official hostess at the sailing site. Her father, Colonel Campbell Jones, was director general of the Olympic yachting events. Whether she was teaching him to dance the Bump or they were off the dance floor drinking fruit cup and eating doughnuts, Andrew kept an arm firmly round her waist and the Canadian nation was convinced that it was at last going to have a representative in the Royal Family. Alas, the romance did not blossom although the pair dated several times after that right up to a visit he made to Florida in 1980.

Sandi said that the Prince was just like any teenager on the block: 'He is a real character who always likes to make people laugh. He loves girls. He likes jazz, Elton John, the Eagles and Olivia Newton-John. I guess he is really attractive to women. He really liked to be where there were women, I think because they didn't give him a rough time. When he was at the home of people acting as his guardian in Canada he tended to go into a room where the ladies were, while I went in a room with the men. Whether they were grandmothers or little girls, he always gravitated towards the ladies and was utterly charming to them. He knew they weren't trying to analyse or compete with him. But he always had problems with boys because he felt they were rivals. They refused to accept him for what he was.'

In her heart, Sandi knew that she had lost her Prince when she travelled to Britain in 1978 with her school choir and was invited to the Palace by Andrew who proceeded to introduce her to his latest girlfriend. The girls loved Prince Andrew and his reciprocation of the feeling soon earned him the nickname, Randy Andy. One of the Gordonstoun girls he took home to Windsor Castle was Clio Nathaniels. She gave way gracefully to Julia Guinness, a daughter of the prominent brewer, who later regaled her fellow pupils with the tale of how her tie-less royal date almost got barred from Annabel's. Ever anxious to impress the girls, when he promised to take Julia to dance at Annabel's he was reminded at the door that even his father obeyed the Mayfair club's rule to wear a tie.

Despite his close attention to the girls, Andrew left Gordonstoun in 1979 with a creditable record. He passed all three of his A-level subjects – English, History and Economics/Political Science – sufficient to win an Oxford or Cambridge place if he desired. He had also demonstrated some qualities of leadership as head of his house, Cumming, and of his service, the Air Training Corps. He had learned to fly a plane and won his parachute wings. But Andrew was best remembered at the school for his prowess in sport. He played cricket for the first XI, rugby, tennis and squash and also learned to pilot a glider. Within days of leaving the school, in his capacity as the deputy heir to the throne, he joined his parents on his first major foreign tour. They travelled to Tanzania, Malawi, Botswana and Zambia before he returned to start his Royal Navy career at Dartmouth where he had been accepted for officer training as a £2400-a-year midshipman.

His taste for beauty queens became apparent when in 1979 he pursued a girl whom Dai Llewellyn – not to mention Wimbledon favourite Ilie Nastase and an Arab prince – had also admired, the former Miss United Kingdom, Carolyn Seaward. Carolyn talked too freely to newspapers about their dates and Andrew let it be known that he dropped her for just that reason. She was most notably followed by model Gemma Curry in 1980 and her cousin Kim Deas, another model, the following year.

But it was the arrival of Koo Stark in 1981 that marked a watershed in Andrew's love life. She was among that small band of women to whom Andrew designated a code-name. When the Buckingham Palace switchboard operator or any other servant requested her name, Koo was told to say 'Fiona Campbell'. Palace staff became used to seeing 'Miss Campbell' around the place, and when they moved up to Balmoral for the Royal Family's holiday at the end of summer in 1982, no one was surprised to see the attractive 'Fiona' in attendance, although her appearance at the Queen's dinner table in a gold ra-ra skirt on one occasion did raise a few eyebrows.

One in Her Majesty's service commented: 'We never minded having Koo around, she had no airs and graces and seemed more like one of us than one of them. More importantly, HRH was always more even-tempered when she was around. Her presence seemed to put an end to his tantrums.'

Andrew's shipmates might have preferred it, therefore, had she been with him when he was at sea. One of them recalled that he 'could be like a bear with a sore head when things weren't going his way'. Pressed on what might exacerbate his irritable condition, the sailor added: 'He was particularly unpleasant with any member of the crew who had overindulged during shore leave. He never missed an opportunity to remind people that he did not drink and would not tolerate bad behaviour from those who did. He was particularly intolerant of drunks.'

It was Prince Philip who finally succeeded in convincing Andrew that his romance with Ms Stark was going nowhere. Although he kept in touch with her by telephone for a considerable time thereafter, Andrew accepted that he had to abandon all hope of settling down with his very nice girlfriend, and he embarked on a series of adventures with women who, if no more suitable than Koo, were certainly less likely to leave any permanent scar.

One of these was a former model thirteen years his senior, Vicki Hodge. He conducted an eight-day affair with her when HMS *Invincible* made a stopover in Barbados in March 1983. Baronet's daughter Vicki and two younger friends, Lucy Wisdom and Tracie Lamb, were holidaying on the island when they were invited to a party in the wardroom aboard *Invincible*. Clearly proud of her royal encounter, Vicki later revealed every detail of it – including his admission that Koo had been his first lover, that he was definitely 'in love' with her and that the Queen had 'really liked her'. During a moonlit moment among the scented flowers, Vicki said he revealed to her that his fantasy was 'to dress up as a frog, go to a party, kiss a beautiful girl and then turn into a prince'. When the girl who was finally to replace the truly glamorous Ms Stark in his affections did arrive, His Royal Highness had neither the time nor the inclination to dress up as a frog.

SIX

Gone with the Windsors

'I am not a person to obey meekly.'

SARAH FERGUSON

The moment Miss Sarah Ferguson of Lavender Gardens, London SW11, took her place for luncheon in the State Dining Room at Windsor Castle, seated next to Prince Andrew and under the reassuring eye of the Princess of Wales, a chain of events began to unfold that would ultimately rock the House of Windsor to its foundations.

Andrew had concluded from his many amorous experiences with women that he was the kind of man who had to fall desperately and helplessly in love if his initial infatuation were to lead to a lifelong commitment. 'It is going to come like a lightning bolt and you're going to know it there and then,' he explained. 'The initial catalyst certainly comes like a thunderbolt. Everything comes into place and there's a channel that's opened up.'

Nothing as elemental as that happened to the Prince that day, 20 June 1985, after the Queen's guests had taken drinks in the Green Drawing Room and filed into lunch in their Ascot finery, minus the hats each and every one of them was required to wear. What did happen before the meal had been completed and the royal party, hats correctly in place, had adjourned for the open carriage procession to the racecourse was that he and Sarah had started a long process of identifying just how compatible they might be. A channel had opened up.

As far as Andrew was concerned, Sarah's part in his life until then had been confined to a walk-on role in various little cameos which, even taken together, formed only a tiny segment of the big royal picture in which he was a star performer. She might have been present on these occasions but she was never the One. This was as true at Smith's Lawn in her tomboy days as it was later on at Sandringham where Sarah had been invited but as no one's friend in particular. The nearest they had got to any sort of physical contact was at a house party at Floors Castle, the 128-room Scottish home of Andrew's friends, the Duke and Duchess of Roxburghe, when, blindfolded for a game of hide and seek, she had found him crouching under a table and pinched his bottom. He saw her clearly, perhaps for the first time, through the lens of his viewfinder when he asked her to pose outside the Vanbrugh-designed castle for photographs he was taking for his private collection. He discovered that, shot from certain angles, she was not only photogenic, she was beautiful.

'There are always humble beginnings, it's got to start somewhere,' said Andrew when Sarah was wearing his £25,000 ruby-and-diamond engagement ring, and he had changed his mind about life-altering thunderbolts. 'We were made to sit next door to each other at lunch.'

'Yes,' said Sarah, 'and he made me eat chocolate profiteroles which I didn't want to eat at all. I was on a diet.'

For Andrew, Royal Ascot had been a very welcome interlude between his naval career at Portland, Dorset, and his first official tour of Canada as the Monarch's son. Foremost, he was determined to enjoy his few days off. He told Sarah that he fancied some of the rich chocolate pudding, but he would eat it only if she had some first. Sarah obligingly finished off her portion only to find that Andrew had been joking. He would not touch even a spoonful. Sarah did the only reasonable thing; she whacked him on the shoulder. 'I didn't have it so I got hit,' he said. 'It started from there.' Andrew's little jape had been his rather clumsy way of flirting with Sarah to see if they were on the same wavelength. They were. To show he had meant no harm, he put his arm around the jacket of her cream silk suit, she laughed, and they set off for a splendid day at the races.

The couple were photographed in the Royal Enclosure which, until recent times, had been a no-go area for divorcees like her mother and father. The press, willing as ever to link Andrew's name with any new girl on his arm, printed the pictures but the *cognoscenti* muttered privately that she was not of the usual pin-up variety to be found in the Prince's portfolio. Diana, sitting with them in the Royal Box, had already realized something about Sarah and Andrew that neither saw for themselves. After her experiences of love and marriage among her parents' circle as a child and with the Verbier Set as a young woman, Sarah, at twenty-five, desperately wanted to settle down with a man who loved her for herself. The affair with McNally, although lingering in her life, was heading towards its final pitstop. Andrew, more mature after the Falklands War, but still searching for self-gratification in the arms of beautiful young lovers, was fast reaching the point of departure between his libidinous past and a more responsible future.

It was Diana, her antennae tuned to the sexual politics surrounding her, who read the signs for them as surely as any matchmaker. She decided that not only were they ready for marriage, they were ready for each other. This meant changing the Royal Family's attitude towards Sarah who, like so many of the young women who had grown up on the fringes of their world, was still regarded as a first-rate reserve but never first choice, never the One.

It was a slow process in the weeks that followed Royal Ascot. Diana made the point to the Queen and Prince Charles that Sarah had been invited to Windsor Castle as a single woman in her own right. She should be treated on merit, not typecast as someone's daughter. The Queen, especially, was receptive. Koo Stark had been unacceptable to her, and Andrew's fling with Vicki Hodge had shown beyond any doubt that he was susceptible to the wiles of a sexually exciting adventuress. The boy needed looking after. What Sarah's pedigree might lack in some desirable ways was just about balanced by her single-minded attitude to fidelity. If she could make Randy Andy tear up his little black book of phone numbers and turn towards family life instead, the Queen would not stand in her way.

Sarah had made her entrance at precisely the time things started to go unnervingly awry for the royal who had, until then, filled an intriguing and necessary role in what Prince Charles came to speak of as the royal soap opera. Princess Michael of Kent, the beautiful and somewhat mysterious divorcee who had married the Queen's cousin, Prince Michael, had revelled in the spotlight of her new-found celebrity despite the minor irritation of being labelled Princess Pushy. She gave great value.

Unfortunately, details of an extramarital friendship she was conducting with Ward Hunt, a divorced millionaire from Dallas, Texas, were leaked to the *News of the World*. David Montgomery, the paper's tough and unrepentant editor, discussed the story with his proprietor, Rupert Murdoch, as the two men stood on the balcony of Murdoch's penthouse overlooking Green Park. When the mass-selling Sunday published chapter and verse on the affair, Princess Michael was forced to curb much of her natural exuberance and return to Kensington Palace as a devoted wife and mother. 'It was deliberately put out by someone with Palace connections to disgrace Princess Michael,' said Montgomery. 'It worked a treat. She was completely subdued by the revelation and she's never raised her blonde locks since. She has virtually disappeared into oblivion since that episode.' A vacancy was thus created for an endearingly outrageous, and eminently headlineable, successor. The press did not have far to look nor long to wait for a suitable understudy to start speaking her lines. The audition had lasted most of Sarah's life.

To Andrew, Diana suggested that he should listen to his heart and allow his true feelings to emerge. Andrew, who had seen the girl he kissed under the mistletoe turn into one of his staunchest friends, took careful note of her advice. Then he jetted off to Canada where he engaged in some more flirting, proving once again that, in secular matters, the Royal Family were no less immune to temptation than anyone else. For that reason alone, to submit to the renewed cries to 'let daylight in' upon the magic of monarchy was inadvisable. It would, unavoidably, illuminate some of the darker corners.

Andrew's paternal grandfather, Prince Andrew of Greece, finished his days exiled in Monte Carlo where he took a mistress, drank and played the tables. He died penniless. 'Royal circles are not protected from character defects and never have been,' said the highly placed royal source. 'The late Duke of Kent was a drug addict and a homosexual. I mean, no handsome young man was safe unless the Duke was completely stoned out of his mind and couldn't perform.'

All of Andrew's great uncles on his mother's side, the sons of George V and the indefatigable Queen Mary, suffered from one problem or another. George, the Duke of Kent, was eventually treated for his cocaine addiction and fathered three children. Henry, Duke of Gloucester, however, was an alcoholic thought fit only to be Governor-General of Australia where, it was imagined, his bibulous conduct would go unheeded. Prince John, the youngest son, was an epileptic who lived most of his short life in a cottage on the Sandringham estate, cared for by a nurse. He died, aged fourteen, virtually unmourned. David, the eldest son who became Edward VIII, was addicted to adulterous relationships with other men's wives. When he abdicated the throne to marry, his bride, Wallis Simpson, was a divorcee who had perfected the art of love-making in a Shanghai brothel. The Queen's own father, Bertie, who became George VI, was addicted to the cigarettes which killed him at the relatively early age of fifty-six. He also endured a crippling stammer which he fought all his life to conquer.

Andrew's aunt, Princess Margaret, was a heavy drinker who had been treated for alcoholic hepatitis. Like her father, she was strongly addicted to nicotine. At her best, she was gracious and relaxed; at her worst, insufferable. 'She visited the home of a friend of mine and drank whisky and Malvern water for three and a half hours,' said a lady of letters. 'She used my lighter to light cigarettes one after another. The protocol she insisted upon made me feel very uncomfortable. We all had to stand every time she went to the loo, and no one could leave until she decided it was time to go home. Once she departed, the tension that had built up was so unbearable that the hostess's husband, who had drunk very little, became absolutely paralytic in a matter of minutes.'

'The point I'm making is that it is a misconception to think of royal circles as being non-sexual, or as being protected from life in that respect,' added the highly placed royal source. 'They're just not. Okay, so Sarah had a freedom that Diana only glimpsed in comparison. But let's not forget that Diana had a very free life from the ages of sixteen to nineteen. She was living in her own flat in London and going away practically every weekend with her girlfriends and boyfriends. She wasn't quite as protected as people think. She did get a little glimpse of it herself.'

.　　　.　　　.

When Andrew returned from his sweep through New Brunswick, Nova Scotia and Ontario, he sent flowers and a note to Sarah's home. She accepted an invitation to the ballet at Covent Garden and visited his bachelor quarters at Buckingham Palace for dinner. Wisely, she kept quiet about the moves Andrew was making in her direction. 'The first rule at the beginning of a royal romance is to say nothing to anyone,' stressed Diana's tennis friend. 'It seems to happen instinctively. Girls who are open about their boyfriends suddenly clam up as soon as a royal takes an interest in them.'

It was from a position of some strength that Sarah joined Paddy McNally for a holiday at the villa of Michael Pearson in Ibiza. Some of the Verbier Set were enjoying his summer hospitality as well and they noted that Sarah was no longer under McNally's spell. Her bikini bottom fell off during a high dive into the pool. McNally laughed out loud. Sarah scolded him in no uncertain terms. She rode a bicycle round the pool. It got out of control and she crashed into the pool. McNally did not laugh. For a guest's camera, Sarah, wearing a panama hat and polka-dot sundress, nuzzled up to McNally. When she left Ibiza, however, she was far more liberated than she had been at any time in the past three years.

Back at work, Sarah carried on as though nothing unusual was taking place in her life. She was working on her most challenging project for Richard Burton so far, a book on the Palace of Westminster, which was being written by Sir Robert Cooke, a former Conservative MP who was dedicated to the history of the majestic Gothic pile. She kept in touch with her father's friend Bryan Morrison, whose no-nonsense East End approach to life endeared him to her. 'I took her out to dinner a few times after she had broken up with Paddy McNally,' said Morrison. 'One particular night we were dining in Michael Chow's old Italian restaurant near Harrods. She mentioned to me that she wanted to settle down with a nice young man. She'd run around for years and she wanted a more stable future.'

There were other invitations from Andrew, notably to Floors Castle, scene of the royal bottom-pinching. Jane Roxburghe, the sister of the Duke of Westminster, whose £3500 million fortune made him the wealthiest man in Britain, had already played hostess to another of Andrew's lovers: Koo Stark. As Christmas approached, Sarah's blue BMW, now sporting an owl on its bonnet, a gift from Prince Andrew testifying to her nocturnal lifestyle, was to be seen parked inside the gates of Buckingham Palace. Andrew gave her another, more significant present, a Russian wedding ring in three colours of 24-carat gold, a pre-engagement symbol among Sloanes and their beaux to indicate they were spoken for. Off came the many rings she invariably wore and on went Andrew's pledge of love.

Sarah spent Christmas with Ronald, Sue and the children at Dummer Down Farm. 'By Christmas, I knew she was very happy,' said Sue. 'She came home positively glowing with happiness.' Sue had been desperately fending off the inquisitive with a neat reply: 'If I so much as open my mouth on that subject, I'll be cast as the wicked stepmother'. Ronald, who normally talked openly to the press, would only say that speculation about an engagement was 'premature'.

The Queen invited Sarah to join her family for the traditional New Year break at Sandringham, not as first reserve but as Andrew's very particular girlfriend. Motorists tootling along the public lanes which criss-crossed the Norfolk estate were delighted to catch a glimpse of Andrew, shotgun slung under his arm after a morning's pheasant shooting, strolling hand-in-hand with Sarah, who was decked out in country rig of Barbour jacket, fur-trimmed hat and green wellies.

Having seen her plans proceed so smoothly so far, Diana decided it was time to tip off an expectant public to the fact that Sarah was a royal in-waiting. She had grown skilful at manipulating public opinion through the press during her romance with Charles. Now she gave Sarah the benefit of that experience, plus some fashion advice she had learned the hard way. No one could forget the see-through skirt that Diana, oblivious to the camera's voyeurism, had worn to work one day, nor the noticeably lowered hemline of the royal blue engagement suit. With Andrew's agreement, she invited Sarah to join her and Prince William on a visit to HMS *Brazen*, which was moored in the Pool of London prior to taking part in NATO exercises in the North Sea. Andrew escorted the trio around the 3500-tonne frigate, showed them his helicopter much to William's delight, but failed to kiss Sarah goodbye, much to everyone's disappointment. Once smitten, twice shy.

Still, Diana had made her point. Thanks to her influence, Sarah really looked the part in a smart black and white coatdress worn over a white shirt with pussycat bow, gold and crystal earrings from Butler & Wilson and comfortable but flattering court shoes. Her usually back-combed hair had been coiffeured at Michaeljohn and she had taken particular care with her make-up. She looked poised and elegant. The Russian ring, however, was missing. Sarah had removed the evidence to prevent anyone going even further in their speculation.

By now, the Queen and Prince Charles were convinced that Sarah was the One, and Prince Philip was responding to persuasion. Diana got on well with her father-in-law, noted for his grumpiness in such matters. Sarah accompanied Charles and Diana on another trip which would provide good publicity for her, a skiing holiday at Klosters. The party included Major Hugh Lindsay, the Queen's Equerry, and Jane and Guy Roxburghe. Sarah and Diana posed together in similar blue ski suits, shared a furry white headband, giggled a lot, and Sarah showed her athletic skills by racing Charles down the highly dangerous black Wang run. Diana stuck to the nursery slopes, but in other ways she was a fast learner.

Very cleverly, the Princess of Wales was taking the first steps along a course that would eventually give her a position of great power inside the House of Windsor. Only twenty-four, she had provided Charles with not only one heir but two, which guaranteed her a secure role as a wife and mother, however much she and Charles drifted apart. In some royal circles, she was referred to not as the Princess of Wales, but as the mother of the future King William, the King Mother. She had seen the Queen Mother in action as the royal matriarch, very much spiritual head of the family. Her husband Bertie, George VI, a shy man with a nervous stammer, had never wanted the crown but it was the Queen Mother, then Duchess of York, who persuaded him that history was within his grasp. She had learned a great deal from her mother-in-law Queen Mary, who manipulated her husband George V so successfully that his subjects regarded him as a great and wise monarch. Mary's mother-in-law, Queen Alexandra, was another inspiration for Diana. A strikingly beautiful woman, she maintained a gracious air of quiet calm while all around her knew that King Edward VII was seeing other women.

With Sarah safely tucked up in her chalet, Andrew indulged in some more flirting before *Brazen* sailed north on her six-week tour of duty. To keep everyone guessing, he and two other officers took three stunning girls to a West End show, dined them in a restaurant and Andrew's dancing at Tramp suggested he was very much unattached. This was a necessary diversion. The Palace secretariat needed time to complete the discreet but immensely thorough check it had ordered into Sarah's background. Such vetting was standard practice when an outsider was about to enter the royal ranks. 'It is organized by the Palace secretariat, possibly without the extent of it being known to the monarch,' explained royal author John Parker. 'They're given a wink and a nod and they get on with it.' When George V asked: 'Who is this woman?' about Wallis Simpson, the secret service did an enormous check on her called the China Report which showed that she had been working in a Shanghai brothel in 1924–25. It remained confidential until after her death. The report on Princess Michael revealed to the Queen that her father, Baron von Reibnitz, had been an officer in Hitler's hated SS during World War II, an uncomfortable fact which was unknown to the then Marie-Christine and one which remained a well-kept secret for years.

Sarah had flown to Switzerland just before Christmas to remove all her personal belongings from McNally's chalet in Verbier and his home in Geneva. She was acutely aware of the damage that letters, photographs and the other minutiae of her life could cause if they fell into the wrong hands. She did not know it then but she was already too late.

Sarah arrived back from Klosters to a near riot among photographers at Heathrow, and there were more outside her office in St George Street when she went back to work. From a window high above Maddox Street around the corner, Terence Donovan watched her dash to and from work with cameramen in pursuit. The famous East End photographer had never met Sarah, but from his personal observation he thought she handled the situation brilliantly. It was stressful, though. She lunched with Sir Robert Cooke to discuss progress on his book. Cooke was soldiering on bravely with his work despite the crippling effects of Motor Neurone Disease from which he suffered. Sarah cheered him up, although he was disconcerted when a battery of cameras opened up in his direction as they left the restaurant.

Brazen was in Devonport on 19 February and Andrew was surprised to receive an order to take his helicopter up. When the Hussey, as he called her, was airborne over the frigate, the captain ordered the Royal Standard broken out and a strip of flags signalling HAPPY BIRTHDAY HRH was run up. Jane and Guy Roxburghe had invited him and Sarah to visit sprawling Floors Castle again that weekend, although Sarah had already accepted a prior invitation to stay with Bryan and Greta Morrison at their home near Maidenhead. She knew, however, that they would understand if she cancelled. 'She rang up a few days before and said she had been invited to a house party – a real fun thing,' recalled Morrison. 'We learned subsequently that Prince Andrew was there. We were among the first to know they were getting married.'

Using the alias Miss Anwell, Sarah caught a plane to Newcastle-upon-Tyne and was driven the fifty miles to Floors Castle on the banks of the Tweed near Kelso. Andrew, who had driven from HMS *Brazen* which was docked in Sunderland for a five-day goodwill visit, joined her there. Freezing weather kept the couple indoors most of the time, but they did manage to walk the Duke's dogs in the grounds. Snowfalls had turned the trees a ghostly white and they chased each other through the drifts, throwing snowballs.

The Roxburghes had placed the couple in adjoining bedrooms with four-poster beds. Around midnight Andrew went down on both knees and asked Sarah to marry him. She accepted. 'When you wake up tomorrow morning, you can tell me it's all a huge joke,' she told him. They toasted their betrothal in champagne. Andrew was not joking and he did not change his mind.

Sarah's peace of mind was short-lived. A newspaper story as dangerous in its own way as an avalanche was about to descend on tiny Kelso. Under the headline ANDY GIRL IN COCAINE CASTLE, the *News of the World* splashed allegations about the lifestyle of some of her Verbier friends right across the front page on Sunday, 23 February. The story was based largely on an affidavit sworn by a chalet girl who had worked at McNally's place, nicknamed the Castle. McNally responded immediately. The informant, a drug user, had worked for him for a few weeks in 1981 'before I started going out with Fergie', he said, adding: 'I sacked her for obvious reasons.' He picked up agreed damages of £35,000 from the newspaper.

After lunch on Monday, Andrew dropped Sarah off at Newcastle Airport on his way back to Sunderland. An unmarked police car was waiting to drive her straight to the terminal building to catch her return flight to Gatwick. Plain Miss Anwell got back to Lavender Gardens a much changed young woman, a Windsor-in-the-wings.

· · ·

An official announcement of the engagement had to wait until Andrew got the Queen's consent to marry after Her Majesty returned from a trip to Australasia with the Duke of Edinburgh. Sarah faced some awkward moments in the intervening three weeks. 'I remember coming home from South Africa, my marriage had fallen apart and I called round to see Vanessa and the children,' said Dai Llewellyn. 'Fergie, who is my daughter Arabella's godmother, was there so I just slapped her on the back and said: "Hi ya, how's Paddy?" That was met with deathly silence. I hadn't heard about her and Prince Andrew.'

Neighbours in Lavender Gardens noticed that a green Jaguar was regularly parking outside No. 40. They speculated that the man sitting in it for hours on end might be a private detective on the trail of a philandering husband or perhaps a burglar staking out the premises. When they discovered that he was, in fact, Prince Andrew's bodyguard and that the Prince was visiting Sarah, they were overjoyed for her. The address leaked out and carloads of newsmen joined the watch. Carolyn Beckwith-Smith, who had known about the romance ever since Prince Andrew started telephoning, helped Sarah to dodge the Press by acting as a decoy. 'She was Sarah's closest confidante throughout the court-ship,' commented a friend. 'They worked out a number of tricks to fool everyone. They arranged that when Sarah went in one door she could escape through another to avoid publicity.' If she were cornered, she told reporters: 'I'm just a normal working girl and I've got a job to do.'

Princess Diana, veteran of the Siege of Coleherne Court before her own engagement, stepped in to help. Andrew was on shore leave and she invited them both to spend the night at Kensington Palace. The Prince had finished his spell on HMS *Brazen* and was staying at Buckingham Palace before joining an officer's course at the Royal Naval College in Greenwich. When Sarah did visit the Palace, she parked her car at the tradesman's entrance and, as Diana had done before her, took the service lift up to the second floor.

Andrew saw the Queen at Windsor Castle on Saturday, 15 March, and although he required her consent to marry, it was pretty much a formality. Sarah waited at the Castle until she was invited into the Queen's chambers where the young couple discussed their plans with Her Majesty. With her blessing, the engagement was set for the first practical date, Wednesday, 19 March – the day after the Chancellor, Nigel Lawson, presented his Budget to the House of Commons. It was a very happy Sarah who went out to celebrate with her new fiancé that night. They drove to Beaconsfield, where Andrew's photographic guru Gene Nocon and his wife Liz were holding a small dinner-party in their neo-Georgian home.

'They had just come from Windsor Castle and were very happy,' recalled Penny Thornton, the astrologer, who was one of the guests. 'I had first met Sarah over lunch with Liz Nocon and I'd always liked her. I thought that night she was much, much more attractive than in her photographs. They seemed to show all the podginess, but she wasn't really half as chubby. When you saw that wonderful flame-red hair, there was vibrancy about her, a loveliness. She was a real Scarlett O'Hara. It was stark, staringly obvious that they were very much in love. They were very physically attracted to each other and that always generates a tremendous aura.'

However, Penny knew from Sarah's and Andrew's birth charts, which she had prepared back in January for a book she was writing called *Romancing the Stars*, that the couple were not particularly suited in astrological terms. 'Sarah isn't a typical Libran at all. A woman always works through her Moon sign, and Sarah's Moon is in Aries so her instinctive self is very Arian, very assertive, forthright, impulsive, generous, warm-hearted, but foolhardy. She's a sort of Libran masking as an Aries. Where most people crumble up, she goes into overdrive. She thinks, I've got to make myself liked. She's such a contrast to Princess Diana. They're two totally different people.'

Using the Windsor Castle telephones, the couple rang their closest friends and relations to tell them the news. Her sister Jane was deliriously happy, even more so because she had just given birth to a daughter, Ayesha, an event which wiped away her earlier heartache. Ronald was due to fly out to Australia on the day of the engagement to see his new grand-daughter. Sarah arranged to meet him for lunch at the Causerie in Claridge's. Everyone was sworn to secrecy.

Sarah lunched that day with her future mother-in-law while Andrew attended the All England Badminton Championships at Wembley. The Queen loved to talk about royal weddings on such occasions; a favourite anecdote was how her own bridal bouquet had gone missing at the crucial moment and was eventually found in an airing cupboard. Sarah spent the night at Dummer Down Farm where she was asked on her arrival: 'How did the meeting go?' 'That would be telling, wouldn't it?' she teased. She guarded the Queen's confidences like the Crown Jewels.

With only twenty-four hours to go, Sarah packed her bags and, with the help of her stepmother Sue, loaded up the BMW and drove away from Lavender Gardens. She arrived at her office in St George Street at 10.30 a.m. wearing a French-made cotton pullover decorated with nautical flags. St George Street had become a tourist attraction. Tour operators had been quick to react to the royal romance and had rerouted their buses to show sightseers No. 11, where Prince Andrew's girlfriend worked in the same building as his father's military tailors. Nikons clicked away at the ranks of photographers corralled on the steps of St George's Church, noted for its high-society weddings. Reporters interviewed Sloanes visiting Queen's coffee bar and just about anyone else with something to say on the subject. 'I had been here for five years before this happened,' stressed Remo Costa, Queen's proprietor. 'People got jealous – they thought I was cashing in on the name. So I changed it to the Royal Sandwich and Salad Bar.'

At lunchtime, Sarah and Sue went to the Westbury Hotel around the corner in Conduit Street. When an admirer gave Sarah a dozen red roses, she said: 'I am the last person in the world who needs cheering up today.' Turning to Sue, she added: 'This is my Wicked Stepmother.'

After work, Sarah joined Andrew at Buckingham Palace where

they talked excitedly until bedtime. In the morning she awoke with a slight headache and only picked at the sausages on her breakfast plate. She cheered up at the sight of Denise McAdam, the hairdresser from Michaeljohn who had come to tend her tresses. Her engagement outfit, a blue wool-crêpe suit with a pleated skirt and broad leather belt, had been a rush job for the designer Alistair Blair. She looked fresh and elegant in it, although she was nervous when she met the four accredited Court Correspondents who would interview her and Andrew for radio and television. They came across well as a modern young couple. 'We're good friends – a good team. We're very happy.' They said nothing more than was required but it was enough. After the nerve-racking wait, there was a universal feeling of relief that they were finally getting on with it; that the build-up had not ended in another anti-climax. After the interviews, Sarah and Andrew strolled on to the lawns of Buckingham Palace to pose for a selected band of the photographic profession who had, until so recently, made Sarah's life a misery. 'Could you give Sarah a peck on the cheek?' asked one of them.

'Certainly not,' replied Andrew.

'Oh, why not?' said Sarah, wide-eyed and smiling. They got their picture.

For the official engagement portraits, the couple had chosen Terence Donovan, the genial Cockney son of a lorry driver who had watched the paper chase going on beneath his window. 'It came right out of the blue,' he said. 'I mean, I'd never been asked to photograph royalty before. I found them an extremely pleasant couple – very nice to work with but it was exacting. Not only is one half of the team a photographer himself but he also has that extraordinary eyesight that pilots have which makes you look around a bit more yourself.'

At his home in Barcelona, Richard Jeffries, McNally's friend since they met at the home of film director Roman Polanski in 1974, heard about the engagement on *Buenos Dias*, the Spanish breakfast-television programme. His first reaction was one of surprise, even astonishment. 'When I saw her unbelievable discomfort sitting next to Andrew like a large Cumberland horse giving him the odd nudge and then saying, "Sorry", I realized how painfully embarrassed she is about this whole thing,' Jefferies told a friend at the time. 'It's been engineered largely by Fergie and Diana, who needs company in the circles she keeps.' Jefferies was in the extraordinary position of not only being McNally's friend but also Koo Stark's father-in-law, his son Tim, heir to the Green Shield Stamp fortune, having married her in 1984.

'Fergie is quite a nice chick,' he said. 'We've met several times in the last eighteen months. I had a blind date with her when we went to the theatre in London not that long ago.' Still concerned that Andrew was holding a torch for the young American actress, Sarah had pumped Jefferies about her erstwhile rival for Andrew's love. The reason she had been so inquisitive now became crystal clear, and it was in keeping with Sarah's curiosity about the women in the lives of her loved ones. Jefferies, whose nickname in McNally's jet-set world was the Freak because of his hippie appearance, recalled his first meeting with Sarah.

'I was at a wedding at the Ritz Hotel in London when this jolly redhead bounced up and said, "Hello – are you the Freak? I'm Paddy's girlfriend." ' Sarah proceeded to question him about McNally's wife, Anne. 'It was quite extraordinary,' he said. 'I'd never met the girl before in my life and here she was asking me some highly personal questions about a good friend's children and family.' As he got to know her better, Jefferies warmed to her. 'Fergie is very much her own woman,' he said. 'I know that any man who is with her has a really fantastic girl'.

Soon after Sarah had moved out of Lavender Gardens, men in overalls systematically removed every trace of her presence in Carolyn's home. Anything she had carelessly left behind, or deliberately discarded, was gathered up and placed in an unmarked van parked outside. When the mysterious visitors had departed, Carolyn did not have a single picture of Sarah left to remind her of their time together as bachelor girls. The clean-up was the work of secret-service agents acting on a brief from the Palace. The files on Sarah had, naturally enough, revealed her very open affairs with Kim Smith-Bingham and McNally, but the dossier also contained information about her connections with some of the less squeaky clean members of the Verbier Set. Anything, however tenuous, that might embarrass or compromise her had to be found before it fell into the hands of a blackmailer or someone unscrupulous enough to sell it to the press.

Meticulous as the professionals were, the trail they were following in their mopping-up operation was already lukewarm. Sarah had warned McNally months earlier that she did not trust some of the people turning up at the chalet. Her suspicions were to be proved right. A member of the Verbier Set, motivated more by greed than malice, had stolen pictures showing Sarah in some exceedingly uninhibited moments and hidden them away. 'The person who took them was decidedly broke and looking for a way to make a quick buck,' remarked Diana's tennis friend.

The first of the snaps were published in the *News of the World*; later they turned up splashed across seven pages of *Paris Match* magazine under the headline SARAH: LES PHOTOS SCANDALE. These pictures were the ones taken during Sarah's holiday with McNally in Ibiza the previous summer. One showed Sarah, in panama hat and polka-dot dress, snuggling up to a bare-chested McNally. 'I don't know who's selling the pictures but I'm going to find out,' said McNally, confirming that they had gone missing from a drawer at his chalet in Verbier. The most damaging picture in the stolen set showed Sarah taking a bubble bath, her legs over the side and her hair swept up above her head.

'As Fergie was such a character and had a past, a paper like the *News of the World* was going to investigate her fairly thoroughly,' said David Montgomery. 'There was a huge team involved in Fergie Watching and we got many bits of information about her from a variety of sources. In retrospect, I don't think she made strenuous efforts to cover up things.'

At Easter, the Royal Family met at Windsor Castle for the traditional get-together. Sarah and Andrew attended the service at St George's Chapel, where hundreds of well-wishers stood in the rain for hours just to catch a glimpse of the bride-to-be. She had won over ordinary people, but she was losing touch with some of her old friends.

'I wrote to her when she was getting married and I said, "Sarah, don't let anyone change you. You are so lovely as you are. Don't let anyone remould you," ' said Christina Dumond. 'Her letter of thanks was typewritten, but she had added in her handwriting, "It's great to hear from you. Hugs and love, Sarah." She is just a warm, loving girl.' Other influences, however, were now at work in Sarah's life. 'I think she was made to cut herself off from a lot of people,' continued Christina. 'I think she was told, "Sarah, these are not the sort of people one should be mixing with." We would see her around and I'd say, "Let's meet for lunch next week" and she would say, "Yes." Then, all of a sudden, she was off the scene. It was quicker than that, and it was so hush-hush.'

Not everyone was excluded. With the wedding date set for 23 July and the Lord Chamberlain in charge of the arrangements, Sarah joined Florence Belmondo, her friend from Hurst Lodge, at her father's £300,000 villa on the Caribbean island of Antigua to relax and shed a few pounds. 'Miss Sarah keeps coming into the kitchen to see what we are preparing,' said a maid at the villa. Refusing bacon and eggs, Sarah had fresh fruits for breakfast, light salads and seafood for lunch and fish for dinner. Florence took her to the Admiral Inn for the house speciality, kingfish steaks washed down with chilled Chablis. Sarah swam each day in the villa's 30-foot pool, squeezing into a scarlet bikini which gradually loosened up as the days passed. She needed no better role model than Florence, tanned and slender in a bikini, her raven hair tied back in a long ponytail. As the week-long holiday drew to an end, they took a speedboat ride to uninhabited Bird Island and ate a picnic lunch of smoked salmon and fresh pineapple on a white sandy beach. Revitalized, Sarah braced herself for what was to come.

.   .   .

In choosing her wedding team, Sarah showed that her new independence extended to making decisions no matter what the Palace might think. The four key roles all went to women, a first for a royal wedding team. To make the wedding dress, she chose Lindka Cierach, whom she had met through Carolyn Beckwith-Smith, soon to be Mrs Harry Cotterell. Lindka, born in Africa of Polish-English parentage, had set up a studio in Fulham after studying dressmaking and design at the London College of Fashion. She was starting to make a reputation for herself as the creator of stylish, well-made outfits, including wedding dresses. Her beadwork was exquisite. Sarah spent hours working with her on designs for the wedding dress, which, like so many things associated with her name, would startle the fashion world.

For the head-dress and bouquet, she chose Jane Packer, a 28-year-old florist from Essex who had opened a shop in Marylebone with a £200 overdraft. 'I never dreamed for a moment I would be picked,' she said. She got the job after making up a head-dress of lilies of the valley and blue muscari for Sarah's hair for a Covent Garden gala to celebrate the Queen's sixtieth birthday. A few days later Sarah called her to the Palace to discuss the wedding. 'My idea of a bridal bouquet is that it should not be a solid lump but should flow and bend on the way down the aisle,' she said. Her design included a sprig of myrtle from Osborne House overlooking the Solent at East Cowes on the Isle of Wight, which had been grown from Queen Victoria's wedding posy in 1840.

Sarah's hairdresser was 28-year-old Denise McAdam, the personable young woman whose Edinburgh burr remained intact despite constant exposure to the raucous Sloanespeak of her customers. She had become familiar with the special needs of long tresses and tiaras as hairdresser to Princess Anne. Denise was responsible for the bows and jewelled clips which had graced Sarah's recent hairstyles. Finally, there was cosmetician 35-year-old Teresa Fairminer, who believed that beauty was more than skin deep; she had studied how the body functions and how it reacted to certain cosmetic products. She preferred soft lilac or russet hues to the blue eyeshadow and shocking pink lips favoured in Sloanedom. She was to be Sarah's beautician for the day.

When she got a chance, in between visiting the dressmaker and rehearsals in Westminster Abbey, Sarah invited special guests to lunch with her at Buckingham Palace. One of them was Penny Thornton, the Royal Ballet dancer turned astrologer. 'I had asked her permission if I could interview her and user her astrological profile in my book. We had lunch around a small table near the window in the Sitting Room at Buckingham Palace. Sarah had a very hearty appetite; she really loved food, and we had some white wine. We tucked our way through *crème brûlée* together. It was very nice.' Penny tape-recorded the interview and, when the copy was written, Sarah approved it in writing.

Somehow, she found time to do everything required of her. If anyone questioned her ability to enjoy herself, though, she was about to provide them with some classic high jinks that would remove any doubt. Andrew's choice of venue for his stag party on Tuesday, 15 July, was Aubrey House, a walled mansion in Holland Park, which would keep out not only the press but his bride and her friends whom, he suspected, would not let the night pass as a purely all-male event.

Sarah did, indeed, plan to gatecrash the party, and when Princess Diana met her at Jane Roxburghe's apartment in Belgravia for dinner that was their plan. As arranged, Pamela Stephenson and Elton John's wife Renate turned up dressed as policewomen. Sarah and Diana slipped into the two spare wigs and hired uniforms Pamela had brought and, with Sloaney friend Julia Dodd-Noble in tow, they set off to create some mischief. A reconnaissance of Aubrey House, however, proved that it was impregnable; too many plain-clothed and uniformed police on duty.

Determined that their disguises should not be wasted, they headed for Annabel's. So it was that patrons enjoying the nightclub's Gold Card ambience were treated to the spectacle of Julia Dodd-Noble, in ordinary clothes, fronting up to the bar for a drink with four uniformed policewomen. 'For a moment, it seemed like a police raid,' said Lewis Louis, the club's manager. 'Then guests obviously decided they were kissogram girls. One of the staff told them that one or even two kissogram girls might be all right but four was a bit of an embarrassment. One of the four apologized and promised, "We'll be leaving soon." ' They drank a glass of Buck's Fizz each and, giggling fit to burst, retreated up the stairs and escaped into Berkeley Square.

'The wig was hot and uncomfortable and my feet were killing me –

the shoes were two sizes too small', said Princess Diana. They did, however, manage to get the upper hand. When Andrew drove himself back to Buckingham Palace, he was astonished to be challenged by two policewomen patrolling the gates. Before he could lose his temper, he recognized Sarah and Diana. 'You have to have a laugh sometimes,' said the Princess of Wales.

To honour the engaged couple, Ronald and Sue Ferguson organized a dinner dance for nearly eight hundred, including most of Andrew's family and the visiting Nancy Reagan, in a marquee at Smith's Lawn. It was everything Sarah had ever wanted. Loyal and loving friends by the score; her sister Jane and brother-in-law Alex over from Australia; her two grandmothers, Grummy Wright and Lady Elmhirst; celebrities like Elton John, Billy Connolly and Jackie Stewart; Paddy McNally. All were united under the tented roof to celebrate the forthcoming nuptials. She was, indisputably, the One.

At the height of the festivities, Sarah, in a pink Gina Fratini ballgown, took Paddy McNally by the hand, guided him through the excited throng and introduced him to Prince Andrew. The two men chatted amiably for a few minutes, a diplomatic gesture to quell suggestions that McNally was in Verbier, nursing a broken heart. Nancy Reagan provided the only sour moments in a night that saw the Queen dancing until 2 a.m. and Diana dragging Charles home at an ungodly hour. Never relaxed with the understated security which the Queen insisted upon, Nancy's bodyguards kept well-meaning guests away from her table, and she danced only once, with an obliging Prince Charles. She departed unscathed into the rainswept night in a bullet-proofed Cadillac.

For her coat of arms, Sarah chose a bumble bee, yellow and black like the Ferguson tartan, hovering on top of a Scottish thistle. Scrolled around the Highland motif was the motto *Ex Adversis Felicitas Crescit*. Of all the symbols she might have chosen, Sarah picked one with a peculiar significance to someone marrying into the Royal Family. Napoleon Bonaparte had chosen the bee as his personal emblem for his coronation as Emperor of the French. The similarity with Napoleon did not end there. As a love-struck young soldier, Napoleon had penned an autobiographical story about his first love, a young woman of good family. He called her Eugenie.

Drawing his inspiration from the crest, Ted Hughes, the Poet Laureate – emolument: £70 a year and a crate of wine – composed a song called 'The Honey Bee and the Thistle' in which Prince Andrew whisked his bride away in a helicopter. Fergie's Fizz, a champagne cocktail, was the summer's most refreshing drink at the Queen's Inn at little Dummer.

Sarah realized it was time to get her bearings if she were not to vanish completely into the mists of Fergiana, a mythical, candyfloss land which royal-wedding fever had dreamed up. Her picture was everywhere; one of the best a portrait Prince Andrew had taken of his titian-haired bride to grace the cover of a glossy souvenir programme. Her name was on a million lips.

Not everyone, however, was in awe. Jean Rook, the First Lady of Fleet Street, wrote in the *Daily Express* that she looked like 'an unbrushed red setter struggling to get out of a hand-knitted potato sack'. Elsewhere, the Killer Bimbos dissected every facet of her personality and appearance. She was voted Worst Dressed Woman in the World. Even her biorhythms were compared with Andrew's, and not favourably. Sarah collected her thoughts and sensibly took stock.

'It used to bother me when I read criticisms of me in the newspapers,' she said, choosing wedding-eve profiles broadcast on both ITV and BBC as her platform. 'It was a mistake to read them. Now I have stopped.' Turning to the question of the wedding vows, she said: 'Since he is going to be worshipping, I chose to obey deliberately. Someone is going to have to make the decisions. Let the man take the final decision. But I was thinking of obeying in moral terms as opposed to physically obeying. I am not the sort of woman who is going to meekly trot along behind her husband. I am not a person to obey meekly. When I want to, I will stress a point.'

Her figure, a size sixteen compared with Princess Diana's model-like size ten on her wedding day, did not cause her any concern. 'I do not diet. I do not have a problem. A woman should have a trim waist, a good "up top" and enough down the bottom but not too big – a good womanly figure.' She came across as positive and independent, if a little opinionated which, she admitted, she was.

Steadfast as ever, Ronald Ferguson opened up on the subject of the groom. 'I once described Prince Andrew as a real man, and I admire anybody who is professional in their job. He is a really good professional as a sailor and a helicopter pilot, and he proved himself in the Falklands. He is also an extremely nice man. I wanted my daughter to marry someone she is really in love with. That is exactly how it has turned out.'

Londoners prepared for the Wedding of the Year with their usual high-spirited gusto. Visitors to the capital were welcomed all along the Union-Jack-draped route where bivouacs had been set up for a communal all-night party. One man spray-painted his dog red, white and blue. Before she slipped into bed at Clarence House, the bride, in a pair of well-worn jeans, ventured outside on to the Mall. At first, well-wishers failed to recognize her. Then the whispers turned to disbelieving shouts: 'It's Fergie!' She had not been able to resist the temptation of joining ordinary people on the night before the biggest day of her life.

'We spent the night at the May Fair Hotel and next morning the crowd was fifty-foot thick at the Hyde Park end as we drove down the Mall to the Abbey,' recalled Bryan Morrison. 'We had a sticker for invited guests on the windscreen, and as we drove along there was just this indescribable wave of happiness; thousands of people waving at us and that wonderful feeling of love.'

Only a four-minute walk down a broad strip of richly blue carpet separated Sarah from her appointment with destiny. Her head of long, reddish-golden curls bowed briefly beneath its coronet of roses, lilies of the valley and gardenias. Lifting her chin, she gazed through the long silken veil at what lay ahead. No black run at Verbier or Klosters ever seemed more daunting. Her eyes, bright blue in the sudden sunshine, widened perceptibly. Bracing herself against Ronald's arm, she sensed that he was even more nervous. 'It will be all right, Dads,' she whispered reassuringly.

Outside the West Door, Lindka Cierach adjusted the train and prayed it would sail a straight course. The six bridesmaids and page-boys, including Prince William who, if the monarchy survived long enough, would be crowned king in Westminster Abbey, were placed firmly in line. A trumpet fanfare announced her presence to anyone who might have missed it. The glare from 2000 kilowatts of television lighting blinded her. Around the world, an estimated audience of 500 million was tuned in to watch this much hyped union of the Sloane Ranger and her Playboy Prince. On the NBC network in the United States, Lord Althorp, Princess Diana's brother, had been hired to provide a running commentary.

Suddenly, the deeply joyous strains of Elgar's *Imperial March* washed over the bride, sweeping her along as she took her first steps down the blue carpet. The sepulchral gloom of the Abbey, burial place of kings and queens and once a temple to Apollo, had been transformed into a living theatre of dazzling light and rousing, triumphal sound. The Abbey gold plate glinted like myriad suns, and from every cornice tumbled pink and white ribbons. 'Do you know the way?' Sarah asked her father. He nodded towards the carpet. 'I'm following the blue.'

Every eye fastened on the Dress. 'There will never be another like it,' she had promised them, and no one was going to disagree. Not only her honey bees and his naval anchors, nor their entwined initials, ensured its uniquely personal quality. The Dress had a one-off rarity that was simply Sarah. She had chosen ivory-silk duchess satin for the gown, a tight bodice beneath a deep neckline accentuating her slender waist. The waistline itself dropped to a V, moulding her figure even more flatteringly. The skirt, flat at the front, skimmed her hips to fan out at the sides and back. The sleeves tapered down from bows on her shoulders to pearl-edged points beneath the elbows.

Flowing behind like a white stream cascading from a big, fan-shaped bow was the train, 17 ft 6 in long and glistening with anchors and waves scattered among gleaming hearts. As she sailed slowly past the rows of craning heads, the 1800 guests saw that the whole outfit was scattered with crystals and beads stitched to form her armorial thistles and bees. The bows that had become her trademark were worked in both beads and satin ribbon, and the heraldic letter S was spelled out in more ribbon on the bodice and sleeves. Simply Sarah the bride was simply sensational. 'Not so much a wedding dress, more a statement of intent,' said one fashion writer, sketching frantically as Sarah reached the half-way mark. It was 11.33 a.m. on Wednesday, 23 July 1986, thirteen months since the day it all began at Ascot.

Morning showers had drenched the crowds who camped overnight outside Clarence House to ensure the best vantage-points for a glimpse of the bride. Servants from Buckingham Palace moved among them, serving glasses of champagne from silver trays. Sarah was already awake before her 7 a.m. alarm call came through. At 8.45 a.m. she was ready for a light breakfast after a bath. Then she joined hairdresser Denise McAdam and beautician Teresa Fairminer. At 9 a.m. Lindka Cierach was ushered through a side door to advise on make-up. The rich cream colour of the dress called for only a light touch of cosmetics to set off Sarah's fair complexion. At 9.30 a.m., Denise placed the headdress on top of Sarah's head and arranged the veil. Carefully, the bride began to slip into the ivory satin dress which Lindka had created with the help of eleven other seamstresses. The cost, conservatively, was £25,000.

Her mother Susie, in golden yellow silk, and sister Jane, in a green striped top and a split skirt that revealed her shapely legs, popped in and out to check on the progress.

Across the Mall in Buckingham Palace at 10 a.m. the Queen conferred the title of Duke of York on Prince Andrew, making him the fifteenth holder of the title first granted six centuries ago. Unlike Prince Charles's Duchy of Cornwall, there was no money or estates to go with it, but the Queen had another surprise. As well as creating her son the Earl of Inverness, a traditional honour to go with his Dukedom, she also made him Baron Killyleagh, after the sailing resort in County Down, Northern Ireland, which had ancestral links with Sarah. It was a thoughtful gesture from the Queen to mark Sarah's wedding day.

At 10.36 a.m., the Glass Coach pulled into Clarence House where Ronald Ferguson, in his father's 1921 morning suit, was endeavouring to keep the bridesmaids and page-boys – two of them, Andrew and Alice, his own children – in order. The bridesmaids wore peach silk-taffeta dresses; the pages were dressed as midshipmen or nineteenth-century sailors. 'I am so unbelievably proud, but I think later on I will be very emotional,' he said. 'The thing I'm most looking forward to is seeing the dress.' Ronald had left his topper on a piano at the Sheraton Belgravia where he had spent the night. 'I never intended wearing it anyway,' he added.

At 11 a.m., the Queen left Buckingham Palace at the head of the royal procession. Five minutes later, the new Duke of York, his Falklands medal pinned to the breast of his naval lieutenant's uniform, rode out of the gates with Prince Edward, his supporter, beside him in an open-top carriage.

As he set off, Sarah appeared downstairs in Clarence House to kiss her father, who said tearfully: 'You look so beautiful.' Lindka helped Sarah step into the Glass Coach and arranged the train on the seat opposite her. It took four minutes. Right on time at 11.15 a.m., the gates of Clarence House swung open, and the crowd burst into a rousing chorus of 'Here Comes the Bride' as the coach, escorted by eight Lifeguard troopers, started its journey along the Mall.

Now, in the Abbey, television cameras followed Sarah's glide along the blue carpet as she descended slowly towards Andrew who, turning to peer down the nave, saw her for the first time and broke into his famous grin. 'You look wonderful,' he told her as she hitched up her dress to climb the five steps and join him before the Archbishop of Canterbury, Dr Robert Runcie. 'Thank you, darling,' she whispered.

Four-year-old Prince William, discharged from his duties during the service, fiddled with the strap of his sailor's hat, yawned and poked his tongue at one of the bridesmaids. His mother, seated between Prince Charles and Princess Anne in the gold and pink chairs, coloured visibly at first. Then she did her best to suppress an almighty fit of the famous giggles. Ronald, next to Susie in the bride's front row, looked straight ahead. If they exchanged a single word, it went unrecorded; their own wedding had taken place thirty years ago in St Margaret's next door, and the memories were too painful to revive on this of all days. Nor did Ronald and Hector Barrantes, handsome as ever in the pew behind him, acknowledge each other's existence. The Queen, however, had made a point of inviting Susie and Hector to the Royal Enclosure at Ascot and had taken tea with them in a room off the Royal Box. When Hector visited Smith's Lawn, where he had once struck a ball so hard that it broke the scoreboard clock, Sarah had dashed up to him, kissed him on both cheeks and given him a welcoming hug.

As far as relationships were concerned, some of the guests, Princess Margaret and Lord Snowdon for instance, were already divorced from each other and quite a few more were heading that way. Princess Anne and Mark Phillips, Jane and Alex Makim and Elton and Renate John would all seek freedom from their partners in the divorce courts. Nor were all of the guests going to remain free in the literal sense: the American polo enthusiast Peter Brant, for one, who would receive a prison sentence in America for tax evasion. Sarah and Andrew, though, were nothing if not liberated in their selection. Sarah had invited her two former lovers, Kim Smith-Bingham and Paddy McNally, and if Sandi Jones, the Canadian beauty, were Prince Andrew's only former sweetheart in attendance, no one was saying.

A Thames Television camera mounted on the tomb of a forgotten monarch broadcast close-up pictures of a royal couple making their wedding vows for the first time. Andrew spoke in a loud, clear voice. Then it was Sarah's turn. 'However excited I get, I don't want to fluff it – and I won't because I've worked it out,' she had said. 'It's Andrew ACE, Albert Christian Edward.' When it came to the moment of delivery, she stumbled, repeating the Christian bit twice. Everybody loved her for that tiny slip. When she promised to obey, she stole a sideways glance at Andrew, and he grinned again. The wedding ring of Welsh gold slipped on at the second attempt and, at that moment, she became the Duchess of York. Walking down the aisle on her husband's arm after signing the register and almost forgetting to curtsey to the Queen, Sarah caught McNally's eye. She gave him a cheeky wink. Like the last Duchess of

York, the Queen Mother, the bride arranged for her bouquet to the placed on the Tomb of the Unknown Soldier.

Andrew and Sarah, a royal diamond tiara replacing the flowers in her hair, emerged from the Abbey at 12.29 p.m. to a tumultuous welcome. They beat the rain back to Buckingham Palace in the open-topped 1902 State Landau with minutes to spare.

.   .   .

Andrew had chosen Albert Watson, an unflappable Manhattan-based Scot who had done some of his best work for *Vogue* magazine, to take the formal wedding pictures. Helping him was Gene Nocon, who had drawn up a list of possible photographers to take the engagement and wedding pictures. None of the acknowledged royal photographers like Norman Parkinson, Lord Snowdon or Lord Lichfield was on the list. Andrew had invited Watson, whose portfolio included Sophia Loren, Clint Eastwood and Mick Jagger, to lunch at Buckingham Palace the year before to discuss his work. Watson had told the Prince that he had a good eye for landscapes, advice Andrew had taken to heart in his recent work.

Watson had just twenty-five minutes to take the bride, groom and assorted Royals and Fergusons in a variety of groups, but he lost valuable time while everyone enjoyed a drink before filing into the Throne Room. 'We found all the grown-ups drinking champagne, and the bridesmaids and pages bowling their floral hoops up and down the Queen's Gallery,' he said. Somehow, Watson managed to assemble forty-six of the group but one was missing.: The Queen.

'When I looked round, she was being helped up a ladder by my assistant so she could look through the camera herself.' He used a pushbike hooter to attract attention for each shot. 'I hit upon the horn when I had to photograph a group of fifty rather rowdy stuntmen. I had just forty-five seconds to get the main picture. Tongues had to be in and eyes open, it had to be right first time.' Prince William was the main problem 'His tongue would keep on coming out, which can of course be very appealing, but I was doing official portraits. When we did manage to get them all lined up, the pages would start pulling the bridesmaids' hair. The bicycle horn was most useful. It did the trick.' Watson got his 'piece of history' and the bride and groom headed for the balcony in what was, in the eyes of the 250,000 people who packed the Mall, the high point of the wedding: the Kiss.

As they were about to step on to the balcony, the Queen noticed a deep-red stain on the wedding dress. She bent down to inspect it.

'There's only one solution – someone fetch me some soda water,' she said. The Queen knew all about the cleansing powers of soda water. She kept a soda syphon close at hand to squirt on the carpet of her private sitting room whenever one of the corgis surrendered to a call of nature. A bottle of soda water was produced and, as the Queen was about to pour it over the mark, Alex Makim stepped forward. 'Allow me, Ma'am,' he said, and did it for her. 'Thank you,' said the Queen, 'that was very kind of you. I think we've cleaned it up rather well.'

The crowd started chanting as soon as they saw the newly-weds. 'We want a kiss, we want a kiss,' Sarah pretended she could not hear. The roar increased. At 1.50 p.m., they got their kiss, and the Queen and her immediate family joined Andrew and Sarah on the balcony. Ducking low to keep out of sight of the crowd, Nocon shot some unofficial pictures of his own which he 'just tucked away'.

By now, the arrangements were running half an hour late, and the wedding breakfast for 140 was a sumptuous, if hurried, affair beneath five crystal chandeliers in the State Supper Room. The band of the Irish Guards played 'For Me and My Girl' as they tucked into diced lobster decorated with prawns, egg and tomato. Roast best end of lamb followed, garnished with tomatoes filled with mint-flavoured hollandaise sauce, spinach soufflé with mushrooms, broad beans with butter and new potatoes. The dessert of strawberries and whipped cream was in the shape of the Cross of St George on a base of strawberry fool. The guests drank Piesporter Goldtropfchen Auslese 1978, and Chateau LangoaBarton 1976. They toasted the bride and groom in Bollinger champagne. The liqueur was Graham's 1966 port.

The Duke and Duchess left the Palace in a shower of confetti at 4.20 p.m. in the horse-drawn landau, accompanied by a giant teddy bear swathed in pink and blue ribbons, for their trip to the Royal Hospital, Chelsea. Sarah's going-away outfit was a two-piece green, blue and cream floral-print suit in silk Jacquard crêpe de Chine. She broke with tradition and went hatless. Andrew had changed from his uniform into a less stifling grey lounge suit. A red Wessex helicopter of the Queen's Flight lifted them from the hospital grounds to Heathrow Airport, where they boarded a British Aerospace 146 jet bound for the Azores. Andrew had hoped to keep the honeymoon destination – a trip around the islands in *Britannia* – a secret from his bride, but the news leaked out in Lisbon. There was, however, to be no shortage of surprises for either of them in the hectic months that followed. One of the songs the Irish Guards had played was 'We've Only Just Begun'.

SEVEN

The Galloping Major

'Everybody else was at it, and Major Ron wasn't.'

BRYAN MORRISON

The Very Important People who booked suites at the big hotels on Park Lane for certain men-only affairs liked to make sure everything was done in style. Banqueting menus and wine lists were consulted well in advance, the finest liqueurs assembled in cut-glass decanters, Havana cigars neatly arranged in their humidors, speeches prepared and shoved into breast pockets, obliging madams alerted by telephone.

One such festive black-tie occasion was held at a Mayfair hotel as a stag night before a high-society wedding, and one of the guests was Major Ronald Ivor Ferguson. A retired soldier who had seen service in Aden, Cyprus and Germany during twenty years with the Life Guards, Ronald was hardly a prude. More to the point, his own experiences among the polo set qualified him more as a man of the world than many of those present that evening.

'There were about a dozen men drinking cocktails, laughing and joking when I arrived,' said one of the invited guests. 'We sat down around a big table and the waiters started to serve the first course. Before it was finished, the door opened and a girl of the hostess/prostitute variety appeared. This girl came into the room and another tarty type took her place in the doorway. There were appreciative murmurs from the other guests, and everyone looked at the bridegroom. More and more girls came in until there were at least a dozen, and everyone was clapping and cheering. One of the hookers went under the table and made her way to the groom. There were bedrooms off the dining-room, and some of the men drifted away with the girls before the main course had been eaten.'

Not every one joined in this unexpected bacchanalian interlude. Bryan Morrison, for one. Without making a fuss, he folded his napkin and slipped out through the door of the suite. 'I like women but I don't like brass,' he said. 'I was half-way down the corridor heading for the lift when I heard someone shout my name. It was Major Ron, who said, "Wait for me, Bryan! I can't stand that kind of thing."

'It's a story that should come out because it actually shows the world how wrong they are about Ronnie Ferguson,' said Morrison. He was speaking over lunch at Morton's, the club across Berkeley Square from Annabel's, after another of the Major's more recent peccadilloes had appeared in print. 'It illustrates the fact that he's not the randy bloke everyone thinks he is. Everybody else was at it and he wasn't. I can't mention the other people who were present, but it was a stag night and a lot of VIPs were there.'

There was, however, another establishment not too distant from Park Lane where Ronald did not make his excuses and leave with quite the same resolve. He had been a member of the Wigmore Club at 67 Marylebone Lane, a narrow artery linking Wigmore and Hinde Streets in the West End, for years. To Westminster City Council, the Wigmore was a registered sauna and massage parlour catering for a select clientele of parliamentarians, sportsmen, actors, film directors and businessmen.

'It was a very nice massage parlour with bloody good masseuses,' said one Mayfair professional man who often used its facilities to relieve stress and fatigue. It was also a brothel. The same masseuses offered customers a range of sexual services for money.

'I was taken there on my fortieth birthday by Major Ron and two others,' said Morrison. 'It was a very well-laid out place, and nothing other than a massage happened to me. Nice girl. I didn't ask for it and didn't get it. It would be stupid of me to suggest that nothing went on; I'm sure the odd thing did take place, and Ronald got caught.'

The sex scandal that broke in the summer of 1988 had serious repercussions. Unknown to Sarah, the storm clouds were already gathering when the Yorks attended a performance of *Back With a Vengeance*, which starred their friend Barry Humphries as the ghastly Dame Edna Everage. Elton John, Pamela Stephenson, Billy Connolly, Bob Geldof and Paula Yates were among the audience. So was Major Ron, now a media star in his own right, having revealed a talent for lively and informed conversation on chat shows in Australia and the United States.

With malice aforethought, Dame Edna coaxed the unfortunate Ronald on stage where he was dressed in a black leather jacket swathed in swastikas and chains. A puce Mohican hairpiece completed his transformation into an ageing, and distinctly undignified, Hell's Angel. Not a few of Sarah's friends in the first three rows of the Strand Theatre squirmed in embarrassment for her and, when pictures of his impromptu performance appeared in the press, newspapers crackled indignantly.

The following Sunday, the *People* newspaper, whose proprietor was Robert Maxwell, published its revelation that Ronald Ferguson had been availing himself of more than a massage in the cubicles of the Wigmore Club. Sarah, six months pregnant with her first child, and Sue, now the mother of three children, were devastated. There was never any question of Sarah not standing by her father whatever shame and grief he had visited upon his family. 'Well, he's my Dad,' she said, but she was deeply distressed.

'I will stick by him through thick and thin,' said Sue.

The Queen was furious with her former Commander of the Sovereign's Escort. She remained half a mile away from him at the Royal Windsor Horse Show and only agreed to see him in public after she had discussed the matter privately with Sarah. Four long weeks later, Her Majesty relented and agreed to meet Ronald at the Guards Polo Club. Smiling warmly as she entered the Royal enclosure, she shook hands with Ronald, who bowed before guiding her into the Royal Pavilion. Charles had already shown his loyalty to his polo manager by posing side by side with him after chukkas at Smith's Lawn on the day the story was published. Diana, though, could not hide her disgust. As Ronald approached her, she bundled William and Harry into her Jaguar XJS and drove off to Windsor Castle to avoid being photographed with him.

The only person who stood to gain from the disclosure was Robert Maxwell, whose motives, suspect at the best of times, were more personal than financial in matters concerning the Royal Family. Of all his improbable dreams, the one he had cherished most dearly was to become a personal friend of the Queen. To him, a barefoot boy from the Carpathian Mountains of what was then Czechoslovakia, royal patronage was the ultimate token of acceptance in a society which had hitherto consigned him to the fringes, sometimes quite forcibly. The establishment hated Maxwell and the contempt was mutual. 'The aristocracy use lavatory paper like me,' he used to say.

So far, Her Majesty had wisely managed to sidestep the advances Maxwell had made in her direction. When he placed an enormous arm around her to give her a little hug at the 1986 Commonwealth Games in Edinburgh, she pointedly turned away and ignored him for the rest of the evening. Maxwell was used to such rebuffs, though not from the very few people he idolized. It had been his fervent desire to be of service to the Queen. Now, in his twisted way, he decided to show Her Majesty that people around her, even her in-laws, were merely flawed mortals. He, Robert Maxwell, was the Only Man Her Majesty Could Trust.

Maxwell justified the story by arguing that Ronald's behaviour had left him open to blackmail. Maxwell was at the height of his *folie de grandeur* as a press lord after buying Mirror Group Newspapers in July 1984. One of the first edicts he issued to editors at the Tuesday lunchtime meetings of his self-style Politbureau was that they should cease to publish anything favourable about Koo Stark. He called her 'that Yankee' and declared that her affair with Prince Andrew had embarrassed Her Majesty because of her part in an erotic film. Maxwell the keeper of public morals decried such celluloid erotica. Maxwell the voyeur, however, tried to tempt women whom he fancied into viewing 'Mr Maxwell's private collection of porn videos'. Yet Koo's was the first name on his blacklist that later included Samantha Fox, the Page Three model whose topless pictures used to fascinate him, and Bob Geldof, whose fund-raising activities for Ethiopia through Live Aid had eclipsed Maxwell's own publicity-seeking efforts at famine relief.

The Wigmore Club story did not, of course, open any doors for Maxwell. When he encountered the Duchess of York at a concert in the Barbican Centre soon after the scandal had broken, he beamed at her benignly. 'How did your father react?' he asked.

'Very much as you would have reacted,' Sarah replied frostily. 'Tell me, which newspapers do you publish?'

Top. The Ferguson family on Jane's wedding day at Dummer Down Farm in 1976. Bridesmaid Sarah with mother Susan and father Ronald. (*Desmond O'Neill*)
Above. Child star. Sarah aged six with the family rocking horse. (*Press Association*)
Left. Sylph-like Jane, the elegant bride with 16-year-old Sarah who worried constantly about her weight. (*Desmond O'Neill*)

Above. Christmas together for four generations. Top row, left to right: Jane and Alex Makim, Sue and Ronald Ferguson and Sarah. Bottom row: Doreen Wright, Seamus Makim, Alice and Andrew Ferguson and Lady Elmhirst. (*Press Association*)
Right. Loving couple. Sarah with Paddy McNally at the Monaco Grand Prix in 1985. (*Alpha*)

Left. Princess Diana has a tête-à-tête with her friend Sarah at Windsor Great Park in 1982. It clearly shows how close the two women were long before Diana guided Sarah into the Royal Family. (*Alpha*)

Above. Sarah rented a room in Carolyn Beckwith-Smith's Edwardian house in Clapham. (*Today*)
Left. My Wicked Stepmother. Sarah chats with Sue Ferguson at the christening of her niece. (*Today News (UK) Ltd*)

Opposite. Sarah in the Blue Drawing Room at Buckingham Palace on her engagement to Prince Andrew. (*Camera Press*)
Top and Above. The engaged couple together with Sarah's personal coat of arms. (*Camera Press*)
Left. The way the photographer Prince saw his radiant bride-to-be. (*Camera Press*)

Top. A touching moment. Andrew helped to design Sarah's engagement ring. (*Camera Press*)
Above. Andrew's photographic guru Gene Nocon. (*Today News (UK) Ltd*)
Right. Bridal path. A salute for the newly-wed Duke and Duchess of York. (*Tim Graham*)

Left. After the break-up of Ronald's marriage, he and Sarah became inseparable. "Ronnie's little girl" had grown into a poised young woman. (*Today News (UK) Ltd*)

Above. High flier. Sarah the helicopter pilot became known by the call sign Chatterbox One. Her experiences inspired the *Budgie* series of children's books. (*Tim Graham*)

Right. Touchdown. The Flying Duchess loved to jet to the Alps. 'The mountains ground me' she said. (*Tim Graham*)
Below. Really grounded. Sarah takes a tumble outside Harry's Bar and Andrew pauses briefly. (*Rex Features*)

Above. Evening all. Sarah in a stunning golden gown carries on bravely as details of her private life emerge in October, 1990. (*Camera Press*)

Above. Sandringham celebration. At one of the last happy royal gatherings before her marriage ran into trouble, Sarah sits between the Queen and the Queen Mother while Princess Beatrice poses proudly with her little sister at Eugenie's christening in December, 1990. In the back row are left to right: Major Ron, Godparents James Ogilvy and Lulu Blacker, Prince Andrew, Godmothers Julia Dodd-Noble and Sarah's stepmother Susan Ferguson and Prince Philip. (*Camera Press*)

Left. Soon after Sarah brought Eugenie home, she presented her new daughter to the world in this happy family group. (*Camera Press*)

Above. New friends. Steve Wyatt escorts Sarah to the Houston Polo Club after they met at his mother's mansion in the Texan city in November, 1989. Soon after they met again at a shooting party at Constable Burton Hall in the north of England. Their friendship was to make headline news. (*The Houston Post*)

Right. Old friend. Liz Nocon, Prince Andrew's confidante, dined at Joe Allen's after attending his wedding to Sarah in July, 1986.

Left. The Texan trio. Lynn Wyatt with her sons Douglas (left) and Steve at a Houston gala. She introduced her boys to the Duchess of York. 'Steve became Prince Andrew's friend too,' she was to point out later. (*Houston Chronicle*)

Above. Southern comfort. La Mauresque, Somerset Maugham's former villa on the French Riviera, scene of Lynn Wyatt's fabulous themed birthday parties. (*Today*)
Left. Bea's knees. Princess Beatrice enjoys playtime with Steve Wyatt during the Moroccan holiday with her mother in May, 1990. Pictures from this holiday were found at Wyatt's London apartment only weeks before the Yorks decided to separate.

Opposite. Ladies day. It was Andrew's birthday but Sarah took the little princesses and their friends, the Lobel sisters, on a Cornish excursion in February, 1992 as the break-up loomed. (*Jim Bennett*)

Left. Andrew's frequent absences on Naval duty meant that Major Ron often accompanied the Duchess and his granddaughters to social events. (*Today*)

Above. Power dressing. Her clothes often attracted caustic comment but Sarah in her regal finery was a sight to behold. (*Camera Press*)

Left. Term of endearment. Sarah picks up party girl Beatrice from Upton House School in February, 1992 as all eyes focussed on the royal mother. (*Jim Bennett*)

Above. Command performance. No member of the Royal Family would deny that while Sarah was a member, she was a stunning addition to its ranks. She mixed easily with the crowd during the celebration of Her Majesty's 60th birthday. (*Today*)

Right. The Queen liked Sarah's company and the two often shared moments like this in the public eye before the Sovereign learned that her favourite son's marriage was falling apart. (*Today News (UK) Ltd*)

Left. Aly pally. Sarah's close friend Alison Lobel shared her innermost secrets in the traumatic days before and after the separation was announced. (*Express Newspapers*)

Above. Rock of support. Sylvester Stallone was another to whom the Duchess could turn after they met at a Beverly Hills party in October, 1991. (*Phil Ramey*)

Left. Eastern escape. The disappearing Duchess turned up on the Pacific island of Banda after Johnny Bryan organised their flight from Britain in April, 1992. (*Seeger Press*)

Above. Life with Bryan. Sarah's close friendship with her financial adviser Johnny Bryan intrigued the nation after they returned from a holiday in South-East Asia. Two weeks after they celebrated his 37th birthday in Paris, they were pictured together at Lord Weidenfeld's birthday at the National Portrait Gallery. (*News International*)

Right. Striking in a Versace leopard jacket and black mini dress, Sarah steps out from Harry's Bar with Johnny following her. Prince Andrew also attended the dinner hosted by comedian Billy Connolly. (*Today*)

'The *Daily Mirror*, the *Sunday Mirror* and the *People*.'

'Tell me, Mr Maxwell, and what other trash do you own?'

When the opportunity came for him to enter the Queen's presence at a recital of Handel's *Messiah* at the Royal Albert Hall, Maxwell turned down the chance. His wife Betty was puzzled. 'What am I going to tell the Queen?' she asked. 'Tell her I'm a busy man,' Maxwell replied. Later, when Maxwell drowned after plunging into the sea from his yacht *Lady Ghislaine* off the Canary Islands in November 1991, he was eulogized until it was discovered that he had plundered £800 million from his companies and the pension funds of his employees in a suicidal bid to shore up his crumbling empire. Prince Andrew gave him an astonishing send-off at a black-tie dinner with a joke in highly questionable taste. 'Robert Maxwell took an Irish hooker on board his yacht,' said the Prince. 'He told her to toss him off, so she did.'

The unanswered question behind the fodder that Ronald had fed Maxwell by his presence at the Wigmore Club was: What was the Duchess of York's father, a married man with a beautiful wife, doing there in the first place? 'You've got to understand the man,' said Morrison as the treacle pudding was served at Morton's. 'The Wigmore Club was a pretty innocuous place. The reason he was there was because it was the only place he could go where he wasn't involved in an affair with a married woman or an unmarried woman. He thought he was staying out of the public eye. It was a private place to go. He actually thought, wrongly maybe, that he was doing the right thing going to this little massage parlour. It didn't affect anybody.'

Unfortunately, Ronald did not go incognito. He had given his real name when he originally enrolled as a member, he parked his car nearby and carried a briefcase bearing his full name. Everyone inside the club knew exactly who he was and what he represented, and not a few others recognized him in the street either entering or leaving the premises. 'Who shopped him? I don't know,' said Morrison. Traders in the area, furious about patrons' cars blocking the narrow lane, had complained to Westminster City Council.

Nigel Neilson, however, believed that dirty tricks were to blame. 'Some of the people in polo had got it in for him,' he said. 'There's no question about it – he was set up.' Neilson knew a lot about the sensitive politics involved in dealing with the Royal Family. He had been largely responsible for transforming Prince Charles's image as a teenager. 'Charles was always being shown as a chinless wonder with big ears,' said Neilson. 'I had met him and thought he was a rather good chap. It made me cross. I arranged a dinner party at my flat in Notting Hill and invited Charles and directors of the big oil companies. I told the Palace, "It mustn't be Prince Charles's party; I'll be the host." Somewhat reluctantly, they agreed. We ate, drank, told stories, and I played the guitar and sang. It went off well.' In this unorthodox way, Neilson became the first unofficial PR to the House of Windsor.

He met Ronald Ferguson through polo when Lord Cowdray, among others, was trying to breathe some life into the game. 'It wasn't considered very exciting,' said Neilson, 'so we organized an International Day at Smith's Lawn and the public loved it. Thousands turned up. Sarah's father was really the man who pulled everything together. He was a tremendous disciplinarian and a great worker. Unlike some of the old gentlemen in polo, he was an absolutely first-class organizer. Frankly, there was a lot of jealousy because Ronnie organized International Day and very good he was, too.'

'Why did they have to pick out me?' Ronald asked his press chum James Whitaker of the *Daily Mirror*. 'There are five hundred well-known people who go to that club – and plenty who will be worried at breakfast. But why do I have to ask? It's obvious why they chose me.' In fact, the tip-off to the *People* came from one of the masseuses working behind the green door of the Wigmore Club.

It was becoming obvious that Ronald's behaviour in attracting attention to himself in such a cavalier manner had something to do with the way he saw himself. He needed to be appreciated. It did not stop there; Ronald's next action infuriated his friends and delighted his enemies. When the *Sun* published a cartoon showing a horse stretched out on a massage table in the grip of a topless blonde with the caption: 'We don't see the Major any more, but his horse is still a regular customer,' Ronald immediately dashed off a letter to the editor, Kelvin MacKenzie; not to complain about bad taste but to ask, 'if I could have either the original or a copy of your excellent cartoon in today's paper'. The letter was written on notepaper headed Guards Polo Club – President HRH Prince Philip, Duke of Edinburgh. MacKenzie gleefully reproduced the letter on his front page, adding to the belief that Ronald was incredibly naïve in areas were experience should have taught him to tread with utmost caution.

After heated discussions behind closed doors, Ronald eventually resigned his £28,000-a-year job as deputy chairman of the Guards Polo Club, and he lost his seat on the committee of the Hurlingham Polo Association, the game's governing body. He also disappeared from the

International Polo Committee.

The loss of International Day, which Ronald called 'my personal baby', hurt him deeply. 'The wrench of handing one's baby over after such a length of time was horrendous,' he said. He still retained the loyalty and trust of Prince Charles, whom he continued to serve as unpaid polo manager.

'Charles does not easily abandon old friends just because they are going through bad times,' said a close aide.

'As a friend, Prince Charles has been immensely loyal to me and I am totally dedicated to him,' said Ronald. 'One has discovered a few truths. I have a lot of acquaintances and very few friends. There were those who disappeared when times were bad. Those who remain I would trust with my life.'

One of them was Bryan Morrison, who had become rich through his involvement with pop music. George Michael, Pink Floyd and the Bee Gees all had reason to be grateful to Morrison's entrepreneurial skill – and he had millions in the bank to testify that their ventures had been mutually beneficial. He had opened the Royal County of Berkshire Polo Club with Norman Lobel to make the hitherto elitist sport available to a wider circle. The manager's job he offered Ronald was a godsend, but typical of their relationship. The two men had become friends after a most unpromising start.

'I met Ron at the Guards Polo Club when there was a kind of Them and Us attitude, although everyone was extremely friendly,' he said. 'The kind of feeling people have about polo now didn't exist then. The situation in those days was that the high-goal patrons and their players used one field, and all the rest played on another. I played on the other field. We were the Low Lifes. One day I got my gear on and rode on to the polo pitch smoking a cigarette. I was idly hitting the ball about when I heard this shouting and, bearing down on me from four pitches away, was the Galloping Major. I'd never seen him before. He pulled up in front of me and bellowed, "Put that out! How dare you smoke on one of my pitches." I didn't say anything, just gave him what I call my F.U. Stare. He was still screaming at me so I said, "Look, all you gotta do is tell me. Don't go potty, just explain it to me."

'When the confrontation finished, a few people said, "They'll throw you out of the club for that." I arrived two days later for chukkas and, sure enough, my name was missing from the board. I thought, I've been thrown out. Then Ginger, who organized the polo, rushed up and said, "Bryan, what are you doing here? You're playing Up There." I'd been invited to play on No. 2 with the big boys. I went up and Ronnie said, "Welcome. Nice to see you." We've been friends ever since because I stood up to him and no one else did. I mean, he ruled it.

'Ronnie is a strange man. He appears to be an ogre, but he would do anything for a friend. I remember when my daughter Katrina was born prematurely, the hospital didn't have one vital piece of equipment. All through the evening, everyone was in a panic. Ronnie rang up about ten o'clock to see how my wife Greta was and I told him about the problem. He chased around Berkshire for this piece of equipment, found it and delivered it to the hospital at 4 a.m. That's the kind of person Ronnie is.'

Morrison had just helped Ronald out of another tight spot following an allegation, published on 19 April 1992, that Charity Commission investigators were enquiring into the previous year's Ladies International Polo Tournament, which Ronald had helped Lesley Player, an opportunistic 33-year-old beauty, to organize at Morrison's club. Sarah was being escorted around the Far East by Johnny Bryan after the separation when the *Sunday Times* published a story stating that the investigators wanted to know why, of £80,000 paid by sponsors, only £2,100 went to the Princess Royal's favourite charity, the Save the Children Fund, after the week-long event. The black Rolls-Royce-driving Ms Player was head of the company Platinium International, which had set up the International Ladies Polo Association to break, she said, male domination of the sport.

Morrison stood by the Major in the face of the allegations, which threatened to cloud his polo career once again. 'I've known Ronnie Ferguson for fifteen years and would never doubt his honesty for a single moment,' he said. He produced documented evidence that the charity had received all the money to which it was entitled and added: 'Ron is being pilloried for something he is just not guilty of. It was never set up as a charity event, and the amount that went to charity was more than £8000. His life is a bit of a mess at the moment. He is obviously very worried about what's going on with his daughter, and he is trying to do the right thing. The other day he asked me, "Am I doing you too much damage?" and I said to him, "Yes, you are unfortunately doing a lot of damage." However, I'm very pragmatic, and we enjoyed great publicity on the way up. So I've got to take a bit of the bad somewhere along the line.'

The Charity Commission exonerated Ronald and published a statement making it clear that it was satisfied with the financial arrangements. But the *Sunday Times* investigation had thrown up Ronald's dalliance with Lesley Player, for whom he had pledged his undying love in a series of intimate messages which found their way into the *News of the World*. He had sent her flowers with love notes pinned to the wrapping and left messages of devotion on her answer-phone. Those who worked at her office could not help but observe that on one bunch of flowers a message in clear view read:

I had almost given up on love until you came into my life. Never have I known someone so genuinely caring, someone who with just one touch could make me feel a thousand things I never felt before. Never have I trusted someone so completely, given myself to someone so totally, loved someone so strongly.

At a meeting in Morrison's office, Ronald told his boss that he was not the author of the compromising message. 'Bryan you know me, you know I can't write,' said Ronald. 'Those words were printed on the front of the card by the manufacturer.' But inside the card, dated 11 September, 1991, Major Ron had written: 'Lesley My Darling, I can say no more – like you I spent some time to find this. I am yours now and forever. Yours very lovingly R.' He signed off with three kisses.

On Player's answer-phone, he left the message: 'I just do so long to spend the odd moment with you. I mean, even if it's just an hour or an hour and a half on Friday, that's something. I just want to be alone with you without any hassle. I can make it any time. I do miss you quite dreadfully, quite dreadfully. I love you so desperately. Goodnight, my darling.' Before returning home to Sue after a polo meeting, he left another message: 'Right the way through, all I could think about was sort of you, and you and so on. I wish to hell I was coming back to you now. I love you, my darling, and I hope you are okay. Good night, my darling.'

For her part, Ms Player claimed that she had a trusted friendship with Ronald's daughter the Duchess. 'I know her extremely well and have had Sunday lunch with her and Andrew at their home,' she said. 'I've been to Buckingham Palace and she has even celebrated my birthday with me in Geneva.' Ms Player denied suggestions that she had posed as the Duchess's lady-in-waiting: 'I have never said I was her official lady-in-waiting, but I have most certainly acted in that capacity unofficially as she, her father, her bodyguards, secretary and other people know only too well.

'Sarah and I became good friends after being introduced by her father at his home. She came in wearing a headband, track suit and trainers with her children. It was pouring, and they were all soaked. Ronald introduced us and we shook hands. I was going to bow but it didn't seem right. The circumstances, the rain and everything and her looking nothing like a duchess, made bowing seem a bit silly. After that, we went from strength to strength and she began putting a lot of trust in me. You'd have to pull my toenails out before I would dream of saying what I know about her and her life.'

Declaring that she had last seen the Duchess just before the separation, Ms Player added: 'Andrew was at the house and we all sat around the large table – the children as well.' She said that when she originally set up her International Ladies Polo Association, Sarah 'agreed to be patron and was delighted when I suggested a charity ball and fashion show at the Langham Hilton Hotel in London in aid of Motor Neurone research. Sarah is the patron of a Motor Neurone association and agreed to attend the ball with her children.'

'The problem is this,' said Morrison, summing up the Player association. 'If you are in the public eye and you write letters like that, then you have to take it on the chin. With regard to Lesley, Ronnie's done whatever he's done, but what really irks him is this assumption of theft which is totally untrue.'

As a result of injuries incurred on the polo field, Ronald's body creaked, his knees were wobbly and his front teeth were screwed into the gums. Both his nose and his neck had been broken, his face smashed, his ribs cracked and his fingers and toes had been crushed and mangled beneath horses' hooves. He had been hit by flying polo balls and swinging mallets. But nothing had prepared him for the pain of being rejected by a woman to whom he had given his heart. Fortunately, when Lesley Player ultimately rebuffed his advances, his wife was at Dummer Down Farm to forgive if not to forget.

EIGHT

New York, New Yorker

'People are beginning to call me Ma'am.'

SARAH, DUCHESS OF YORK

L ong before she qualified as the disco queen of baroque 'n' roll, Sarah had to go through a period of adjustment to life as the new Duchess of York. She faced up to the realities of her exalted station immediately the honeymoon was over. This was not easy. The transition from Sloane Ranger to royal fiancée had happened in nine months; from royal bride-to-be to royal wife in only four months more. It had been as bewildering as it was exciting; a magical but confusing journey to a destination her friend Diana had reached precisely five years before her – and had lived to regret.

In truth, the distance Sarah had travelled from the little house in Lavender Gardens to the Palace on the Mall was a lot further than the few land miles she had so often driven in her second-hand BMW. The change had been instantaneous. Less than twenty-four hours after the engagement, the BMW had been left behind at the Palace while she was driven to work sitting in the back of an official Jaguar. Prince Andrew's personal detective, Inspector Geoffrey Padgham, sat beside her as a temporary bodyguard. Armed police piled into a brown Rover which took up the rear as the Jaguar swept silently through St James's and into Mayfair. Outside the Queen's coffee bar, a dozen uniformed police lined up along little St George Street while she worked in her office. Inspector

Padgham made any coffee that was required.

It had continued like that ever since. She had expected things to be markedly different, but the reality of living right at the centre of such a dramatic upheaval took her breath away. No one and nothing could have prepared her for the conversion she had experienced from Sarah Ferguson into Her Royal Highness. Through holy matrimony, her apotheosis into a royal icon like Diana was complete. She woke up in the East Wing of Buckingham Palace and shivered at the thought of it.

Protocol decreed that she was afforded the Palace's special brand of obsequious courtesy to her face. What was being whispered out of earshot, and stated more openly below stairs, was another matter entirely. Sarah realized very quickly that she would have to adapt to living and breathing royalty every waking hour of her life. Royalty, she soon discovered, never took a day off; it followed her everywhere, as stifling as an invisible cloak. She was living in Andrew's bachelor quarters on the second floor and working in a small, makeshift office. The prestige was enormous, the reality something quite different.

Unimaginable clutter was everywhere: her clothes, his photographic equipment, an exercise bike, unopened wedding presents, the books and papers of her publishing work. There simply was not enough storage space. Even wardrobes placed in the red-carpeted corridor outside were packed to overflowing. The apartment consisted of a sitting room, bedroom, a dressing room and a study which Sarah used as an office.

Considering the size of Buckingham Palace, it was cramped after the luxury of the honeymoon cruise in *Britannia* around the Azores. She and Andrew had slept in a double bed, normally stored in the hold, and pleased themselves what time they rose in the morning – if, indeed, they chose to leave their spacious stateroom at all. They danced to 'Lady in Red', the Chris de Burgh hit which had been the theme song of their courtship. Sometimes, they joined the captain, Rear Admiral Sir John Garniere, and his officers, for meals or went ashore for a barbecue on a lonely beach. They passed the days sunbathing on the deck, swimming and water-skiing – until Sarah injured her left knee in a water sports accident. It was their time together, and they made the most of it before the Royal Family joined them for the traditional cruise around the Western Isles of Scotland.

When he briefed Sarah about living in the Palace, Andrew adopted the *laissez-faire* attitude that his father had been forced to accept over the years. He knew from long experience that the one thing no one could buck was Buck House. He explained this, then went on a weapons training course at Yeovilton in Somerset. 'A career in the armed services is wonderful for any person,' he once mused, 'so long as they're single.'

A shore widow for the first time, Sarah breakfasted alone on yoghurt, coffee and croissants unless Diana came over for an early-morning swim in the Palace's basement pool. 'Diana initially welcomed Sarah's presence in the Family because of the interaction between them,' said the highly placed royal source. 'Diana is very competitive, but she was aware of the power of the courtiers, and she warned Sarah about some of the things that had happened to her. Sarah, who is more of a team player, reciprocated by urging Diana to be more assertive. Her attitude was "You hold your end up and I'll hold up mine." She thought she could handle it even if Diana was cracking under the strain. It worked well for a while, but Diana's own marriage was under increasing pressure. Arguments with Prince Charles, mainly over his friendship with Camilla Parker Bowles, were followed by long, brooding silences. Diana had plenty of worries of her own.'

One thing Diana did help Sarah to accept was to allow the servants – or staff as the royals insisted on calling them – attend to her slightest needs without demur. Her maid poured the hot water for her bath, leaving her to add the cold, as was the Palace tradition. Her robe would be folded and placed on a corked mat stool beside the bath in such a way that when she stepped out of the tub, she could sit on it and pull it up around her. Such points of fine detail had been worked out by lackeys down through the generations.

Sarah tried to forget who she was and concentrated, for the time being, on what she was: Her Royal Highness the Duchess of York, the Queen's daughter-in-law. She began to surrender her independence. If she was not careful her self-pitying thoughts began to tell her that she was more a possession than a person. The words formed in her mind for the first time: 'I am owned.'

Around this time, Penny Thornton telephoned the Palace to speak to Sarah. 'I'd finished *Suns and Lovers*, the hardback version of *Romancing the Stars*, and I wanted to send her a copy,' recalled the astrologer. 'I mean, I was speaking to someone I'd known. Once you're an astrologer, you're looking at the deeper layers of a person and you get to know people quite well. I rang up and said, "Hi, how are you, Sarah?"

'I suddenly realized there was a difference in her voice and I thought, Oh God, there's a change. So I said, "Gosh, what do I call you now?" And she said, "People are beginning to call me Ma'am." I said, "Right! Fine! Okay! Well, I'm terribly sorry I rang. I'll just drop the book in at the Mews." I thought, crikey, it's a whole new ball game now. But she said, "No, no, no, there's no need to drop it in at the Mews. We'll have lunch. How does next Thursday suit you?" I said okay and we made an arrangement to have lunch at the Palace. Two days later her lady-in-waiting cancelled it. I just sent the book and we haven't spoken for six years.

'It was almost as though, and I understand it in a way, she had arrived; she was married and she had to think very carefully what she was doing. I think she made a very concerted attempt not to put a foot wrong and, therefore, it might have been deemed very risky to have a friend who was an astrologer. More than that, an astrologer who had been looking at her astrology for a piece during the time she was in a relationship with Andrew before the wedding. It was a hot potato. The Palace could have intervened, yes – but we did speak directly and I did notice the difference in her voice. I think it became very difficult for her after that.'

Nor were the courtiers and members of the Palace secretariat singling Sarah out for special treatment. By tradition, they exercised a certain petulant equality towards every outsider who married into the Family. No one was welcome. 'It's part of the system that has grown up, realistically, since Victoria's day – but it was in place even then,' observed royal author John Parker. When Prince Albert came to Buckingham Palace, he was known by the courtiers as 'That German' and the aides he brought with him were known as 'German spies'. Prince Philip found exactly the same thing when he tried to reorganize the management of the Palace. He came up against a wall of courtiers who, for reasons of job security, did not like other people looking over the fence. These jobs are traditional and go back into the dim and distant past. People who get them do so almost by hereditary means. If they allowed other people into their little world, they would lose some of their power.

Philip called the Palace machine a rumbling old juggernaut and, using his naval expertise, common sense and the help of his aide Mike Parker, tried to tackle the problem soon after the Queen's Accession. 'The first thing they did was to count the number of rooms in Buckingham Palace,' Parker continued. 'Then Philip wanted to know why, when he ordered a sandwich, it took four flunkeys to deliver it. Even with quite minuscule things like that he had the door slammed in his face.'

When Princess Margaret married Antony Armstrong-Jones after their secret courtship in the Little White Room of his home by the Thames, he was given a similar reception. 'The Palace inner circle looked upon him as a bit of a beatnik. They didn't like him at all. He actually broke it down by his manner – he was a very nice bloke in the way he dealt with the Palace.'

More recently, Mark Philips was so nervous in the presence of courtiers that he could never really get in. He was arranging his diary on one classic occasion when one of the courtiers said to him, 'I need to see your diary to compare it with the other diaries in the Palace.' Mark didn't want to do that. He said, 'No, these are my private arrangements.' He was told brusquely, "Well, no, you can't have private arrangements. The Queen is going to Australia on such and such a date, and she needs to know what you are doing at that time.' So he had to conform and he always did, but he was very nervous about it.

Diana knew what to expect largely because she was more royal than the other outsiders; her father, Earl Spencer, had been the Queen's Equerry. He talked to her for hours about life at the Palace. Nevertheless, there were plenty there who tried to mould her and get her round to their thinking. But, they didn't like the Duchess of York at all. She was totally on the periphery of the royal circle and, in their opinion, not really royal enough to be included. She had her own walls to knock down.

The problems, however, did not all stem from the upstairs-downstairs guild of courtiers and staff of the Royal Household. Princess Anne had always held centre stage as the youngest female royal, a position she actually hated but one that was hers by birth just the same. When first Diana and then Sarah made their breathless entrances before an enraptured audience, the spotlight turned away from Anne – and stayed away. 'Initially, she was very jealous of her two sisters-in-law,' said John Parker, whose books include a biography of the Princess Royal. 'When these two glamour girls came along and edged her out of it, it did rankle a bit. She was doing all this charity work for the Save the Children Fund, and they were attracting attention away from her efforts. She wasn't getting any publicity at all by then. She was travelling abroad on difficult, dusty journeys through areas of serious deprivation in the Third World and the media were ignoring her.'

Diana and Sarah had only to change their hairstyles – or their hairdressers – and they rated the front page of the popular papers. 'In fact, Diana's hairstyle got in the way of the State Opening of Parliament,' added Parker. 'It was the first time she had attended, and there was a helluva row back at the Palace because all the pictures the next day centred on Diana's new hairstyle and none focused on the Queen performing her sovereign duty. Prince Philip explained to Diana quite angrily, "This isn't done. You don't put a new hairstyle on when we go to these important dos. It's the Queen's day, not yours." He virtually used those words. These are the sort of things the Duchess of York came up against very quickly but she didn't necessarily heed the warning.'

She did, however, try to act like a Duchess in name at least. No one could accuse her of not trying to fit into the role which, to anyone who had known her long, felt as comfortable as a tight shoe. She had always treated people with a cheery familiarity and she did not, at first, want to change that. Before the wedding, she had told Bryan Morrison: 'I want you to tell me if I ever become too royal.' An occasion arose that convinced him the time had indeed come to remind her of her words.

'We went to a restaurant and there was a lot of fawning from the management and the waiters,' he recalled. 'Then people came out of the kitchens and lined up to greet her. I don't think obsequious is the right word; it was that royal thing and she was accepting it.' When Morrison recalled her words, Sarah told him imperiously: 'I don't remember saying that.'

She began to react against over-familiarity, even if she had encouraged it in the first place. Salesgirls at Bellville Sassoon off the King's Road had known her long before she married into the Royal Family, but they discovered they had to be careful when she came into the salon. 'She could be matey but they couldn't be matey back,' said a designer who worked there. 'Once, when a girl called her Fergie, she sent for a senior person and said, "Please tell that girl I am the Duchess of York," She had always hated that boyish nickname; now, for the first time in her life, she was in a position to stop people using it.

When Sue insisted on curtsying to her before taking her leave after they had lunched at the Oyster Bar in Sir Terence Conran's Bibendum at South Kensington, people thought her Wicked Stepmother must be joking. She was not. Sue confirmed that she was merely observing the recommended protocol. 'In public, all ladies curtsy to a member of the Royal Family and her relationship with me makes no difference,' protested Sue. 'I mean, it's etiquette.'

Such bowing and scraping, however, had no place in the modern manners practised by the people Sarah liked to hang out with in the Cosa Nosheries or at Annabel's and Tramp while Andrew was away. Most of them had known her too long by various terms of endearment – Fergie,

Ginge, GB, BJ and Lollipop among them – to pay anything more than lip-service to her altered status.

The strata from which Andrew chose his friends was markedly different. Protracted absences at sea, including the South Atlantic Campaign, had meant that he had lost touch with many of his contemporaries from Gordonstoun, but he did keep in touch with at least two: Charlie Young, who had helped to organize his stag night, and Peter Neilson, son of Nigel Neilson, the public-relations boss for whom Ronald Ferguson had worked.

'Peter had known Prince Andrew since Gordonstoun and he set up the discothèque at Windsor Castle for his twenty-first birthday party,' said Nigel Neilson. 'Soon after Andrew and Sarah were married, they came up to stay with me at my family house, Catton Hall, beside the Trent in Derbyshire. They stayed overnight, and Andrew went out shooting pheasant. They were perfectly normal and very nice: a loving young couple. They also came down to my farm, Holywell, near Petersfield in Hampshire, and they couldn't have been easier to entertain.'

Andrew preferred these more traditional country weekends where everybody called him Sir without flinching to slumming it with the Sloanes, many of whose partners had gone to Eton and Oxford and tended to have a different set of values from a serving member of Her Majesty's Armed Forces, albeit one with impeccable social connections. He found his wife's outgoing behaviour towards *hoi polloi* intolerable, and on more than one occasion he let it show. 'There was a cameraman in Switzerland called Boris whom Sarah respects a lot because he's such a superb skier,' said one who witnessed Andrew's boorish behaviour. 'They were walking down a Swiss street when she saw Boris and called out a friendly greeting. Andrew was absolutely livid. He told her very loudly to shut up. He tried to kill all the friendliness in her towards people who were not on their level, and she was obviously uncomfortable with that.'

'Sarah couldn't quite grasp Andrew's double standard,' confirms Diana's tennis friend. 'He was perfectly happy to chuck bread rolls and tell filthy stories in the comparative safety of a private dining room, but he didn't want the plebs to forget he was a royal – and so was she.'

'Most members of the aristocracy have a risqué sense of humour,' commented the royal insider. 'It's a very acceptable and valid part of the royal way of life. Only prigs of the old school believe the Royal Family should behave like stuffed shirts; everyone else is allowed to be human, but they're supposed to be demi-gods.'

The Yorks never seemed closer than when they were larking about like two overgrown children, as they did with gusto before the television cameras started rolling for a royal version of *It's a Knockout*, a rumbustious show of the custard-pie-in-the-face variety. Prince Edward, who had agreed to take part in the BBC fund-raising venture, recruited Andrew, Sarah and Princess Anne as leaders of celebrity teams which included Jane Seymour, Christopher Reeve, Sheena Easton, Chris de Burgh and Meatloaf. The night before the show was recorded at Alton Towers Leisure Park in the Midlands, the participants sat down to dinner at Bagshaw's Restaurant.

'Fergie always deteriorates when she's in the company of Pamela Stephenson,' stated one who saw the frivolity. 'The Duchess threw sugar into Andrew's hair and, suffice to say, things got worse after some of those present had consumed enough Moët et Chandon Dry Imperial.' Andrew, who joined in the fun, found it hilarious. The show itself was pure knock-about slapstick with a medieval theme, hardly royal at all. When it was shown on television, Diana was not only thankful she had stayed safely in Kensington Palace, she was openly hostile. She had learned a lesson from her own behaviour when she and Sarah had marched around the Royal Enclosure at rainy Ascot and prodded men and women on the bottom with their furled umbrellas. She had been the ringleader on that occasion but, once the pictures appeared in print, she realized the enormity of her mistake. Chastened, Diana now began to distance herself from her sister-in-law in subtle ways.

'I don't think Diana turned on her,' stressed John Parker. 'She got wind that Sarah was doing all the wrong things and stepped back a bit. Courtiers were saying, "Give her enough rope and she'll hang herself." Diana tried to give her advice and help, but, basically, she ballsed it up. Fashion was one of the big areas of contention. Sarah had worn some outrageous clothes even at the beginning of her entry into royal life and nobody actually said, "Look, you can't do this." They let her get on with it.'

'It's a mistake to see the Duchess as a poor little girl being crushed by senior members of the Royal Household,' said the well-informed royal watcher. 'They were always prepared to lie and cheat to protect her. She simply wouldn't listen to their advice. Innocent girl? Nonsense! She wouldn't accept guidance.'

'Sarah has all the characteristics of a headstrong Aries; it gives her strength, it gives her determination, it gives her fire,' observed Penny Thornton. 'I think this has been expressed right through her life in the way she's come at situations. I would also say that you often find someone who is very insecure being very extrovert. She thinks, I've got to do something to make people notice me. She isn't content enough to say, "Here I am"; she hasn't got the confidence to do that. Her confidence comes from what she can do, which is why she takes up helicoptering. "Look, chaps, I may not be worth much myself but, look, I can fly a helicopter. You've got to say these things are great because they are, aren't they?" Everything she's done comes out of that deep insecurity. She doesn't feel enough in herself, but this will change.'

Sarah had taken to the skies soon after her marriage to keep a promise she made to Andrew at the time of their engagement. She wanted to share in his working experiences, she said, and learning to fly was the only way to do it. Her first lessons were in a fixed wing Piper Warrior with Colin Beckwith, chief instructor with a private flying school. They took off from RAF Benson, home base of the Queen's flight in Oxfordshire, where air traffic controllers soon had a codename for the flying Duchess: Chatterbox One. On one occasion, she and Captain Beckwith soared over the West Country cliffs to see Andrew's naval base and, it was claimed, a memory of this flight inspired the setting of the *Budgie* books she was to write. Rightly proud of her achievement, Sarah became the only female member of the Royal Family to be presented with a private pilot's licence after her first solo flight in early 1987. She was named Pupil of the Year.

After that, it took her only forty hours of flying time under the expert tuition of Kevin Mulhearn, a former navy pilot, to master Andrew's own speciality, the helicopter. Lord Hanson, head of the Anglo-American Hanson Trust, had offered her free lessons as a wedding present, and she availed herself of the chance to learn in one of his Bell Jet Ranger craft. By all accounts, she became a very able pilot and her self-esteem soared accordingly.

Flying, working, shopping and exercising all helped Sarah overcome the loneliness of being a shore widow, but she missed Andrew terribly. When he did come home and began to display early symptoms of weekend sloth, it became a growing source of irritation to his wife. Tired out after five days of daytime lectures followed by hours of studying at his naval base, he found it difficult to keep up with Sarah's abundant energy. She was said to have complained: 'He comes home on Friday, we have a row on Saturday, and he goes back on Sunday.' The couple rented a five-bedroomed Georgian house called Chideock Manor in Dorset to cut down Andrew's travelling time, but they spent only a few weekends there. It was furnished to other people's taste and was too remote and impersonal for Sarah's liking.

Her solution to the problem was to take holidays with or without Andrew. She was just as likely to be found skiing in Klosters, shopping in Paris or sunbathing in Barbados as she was at Sandringham or Balmoral. When the Yorks made an official visit to Ontario, Manitoba and Alberta, Sarah said: 'I like to combine work with fun.' Then they took a thirteen-day break in the Canadian wilderness, some of it spent canoeing down the turbulent Hanbury River. But the Couch Potato Syndrome became more noticeable at their next official port of call, Mauritius in the Indian Ocean, which they visited for a Festival of the Sea.

'Part of it was work – they planted so many trees there must be a forest there now – and then there were a few days off,' said Mike Lawn, the royal photographer. 'They were put up at the Touessrok Hotel which owned a private island just offshore. The hotel went to enormous lengths to make them comfortable, even setting up portable loos behind the trees, changing cabins, a barbecue, gear for water-skiing and boards for surfing. But Andrew never went out of the hotel, let alone visit the island. In fact, I'm told he never left his room. He just stayed in reading books and watching videos on TV. The Duchess came out once – one day when it was raining to go shopping. She looked fed up. Some of us concluded then that the marriage couldn't last. He can be a miserable so-and-so and she's so full of fun it's not true. She can make people happy just by being around them – with him, the reverse is true.'

Even if Andrew wanted some understandable peace and quiet at home, Sarah's capacity for enjoyment remained undiminished. She cut a huge cake and drank champagne to celebrate her twenty-eighth birth-day at a party which Princess Diana, Viscount Linley and Christopher Soames held for her at the Tai-Pan Chinese restaurant in Knightsbridge. She and Andrew left clutching carrier bags bulging with presents. Diana attended on her own, a frequent occurrence.

The Yorks and the Waleses, plus Prince Edward, did manage to organize a rare night out together for Charles's birthday a few weeks later. They tucked into smoked salmon and caviare and drank five bottles of Moët & Chandon at Annabel's. Andrew picked up the bill of £660. Such public displays of family unity were few and far between, and this one only went ahead because the Italian President was forced to cancel a State visit to London. 'Both Diana and Sarah had problems with their husbands, though for different reasons,' remarked Diana's tennis friend. 'Andrew wanted to see Sarah but the navy kept them apart. Charles didn't want to see Diana – and he made damn sure of it. If the two women had been closer, they might have been able to help each other come to terms with their spouses' absenteeism.'

Sisterly relations, in fact, were growing more strained between the two royal superstars. The much-hyped rivalry began to take on serious overtones when it became apparent that Sarah was no longer following her avowed intention of ignoring anything wounding in the newspapers. One vignette proved that, even if Diana did not rate the Duchess as a fashion competitor, the reverse was not necessarily true.

'Why did you wear that Elizabethan dress the other night?' a reporter asked her at a charity benefit at Claridge's, referring to a gown which had been described as a half-hearted imitation of a Mary Queen of Scots dress which Diana had worn the previous week.

'It was not an Elizabethan dress or Tudor,' said the Duchess, instantly colouring. 'And it is not new either. I wore it earlier this year at a banquet. It was designed for me by Alistair Blair so there's nothing special about it, okay? If you don't believe me, check your picture file.' That should have been enough, but two minutes later she was back, even more unduchesslike. 'By the way, that dress. I wore it at a State banquet for the Saudi Royal Family. I think it was for King Fahd.' Turning to her lady-in-waiting: 'What was the date? March, wasn't it? And it was here at Claridge's, too, So it wasn't new. You can ring Alistair Blair and ask him.'

Dragged into this heated imbroglio over a mere dress, Blair's fashion house confirmed that it was, indeed, neither Elizabethan nor a copy of Princess Diana's outfit. Sarah had made her point. Her naivety in allowing herself to be drawn into such a foolish exchange, however, had shown that behind the streetwise nods and winks her insecurity was plumbing new depths. For a royal, she was still far too vulnerable to the barbs of Fleet Street's Killer Bimbos.

Her pride wounded, Sarah refused pointblank to surrender to the dictates of others. She kept on experimenting with even more challenging outfits by Yves Saint Laurent, Edina Ronay and Lindka Cierach. If her fashion ideas ruffled the conformists in Britain, they did not go unapplauded elsewhere, particularly among Americans. 'Since she married Prince Andrew, the dynamic Duchess has metamorphosed from a tomboy in the shadow of Princess Diana to a bold belle with her own sense of style,' noted the newspaper, *USA Today*. 'She shows off her best assets – shapely legs, bare shoulders and lush red hair – in knee-length daytime suits (complete with gloves), strapless evening wear and a legion of hairstyles. It doesn't matter that Fergie's fashion statements sometimes end up with a question mark. When a personality sparkles like hers, she could wear a lampshade and still light up a room.'

The admiration was mutual. The more Sarah turned to the United States, the more it enhanced her self-confidence and reinforced her sense of identity. Unlike so many people at home, Americans, she felt, appreciated her for herself. She had made her first visit to the US as a teenager when she holidayed with Clare Wentworth-Stanley, a commissioning editor for *Tatler*, on the island of Nantucket, just across the water from Martha's Vineyard in Massachusetts. Now she started a deep, reciprocal love affair with American society which, she discovered, could provide her with so much more than what was on offer in Britain. Fashion might have been the catalyst, but it was only an external sign of a much bigger change.

.　　.　　.

To Sarah, modern American cities like New York and Los Angeles held far more exciting prospects than London. They epitomized Supersonic Swank and she was willingly seduced: Concorde across the Atlantic; Broadway and Beverly Hills; wall-to-wall celebrities; New Money values; Gold Card shopping binges; plush suites in ritzy hotels; twenty-four-hour room service. She became a dedicated convert to the wannabe version of the American Dream.

Americans were high achievers whose acquisitive energies matched her own and easily exceeded those of the go-getting yuppies thriving in Margaret Thatcher's Britain. Her swing to Americana was merely a natural progression of that same credo. In America, her title was priceless. Oscar Wyatt Junior, the workaholic oilman who was to take a shine to Sarah, said: 'She's a straight-up girl, very direct.' He explained the English malaise simply: 'I don't think people over there have enough to do.'

Sarah did, though. The impression she gave of 'always being on holiday' was misleading once it was understood that, even then, she rarely relaxed. She lived in a state of almost perpetual motion, skiing, swimming, playing tennis, partying, shopping, dropping in on friends. Her diary was so full that long-standing chums were hurt when arrangements they had made with her were cancelled at the last minute. She had made the dates personally; it was a lady-in-waiting or secretary who rang to call them off. When Sarah worked, she had to devise a routine which embraced not only her official engagements and the charities she supported but her publishing job as well. Her working days in London often began at 6.30 a.m. and finished after midnight. The famous bow in her hair spinning like a propeller, she took off for the United States.

'Sarah has a natural feeling for the liveliness and freedom of America,' said Penny Thornton. 'It's almost like getting on to a bigger stage in a bigger country. There's a tremendous love of life and a need for fun in her, and although her roots are in England, there's a stuffiness and a certain sense of being pilloried here. America has a natural pulling power for her.'

'I do love Americans, actually, because they are free in themselves, aren't they?' Sarah said once Barbara Walters, the celebrity television interviewer, was able to interrogate her on the subject. 'They have a very much more relaxed attitude than the British people. I certainly can relate to it because I'm a little wild.'

She and Andrew paid their first visit to the States as a married couple to see Susie and Hector Barrantes at their summer home on Peter Brant's White Birch Farm at Greenwich, Connecticut, in September 1987. She fitted in easily with the New England polo-playing set and, after duty called Andrew back to Britain, she was the star attraction at the annual ball of the Greenwich Polo Club on Brant's estate. Brant, an art connoisseur noted for his tough dealing, had a fine collection of Andy Warhol paintings, including his Marilyn Monroe and Mona Lisa.

Sarah's first opportunity to sample America at its most lavish arrived with Andrew Lloyd Webber's plans to export his phenomenally successful musical *The Phantom of the Opera*. Sarah accepted a solo invitation to join the advance guard of this latest British invasion of Broadway in January 1988. She took Concorde to New York, a limousine driving her up to the steps of the aircraft on the Heathrow apron. She was two months pregnant with Beatrice, but no one was supposed to know, at least not officially.

Travelling with her were Lt.-Col. Sean O'Dwyer, her Private Secretary, Helen Hughes, her old friend, now lady-in-waiting, and a detective. On Concorde were her kind of people: Elton and Renate John, Ringo Starr and his actress wife Barbara Bach and George Harrison's wife Olivia. The rock world's glitterati were attending a party ex-Beatle George was throwing to celebrate a revival of his musical fortunes in the US. 'George is No. 1 in the States with "Got My Mind Set On You" so he's invited all his mates out there for a big party,' said Ringo. It was the sort of thing they did all the time. Self-made and self-assured, the millionaires of rock 'n' roll were typical of the showbusiness crowd Sarah had gathered into her circle. After landing at JFK, Sarah was airborne again just seven minutes later in the helicopter of developer Donald Trump. She flew to New London in now-familiar Connecticut to tour the Eugene O'Neill Theater Center with Michael Douglas, one of its trustees.

That night, she dined at 1 Beekman Place in the Manhattan apartment of Henrik de Kwiatkowski, a Polish millionaire with a passion for polo, and his wife Barbara – one of Lynn Wyatt's dearest friends. Sarah had visited the Kwiatkowskis' home next to White Birch during her trip to Greenwich and been entranced by the country-style décor in what had previously been a tumble-down block of stables. As Sarah and Andrew were planning their own home at Sunninghill Park, she invited Sister Parish, co-owner of Parish-Hadley Associates, the interior decorating firm responsible for the work, to join them for dinner. Susie and Hector, and Sandy and Peter Brant were among the guests. The Brants were the parents of triplets, a boy and two girls, but there was plenty to talk about in addition to furnishings for Sarah's new nursery. The host, for instance, was an interesting character.

Kwiatkowski, short and stocky with grey-black hair, had fathered six children by his first wife before he fell in love with Barbara Allen, a woman thirty years his junior who was divorced from Joe Allen, Brant's partner in certain cinematic ventures with Andy Warhol. 'Barbara is a fabulous, crazy, wonderful girl,' said author Dominick Dunne. 'She had been the girlfriend of some of the richest men in the world, among them the Niarchoses, both the son and the father. She was one of the girls in the Andy Warhol Set. Henrik divorced his wife, married her and they have a child who is the apple of his eye. She's sexy and she's wonderful and, before her marriage, she was romanced by Steve Wyatt.'

It was doubtful that Sarah knew much, if anything, about the Texan Lothario at this stage, but her initiation into the milieu of the New England gentry where money mattered more than sentiment had thrown up so many fascinating characters it was hard to keep track. The fact that Kwiatkowski was a close friend of Prince Charles did not stop him outbidding the Queen when the coveted Calumet Farms, one of the most famous racing stables in Kentucky, came on to the market.

There were more big names to meet when Sarah played her role as guest of honour at a gala performance of *The Phantom* a few days in advance of its official Broadway première. The sponsors of the evening, *People* magazine, had booked Sarah into the $3000-a-night Presidential Suite of the Waldorf Towers, the residential skyscraper of the Waldorf-Astoria Hotel. The Towers had once been a home-in-exile to the wandering Duke and Duchess of Windsor. The art-deco hotel itself, situated on Park Avenue 'where wealth is so swollen it almost bursts', was as regal in its own way as Buckingham Palace. When Sarah entered the hotel, she passed under a figure over its portals depicting the 'Spirit of Achievement'. *The Phantom* was being staged at the Majestic Theater and guests including Michael Douglas, his wife Diandra, Donald Trump and Phil Donahue, the television presenter, paid $1000 a ticket for the privilege of attending this royal occasion. Sarah might not be the Princess of Wales, but she had considerable pulling power of her own in the United States. Just in case any of the *nouveaux riches* patrons were uncertain, Lloyd Webber's Really Useful Group invited Lady Lavinia Nourse to instruct them on royal etiquette. 'You may address the Duchess of York as Ma'am – as in Spam,' she told them.

Like London audiences before them, the Americans were spellbound by Lloyd Webber's reworking of the classic horror story. They applauded Michael Crawford, as the Phantom, and Sarah Brightman, as Christine, for a full five minutes after the curtain came down. The Duchess, who had seen the show three times in the West End, told Crawford at a celebration party back stage: 'You made me cry – yet again, for the fourth time, you made me cry.' Mindful of her own condition, she seemed obsessed with the vast stomach of actor David Romano, who played the young tenor Piangi. Playfully prodding it, she said: 'Is that real?'

'Yes, it is real,' Romano assured her. 'Everything about the show is genuine.'

The anger that greeted Sarah when she returned to the Waldorf for the after-theatre reception was real enough, too. A crowd of fifty pro-IRA demonstrators protesting against the British presence in Northern Ireland were chanting anti-British slogans and waving banners, one of which read BLOOD ON THE CROWN. As Sarah stepped on to the pavement, one of the demonstrators vaulted a 4-foot high barrier and lunged at her bellowing, 'Murderer'. He was carrying a 6-foot long wooden pole bearing the Irish flag. An FBI agent flung himself on to the fanatic and wrestled him to the ground before he could get close to the Duchess. Her British detective hurried her inside the hotel where Sarah, shaken but unhurt, shrugged off the incident and went to the party.

After an Edwardian supper, guests danced in the hotel's Grand Ballroom. 'Sarah looked sensational in a black velvet gown and tiara,' said one who had followed her royal progress closely. 'But then she completely spoiled the effect by striding across the ballroom like a milkmaid.' The party carried on in Sarah's suite for Susie and Hector and a select group of well-heeled guests. 'She entertained to such an extent that the sponsors faced a charge of several thousand dollars for extra catering and room service,' said the attendant royal watcher. One who scrutinized a breakdown of the wine bill commented: 'Well, she certainly knows her vintages.'

.   .   .

Pregnancy in no way cramped the Duchess's style. When the Palace finally confirmed it at 11 a.m. on a winter's morning in late January, she was taking a spin down to Hampshire at the controls of a Jet Ranger helicopter. As she hovered over Dummer Down Farm, she saw a large sheet bearing the message CONGRATS MA'AM in red lettering that Sue had hurriedly spread across the lawn. Sarah enjoyed her stepmother's little joke, then returned to Castlewood House, which was now their country home. The Yorks were renting the mansion on the edge of Great Windsor Park from King Hussein of Jordan while work proceeded at Sunninghill.

Fellow officers toasted Andrew in the mess at Portland where he was based as a Lynx helicopter warfare instructor with 702 Squadron. The move to Castlewood had improved the Yorks' home life, and Andrew's career was proceeding to plan. He was about to start a new job as one of the watch-keeping officers on the bridge of HMS *Edinburgh*. This would mean more time at sea for him and more shore widowhood for Sarah. But, the Yorks counted their blessings and all three of them turned out for the première of *White Mischief* at the Odeon Cinema, Marble Arch. As her gynaecologist, Sarah retained the services of Mr Anthony Kenney, whom she already knew, rather than switch to the Queen's Harley Street favourite, Sir George Pinker, who had delivered Diana's and Anne's children.

Kenney was concerned that Sarah was taking too many risks with her health. At Sandringham after Christmas, she had chased her labrador over the sugarbeet fields, jumped a five-bar gate and run across muddy paddocks to keep up with the shoot. 'She knew that her mother and sister had both suffered miscarriages, but it didn't stop her,' remarked a despairing friend. 'It wasn't a difficult pregnancy, only the mother-to-be was difficult. The one concession she would make was to give up horse-riding.'

When the Yorks flew to California in February, Kenney buckled his safety belt in the seat nearest to them on the British Airways 747, and he stayed close to her side throughout the nine-day visit. He slept in a cabin next to Sarah's suite on *Britannia*, which had anchored in Long Beach Harbour to serve as a floating hotel for the royal entourage. Sarah would not slow down. There were too many interesting people queuing up to fête her.

Before she met Oscar Wyatt, Sarah found herself a protégé of his great oil rival, Dr Armand Hammer. 'I think she's terrific,' said the man who already knew Prince Charles well. 'She's a great influence on young Prince Andrew. He was getting a little wild and out of hand.' Hammer fell for Sarah's lively charm at a glittering dinner for 800 in the ballroom of the Biltmore Hotel in Los Angeles. Roger Moore was master of ceremonies, and guests paid up to $10,000. As Sarah got up to address them, it became apparent that Hammer was not the only one to have been smitten. An overemotional senator shouted from a rear table: 'I love you.' The Duchess, in a black low-cut Yves St Laurent dress, riposted cheekily: 'I'll see you later!' There was a gasp of astonishment; one-liners like that were a hitherto unknown factor in the royal reper-toire. 'She has a great English sense of humour,' murmured Joan Collins, the *Dynasty* star, who had arrived on the arm of George Hamilton.

There was more fun over lunch during a tour of Hollywood the next day when Sarah sat beside Dudley Moore. 'Milton and Shakespeare?' said the self-exiled British actor. 'They course through the veins of every red-blooded film star now living very nicely in Marina del Rey.' Prince Andrew laughed as loudly as anyone. Before the lunch ended, Sarah was able to add Jack Nicholson, Angelica Huston, Michael J. Fox, Roddy McDowell, Emma Samms and James Bond producer Cubby Broccoli to her growing list of celebs. She had only just begun. Critics began to question whether she might be so starstruck that, to her, royalty was only real-life *Dynasty* with a Crown.

The mishap that Kenney feared took place when Sarah returned to the slopes at Klosters with the Waleses and a group of mutual friends. She had promised she would ski only on powder, but even then she suffered a nasty fall and plunged into a stream. She was unhurt but so shaken that she stayed in the chalet after lunch to talk to Diana, who had had yet another argument with Charles, this time over the safest places to ski. Charles and the others, among them Major Hugh Lindsay, the

Queen's former Equerry, trudged back to the slopes with their ski guide Bruno Sprecher. Ignoring the avalanche warning, Charles led them off-piste near the unpredictable black Wang run. As they neared the foot of the run, an avalanche crashed down on them. Lindsay was buried under the tons of rocks and snow. He died instantly. Another in the group, Patti Palmer-Tomkinson, suffered badly broken bones. The tragic accident deeply affected the Duchess. Her heart went out to Lindsay's wife, Sarah, who was carrying his child. But another traumatic turn of events, wounding in a different way, struck Sarah when her father's visits to the Wigmore Club became public knowledge in the first week of May.

The effect on Sarah was evident in a visible and to her more unsettling way. She started bingeing. Within weeks, she had added two stone to the figure she had fought so hard to get, her blood pressure shot up and her joints swelled painfully. She had started out with the usual cravings of a pregnant woman – in her case, 'a fetish for boiled eggs, toast soldiers and mayonnaise'. Now, in the classic manner of a compulsive overeater, she began to eat her feelings by grazing on whatever food took her fancy. She seemed powerless to control her raids on the refrigerator, even though the results were plain to see.

When the Yorks went to Balmoral for a summer break, the Queen kept a close eye on her daughter-in-law. She knew about the misery Princess Diana had suffered during her two pregnancies. Charles had rarely been on hand to comfort her. This time Her Majesty decided to act. Andrew had scarcely reported for duty on board his new ship, HMS *Edinburgh*, when the Ministry of Defence was instructed to recall him. He was given compassionate leave to return to his wife at Craigowan Lodge, the hunting retreat on the Balmoral Estates. Sarah was complaining of 'fainting, dizziness and sickness'. Andrew called a doctor, who diagnosed stress and advised her to rest as much as possible. The Prince bought her a Jack Russell puppy called Bendicks for company. Then he played a few rounds of golf, a game he was starting to enjoy, before rejoining his ship for an extended tour of the Far East and Australia. Sarah and Bendicks became inseparable.

After six weeks at sea, Andrew was flown home from Singapore on compassionate leave once again to be with Sarah during the birth. In the intervening weeks, she had been involved in a two-car collision on the M4 and although no one was hurt in the accident, she desperately needed her husband at her side. The day after he returned, he drove her from Castlewood to the £250-a-night Portland Hospital in London. She was in a lot of pain and asked for an epidural injection in her spine. Once labour started, Kenney induced the labour. The Yorks' baby, a princess weighing 6 lb 12 oz, was born at 8.18 p.m. on 8 August 1988. Andrew's favourite girl's name was Annabel. He did not insist, though. It would have been taking things too far to name the fifth in line to the throne after a discothèque. Sarah's inclinations were more family-oriented and sentimental. They settled for Beatrice Elizabeth Mary after Queen Victoria's youngest daughter, the Queen, the Queen Mother and the Queen's Grandmother. Mary was also the middle name of Susie Barrantes, who was in London for the happy occasion.

Baby Bea was only six weeks old when Sarah carried out her declared intention of leaving her in the care of Alison Wardley, the young nanny from Manchester she had hired, and flying to Australia to be close to Andrew during Edinburgh's goodwill visit for the country's bicentennial celebrations. The separation of mother and daughter provoked such an outcry in the media that Sarah might have been forgiven for wondering if she hadn't abandoned her baby in some Dickensian workhouse. 'If they bothered to think about it for one second, Beatrice is much better off at home where things are stable,' said Andrew. 'It would have been possible to bring her, but it would have made life so complicated and disjointed it would never have worked.'

'I love Beatrice and she's great, but you've had nine months of looking rather enormous and your poor husband's had to look at you like that,' said Sarah. 'It was his turn for just a couple of weeks; just to make sure that he knew he was very important.'

.   .   .

As the *Edinburgh* sailed around the Australian coastline, Sarah, sometimes with her sister Jane in tow, flew from port to port to greet Andrew upon his arrival. Friends worked up a joke: 'He's the sailor with a wife in every port.' Australia was in a party mood to celebrate its two hundred years of British settlement, and the Yorks were expected to attend an array of official functions. It was a hectic schedule and Jane, who had developed into a beauty like her mother, joined in whenever she could to share the burden. She was delighted to see her famous sister thriving after the birth of Beatrice. Sarah's excess weight had rapidly disappeared, her new clothes were dazzling in the Australian sunshine, and she was revelling in the chance of expressing herself far away from the disapproving eye of Buckingham Palace.

The Makims' marriage, however, was far from healthy. They had recently discussed the possibility of a divorce. Alex did not want to lose

Jane, but events beyond his control were forcing them apart. Ever since the wedding, Jane had been fêted in Australia as the Duchess of North Star. She and Alex had arrived home from the wedding to find their car decked out with the skull of a bullock as a coat of arms and an honorary dukedom inscribed as an insignia.

Jane tried to combine the busy round of social requests that her new status brought in with those of wife and mother while Alex battled to keep the farm going during a severe drought. He sometimes drove his tractor through the night to avoid the sweltering daytime heat. Jane spent more time away from Wilga Warrina at garden parties, fashion shows and functions associated with polo tournaments she was involved in organizing. When she was at home, the house was packed with hangers-on who delighted in hob-nobbing with the nearest thing to royalty the Outback had to offer. Alex, worried about the effect on Seamus and Ayesha, became so desperate that he wrote to Sarah asking if they might speak about the problems in his married life during her tour of Australia.

'Alex joined Jane and her mother Susie, who had flown in from Argentina, for dinner with the Yorks at the Sheraton Hotel in Brisbane,' said Isobelle Gidley, a writer who closely followed the break-up of the Makims' marriage. 'In the dining room, Sarah and Andrew sat facing the main body of the restaurant. They kept everyone amused with tales of their experiences on the tour. As the laughter grew and the waiters swirled about them, the stories turned into jokes. In their telling they got more and more crude. Alex couldn't believe his ears or his eyes.

'The story-telling moved around the table as the wine flowed and Jane urged Alex to tell a joke. He wouldn't. He had caught Prince Andrew's eye and thought that he looked embarrassed. It was hard to believe how the Duchess's staff could respect her when she behaved so crudely. Alex felt ashamed. Sarah was having great fun repeating the punchline of a crude joke over and over. She was pretending a napkin was a pair of knickers and holding it up to her nose. The words of the joke were along the lines of "Past the nose, sweet as a rose".

'Then all the Federal Police and royal bodyguards who were sitting at the next table were ordered to tell a joke by royal command. Several of them did. Suddenly Sarah noticed the fury on Alex's face. She came over and sat beside him. "And how are you, Alex?" she asked. "I gather there is some problem." "Well," he said, "I have written a letter thanking you for the lovely green tie you gave me and I also wrote in it that I would like to have the opportunity to speak to you about our problem." Sarah stared at him intently for a moment, then asked loud enough for everyone to hear: "Don't you think it would be a good idea to try a trial separation." '

The following day, Sarah, Jane and Susie went on holiday together and it was only a matter of time before the Makims were embroiled in a bitter legal battle for custody of their children. Alex had learned the hard way that Sarah no longer regarded him as her Big Bruvva.

NINE

Steve Gets Swanky with Johnny

'Johnny Bryan took to the fast life and he just couldn't get enough.'

WHITNEY TOWER, JUNIOR

S teve Wyatt and Johnny Bryan, Mr Smooth and his inseparable pal Mr Smooth-head, shared a lot more in common than friendship with the Duchess of York. They had gone to high school together in Houston and, after graduation from college, their families became linked in a most unusual and intriguing way.

Lynn Wyatt's only brother, Robert T. Sakowitz, had married Pamela Zauderer, the daughter of a rich New York real-estate developer. But in 1977, Steve's Aunt Pam decided to divorce Uncle Bobby, and it transpired that the man she had fallen in love with was Johnny's father, Tony Bryan. When the case came to court, it was revealed that Robert had discovered the extent of the affair by placing a wiretap on Pam's telephone to try to secure evidence of misconduct. Pam and Tony were married soon after, which made Steve and Johnny distant cousins by marriage. Tony Bryan, who had been educated in England at Ampleforth and then in America at the Harvard Business School, had become wealthy in his own right by building up a big metalworks business called Copperweld. At the time of Pam's break-up, he was married to the Texas heiress Josephine Abercrombie – the second of his four wives. The first Mrs Bryan, now Mrs Lyda Redmond, was the mother of Johnny and his two sisters, Carol and Pamela, whom he called Baby.

Johnny was born in Delaware on 30 June, 1955, but the family moved to New York when he was still a child. 'I've known him since he was a little boy in Long Island, where he was brought up when his parents were still together,' said Whitney Tower, Junior, whose parents, prominent among the upper echelons of WASP society, were close friends of Lyda. 'I lived in Long Island too, and I took an interest in Johnny like an older brother. He was always great fun, always an entertainer. He was mischievous, which I loved, but he was considerate and probably a little lonely because he was sent away to Harvey, a boarding school in Bedford, New York State. Then his parents divorced, and he moved to Houston when his father married Josephine.'

The 'high school' where Bryan forged an unbreakable bond of friendship with Steve Wyatt was, in fact, St John's School in River Oaks, the most exceptional private school in Houston. Steve's athletic achievements – he became captain of the track and field team – and his winning manner made him one of the most popular students of his senior year. After he graduated from the University of Arizona in Tucson, he travelled in South America and Europe before returning to Houston to work in the oil business. He drove a Mercedes convertible and was often seen in smart restaurants such as Tony's in Post Oak, or hanging out at the Houston Polo Club.

Women in his mother's circle were impressed by his spiritual approach to life, which he practised in the shape of metaphysical meditation – 'a sort of religious process where you would appear to leave your body'. 'He wasn't a space cadet like some of his generation,' said an acquaintance, 'He was serious about what he read, books on philosophy and self-improvement, and what he ate – macrobiotic health foods and vitamins.'

Johnny Bryan's own travels had taken him on a tour of academia during which he collected degrees at universities in Boston, Pittsburgh and Texas. Both men enjoyed a love of sport, especially skiing – the Wyatts and the Bryans had homes at Vail, Colorado – golf and squash. They became identified as members of the Texas Longhorns, a jet-setting clique of bachelors dedicated to working hard and playing even harder. 'They are the eligibles,' gushed *Town and Country* magazine. 'They are hard to catch, but worth the effort.' Steve and Johnny enjoyed the chase – and managed to stay single.

A growing problem inside the Sakowitz family which developed into a full-scale feud did not, at first, damage the kinship between Steve and his Uncle Robert. Steve's girlfriend in 1982 was Laura Howell, a blonde, blue-eyed bookkeeper who was raised in the unfashionable oil-refining suburb of Deer Park. He introduced her to Robert, a short man with a long jaw, receding hair and dark eyes, at a charity ball at the Four Seasons Hotel. Later, Robert telephoned Steve to enquire about Laura with more than avuncular interest. 'I called Steven and I said, "Are you dating her seriously?" He said, "No, she's just a really good friend." I said, "Do you mind if I take her out?" He said, "No." '

Robert, who had a penchant for wearing stetsons around the Paris fashion shows, had Laura dressed in the finest fashions at Sakowitz and took her on business trips. She was nineteen years younger than him, and he married her in 1984 after she converted to Judaism. By this time, Steve and Johnny had moved to greener pastures than those on offer in Houston which, after the oil and space boom of the sixties and seventies, was plunging rapidly into recession. Steve's athletic frame and boyish good looks and Johnny's cool, calculating charm, quite apart from their monied backgrounds, made them ideal candidates for the smart set that swirled up and down the avenues of New York City.

The debonair Wyatt soon made friends with the fabulous Barbara Allen, one of the most glamorous women attached to the cosmopolitan set of film-makers, artists, fashion designers, actors, models and extremely rich society matrons who orbited around Andy Warhol. The silver-haired guru of Popism had survived an assassin's bullet in 1968 and considered himself born again in the most literal sense. To dedicated followers of radical chic, he was a walking legend. One of his close friends was Lynn Wyatt, whose devastating beauty had been captured in one of his famous portraits ($25,000 for the first canvas and $5000 for each copy). Lynn and Steve often met Warhol on his nocturnal safaris into the *haut monde* far above the Underground that the artist had immortalized in paintings, films and books in the sixties.

Another integral member of the set was Peter Brant, the art-collecting polo player and a friend of Susie and Hector Barrantes. He had staked Warhol in establishing the movie magazine *Interview*, which had the inspired idea of getting stars to tape-record conversations with other stars about their lives and work. He had also put up much of the hard cash for making *Bad*, a film which followed *Chelsea Girls*, *Women in Revolt* and *L'Amour* in the unconventional genre expected of Warhol's celluloid and canvas Factory in downtown Manhattan.

It was a reunion with his childhood friend Whitney Tower in 1983 that provided Johnny Bryan with the contacts he needed to take a tentative first bite at the Big Apple. Tower was a good friend not only of Warhol's but of Jerry Hall and Mick Jagger, who lived on exclusive Central Park West before moving to a house on West 81st Street. 'Johnny was living and working at Stamford, Connecticut, and I ran into him when he came to New York to go to a couple of parties,' said Tower, a public-relations consultant. 'He called me and I took him under my wing because he didn't know anyone. I was moving into a bigger apartment on 72nd Street right on Madison Avenue, and I said to him, "You seem to be in New York every night. Why don't you get rid of your place in Connecticut and commute in the opposite direction – going out when the traffic is coming in?"

'He moved into my place and stayed two years. He was working for the communications division of Westinghouse – it was called Group W, and they dealt in satellite and cable-television systems. Mick Jagger would come over to my apartment every day or so to play music or whatever, and I introduced him to Johnny. He seemed to take to the fast life pretty quick. A lot of my accounts at the time were nightclubs and Johnny sort of ate up everything that was going on. He took it all in, he loved it. It was like releasing someone from jail – he just couldn't get enough.'

Tower, a 41-year-old public-relations consultant, even introduced Bryan to his only steady girlfriend in New York. Sabrina Franzheim was a beautiful 18-year-old brunette and the daughter of Kenneth Franzheim II, a former US ambassador to New Zealand. 'I visited Whitney's apartment with my sister Pamela and met Johnny for the first time,' said Sabrina. 'We dated for two years before he went to London. We used to dine out together, and he was an energetic, funny and amusing guy.'

When Tower married Pamela at St Bartholomew's Church on Park Avenue, the guest list was so illustrious that quite a few star names were excluded from the reception. It would have meant nothing to the invited Johnny Bryan then, but the date – June 1985 – coincided with Royal Ascot, the occasion fate had chosen to bring Prince Andrew and Sarah Ferguson together over lunch at Windsor Castle. Bryan's career, not to mention his social life, began to flourish – 'with the help of my address book,' joked Whitney Tower. He got an apartment of his own and started to build up his own network. Not without some false starts, he developed the 'edge' that an out-of-towner found essential to survive among street-smart New Yorkers.

When the subject of wing collars came up at a black-tie function one night, Bryan said that he always wore the detachable kind. 'It must be tough getting them starched and ironed,' said another male guest. 'I wouldn't know,' Bryan shot back, 'I wear them once and throw them away.' One of the places he liked to take his girlfriends was Au Bar, a smart East Side haunt. 'He always gave girls a good time, and quite a few were buddies,' said Tower, who smoothed a path for him there. Au Bar, which had been decorated by Emily Todhunter, one of Steve Wyatt's friends, was so successful that Bryan discussed the prospect of setting up a London offshoot with the owner, Howard Stein. Not long afterwards, a British consulate limousine pulled up outside the venue between Madison and Park Avenues, and Sarah, Duchess of York, led her lady-in-waiting, her detective and her detail of State Department bodyguards in for a nightcap. Her friend Johnny Bryan had recommended Au Bar very highly.

Another of Stein's nightspots was Xenon, where Johnny befriended Taki Theodorocopulos, the Greek playboy millionaire and High Life columnist for the *Spectator* magazine. Taki was in the company of Fred Hughes, Andy Warhol's closest friend, and the conversation turned to cable television. Bryan persuaded Taki to invest $50,000 in a company which never made it.

'He was putting together the money for a little company called EnCom Telecommunications and Technology. His partners raised about $2.5 million in early 1985,' said Taki. 'The business was to get into the satellite game. Johnny was secretary and vice president for business development. The company's revenues were just under $6 million – about $8 million less than expected – and the end came in 1989.

'No, I had not been suckered by him. I knew what I was doing. I thought it was a sure thing. I still like him.'

In the not-too-distant future, Bryan walked up to Taki's table at Annabel's in London and introduced his companion, saying: 'Hey, Taki, say hello to the Duchess of York.' For a joke, Taki asked him for his money back. 'As far as I'm concerned, it was an investment, not a loan,' Taki said. 'He convinced me I was going to make millions out of the deal – but that's the way it goes.'

'Johnny is a very good businessman despite his happy-go-lucky nature,' said Whitney Tower. 'He's very knowledgeable – a salesman who could sell you a toupee.' Yet, if Johnny did not find New York's overstated swank intimidating, it was more difficult for Steve Wyatt. He had a more vulnerable side which led one observer to comment that he seemed to be suffering from 'psychological pain'. Johnny Bryan knew all about the heartbreak that lay beneath his friend's self-confident smile and out-going chutzpah. Steve's real father was a New Yorker, Bobby Lipman, and what had happened to him had left an indelible mark on the young Texan's life.

.   .   .

Lynn Sakowitz was born in 1930 and raised as a Southern belle in a colonnaded white house perched above the bayou which ran through Houston. Her father, Bernard, was chairman and chief executive at Sakowitz Inc., which ran the family's highly respected department-store chain. His wife Ann, and later Lynn and Robert, were all directors. As children, Lynn had been very close to her younger brother, whom she called Bub. He was born in 1938, and he called his beautiful big sister Ski.

The family faced the first in a series of crises when Lynn dropped out of Bennington College to marry Bobby Lipman, a handsome young man from a rich New York real-estate family, in 1954. 'He was very self-assured, very effervescent, very gregarious – an attractive guy with a great personality,' said brother Robert. Instead of going to work in his own family's business, Bobby Lipman moved with Lynn to Houston where he was given a job at the Sakowitz store. There were problems from the beginning. Lynn's father decided his new son-in-law should work his way up from the bottom, a time-consuming prospect that did not appeal to Lipman. He drank heavily on his resentment against Bernard and that often led to fights with his wife. Frustrated at Sakowitz, Lipman left the store and moved Lynn and their two sons Douglas and Steven to Florida. The marriage continued to deteriorate until, in 1960, Lynn took the boys back to Houston where, during the next three years, she was to meet, fall in love and marry the toughest diamond in Texas, Oscar Wyatt Junior.

Now a chronic alcoholic, Bobby Lipman discovered drugs after he drifted to London where, in 1968, he killed an eighteen-year-old French student in her Chelsea flat. He suffocated Claudie Delphine Delbarre with a pillowcase during an acid trip. Described as a French actress, Claudie had been working behind a bar when Lipman, who stood 6 ft 6 in tall, befriended her. During his trial at the Old Bailey he said that, under the influence of LSD, he had seen the teenager as a fire-breathing monster, and he had held the pillow over her face until she was no longer a threat to him.

Lipman was sentenced to six years' imprisonment for manslaughter and after his release, he disappeared. Some said he committed suicide, Steve said he was hit and killed by a tram in Vienna. Another school of thought suggested he was still alive and living in penury under another identity.

Oscar Wyatt, who was born in Beaumont, Texas, on 11 July 1924, was the complete opposite of the tragic and hopelessly addicted Bobby Lipman. Big-jowled and massive in size, he was known as a ruthless businessman with a fondness for women. After he was divorced from his first wife Yvonne, she told a friend: 'Oscar is the only man I know who has a mattress strapped to his back for convenience.' Two more wives had come and gone from Oscar's life before Lynn put a stop to his wandering eye. When he decided she was the woman to be his fourth wife, her father Bernard Sakowitz had reservations which Oscar banished by coming up with a $1 million 'reverse dowry'. Oscar was unapologetic about his chauvinistic past. When a female reporter asked him if he had had cancer, he replied: 'Cancer? Hmmm, maybe I have. What was her last name?' And when another asked, 'How are you?', he replied: 'Better than anyone you've ever had.'

There was, however, another side to his gruff, gravel-voiced exterior. 'Oscar is a tender-hearted man,' said one who knows his secret. 'He does good things for so many people that no one ever hears about, particularly in Navasota, the town he was raised in.' Dozens of his employees had Oscar to thank for paying their medical bills or children's school fees in hard times. He gave millions to orphanages, churches and schools on the proviso that he remained anonymous. Born into a working-class family, it was Oscar's never-give-up grit that made him a billionaire in the volatile world of oil, coal and natural gas. He pawned his car to finance the purchase of his first oil well in the fifties, going out on to the streets to sell shares in his newly formed Coastal Petroleum. By the nineties, the burgeoning energy giant was credited with assets valued at $9 billion.

Lynn had little say in Oscar's plans to marry her – he put the plane he was piloting into a dive, pretending to crash unless Lynn proposed to him. Just in time, she asked Oscar to marry her. The World War II air ace accepted, and steered the plane back on course. After their wedding, Oscar adopted Steve and his younger brother Doug, changing their name from Lipman to Wyatt. Later, he fathered Lynn's third and fourth sons, Oscar Wyatt III, known as Trey, and Brad. Oscar proved a loving stepfather and, through him, Steve found a security he had never known in his early years with Lipman.

As the boys grew up, Oscar's fortunes mushroomed, partly through his connection with Saddam Hussein, first established in 1971 when the Gulf War instigator was second in command of Iraq. 'Guys like me like Iraq,' the tycoon was fond of saying. While his reputation as the King of Crude became established internationally, back home in Texas, Lynn had become known as the Queen of Houston. The parties at the Wyatt's mansion, Allington, on River Oaks Boulevard were the highlight of the city's social life. No one who was anyone visited without calling on the Wyatts. There was a strangeness about the mix of Lynn's social world and Oscar's need for secrecy about his global operations and his personal security. Lynn did not mind being in the newspapers; Oscar tried his damnedest to stay out of them.

His oil dealings with the Middle East, vital to America's strategic and economic well-being, gave him clout at the White House when Lyndon B. Johnson, Richard Nixon and Ronald Reagan were in the Oval Office. 'I'd go to hell for William Casey,' he told Marie Brenner of *Vanity Fair* referring to the late director of the Central Intelligence Agency. 'I did all sorts of stuff for him. Casey would call me up and say, "Would you do such and such?" He would ask, "Do you want a CYA memo?" I'd say, 'No, just tell me you got me covered." ' CYA stood for Cover Your Ass, sound advice in the CIA's world of espionage and subversion. Oscar did not, however, see eye to eye with George Bush.

He kept a pistol in the glove compartment of his car, and visitors like Ronald and Nancy Reagan, Mick Jagger and Jerry Hall, Liza Minnelli and the Aga Khan noted that this was not the only precaution Oscar took. They found that the house was the only one in the road completely surrounded by hedges and fences, and a sign warned callers to beware of the dog (there were, in fact, nine pet German shepherds 'trained to attack on sight' according to Houston oil expert Barbara R. Shook). They should remain in their cars and 'someone will come for you,' it added ominously. Another incongruity was the Wyatts' non-membership of the River Oaks Country Club next door in Memorial Park. The club was patronized by the Houston establishment, which resented New Money, and Oscar Wyatt's fortune was most definitely New Money. When Oscar declared: 'Steve and his mother have always gravitated towards theatrical people and royalty,' a member of the country club responded wryly: 'That's because the rest of us wouldn't have them.'

Princess Margaret, who had known the Wyatts for twenty years and stayed at Allington, may have been surprised to hear that. The Wyatts once threw a dinner party in her honour which was held on the same date as the birthday of another guest. 'It's your birthday?' Oscar asked the man. 'Here's your present.' He handed the astonished guest a $3000 watch off his own wrist.

'There's a very strong connection between the Wyatts and the Royal Family,' said Dai Llewellyn, who knew Lynn Wyatt well. 'It goes back many years before they ever met the Duchess of York. Lynn has been to Kensington Palace and, over the years, I think she has met every single one of the royals. In fact, she probably knows more royals reasonably intimately than nearly any other American.'

'You have to be likeable, friendly, bubbly and outgoing in order to succeed at that social game,' said journalist John Taylor, who studied Lynn's Southern style in person. 'Being attractive and a terrific dresser gets you into the ring, but to win you have to be a basically appealing person, and Lynn Wyatt really is just that. She's a lot of fun, and she takes a great deal of interest in other people. She's conscientious and flattering, winning friends, cultivating people by sending them notes and following up, building alliances. That kind of thing.'

'Lynn is a dear, loyal person,' said Whitney Tower, 'and loyalty is the name of her game.' Oscar saw the social world somewhat differently.

'Most of the people you see at those New York social affairs are about as shallow as a saucer,' he said.

The Wyatts, however, entertained on a grand scale at home. When Houston staged the world première of *Urban Cowboy*, starring John Travolta and Debra Winger, the Wyatts invited fifty for dinner – and Travolta turned up for a nightcap with thirty more. 'There were all these crazy people from Dallas and Fort Worth,' Andy Warhol noted about the dinner guests in his famous recorded *Diaries*. 'They were really rich with big rocks and they were really vulgar and funny. Divorced and out for kicks. Barbara Allen and Jerry Hall were making fun of women with jewels in front of their faces.'

Urban Cowboy, which had been filmed in Gilley's, the barn-like saloon in suburban Pasadena, was first shown at the Gay Lynn Theater, named in Lynn's honour. To show that her tastes could be highbrow as well, she became vice-chairman of the Houston Grand Opera, which attracted virtuosi of the calibre of Placido Domingo and Pavarotti. 'River

158

Oaks is the Belgravia of Houston, and Allington is like a French-style château,' said Dai Llewellyn, who was a guest there several times. 'It's so large that it makes the River Oaks Country Club next door look rather small. I had met Bob Sakowitz at Round Hill in Jamaica in the mid-seventies when I was staying with Vere and Pat Harmsworth (Lord and Lady Rothermere). Bob was married to Pam then, and her mother, Mrs Zauderer, had by far the best house there – this enormous tub-like place. She had so many enormous rocks on her fingers you practically had to crank her hands up. Bob and I played tennis together and got into the doubles final.

'When I went to Houston, I stayed with Bob and he was largely responsible for turning me into a wine buff. The bookcases seemed to contain nothing else but books on wine. The two brothers-in-law both loved wine. Oscar has arguably the best cellar in the whole of the United States. In the garden, he has a temperature-controlled mausoleum – a sort of temple to wine. There must be 100,000 bottles of wine there – only vintage La Tours and Lafittes.'

As the Wyatt empire spread, Oscar bought Tasajillo, a 16,000-acre ranch near the Rio Grande on the Mexican border. He took over the magnificent Villa Mauresque, the grandest home on the world's most expensive piece of real estate, Cap Ferrat in the South of France. Lynn revelled in being able to point out to guests – though most, like her good friend Prince Rainier, already knew – that the imposing villa had belonged to her literary hero, Somerset Maugham.

It was there that Lynn staged a spectacular party each year to celebrate her birthday – an event she never ignored, even as the years passed. Guests included her friend Princess Grace, Johnny Carson, Estée Lauder and David Niven. Andy Warhol noted after one visit to La Mauresque: 'Lynn was wearing a dress that was split up the sides and you could see all her breasts and she just had a little bikini on and she looked beautiful.' As Steve grew into the handsome, blue-eyed, sandy-haired six-footer who was later to have such an impact on the Duchess of York, he acquired a retinue of interested women. Unable to let go, it was Lynn who coquettishly described him as her love object.

She did not approve of the relationship he began in 1985 with the curvaceous local mannequin, Denice Lewis. When that relationship foundered on the Colorado ski slopes of Aspen on Christmas Eve 1987, no tears were shed in the house on River Oaks Boulevard. Lynn was more approving when he became engaged to his one-time Arizona college sweetheart, Dorice Valle Risso. He planned to marry Dorice, the daughter of a wealthy Lima industrialist, on 15 April 1989, in an elaborate ceremony 18,000 feet up a Peruvian mountain. But for reasons which she kept to herself, the bride-to-be called the wedding off at short notice.

.   .   .

Steve moved to London in 1985 to make his mark in the oil-broking business with one of Oscar's companies, Delaney Petroleum, based in St James's. Those who encountered him were impressed by his talk of spirituality. He was almost blindingly sincere and told everyone who would listen how he meditated each morning to clear his thought processes. But he rarely explained that his penchant for exploring his own and other troubled souls owed much to the inspiration of brother Douglas, who had fallen under the influence of Manhattan guru Frederick von Mierers and his Eternal Values cult. Mierers's philosophy was supposedly founded on contempt for the trophies of materialism on which such fortunes as the Wyatts were based. After he died of AIDS in 1990, the spiritual leader was exposed as a cheat and a fraud who coaxed money out of Ford mannequins, among other people, to invest in spiritually vibed crystals.

Steve preferred the salving powers of pyramids of the kind lauded by Madame Vasso. Denice Lewis said: 'I was sceptical [about the mystical healing benefits of a pyramid hanging over Wyatt's bed]. But they really worked for me. Steve was my guru and I am sure he was Fergie's as well. Steve believes his ideas will heal you and help you discover your spirituality.' His fascination for discovering the meaning of life sometimes spilled into his professional activities. He sought conversation with spiritual leaders including the Dalai Lama. In 1990, he made a film about religious leaders with Tony Hambro, a member of the banking family. In the South-East Asian kingdom of Bhutan, he was fascinated to conclude that the people there were more spiritually aware, and he returned to London telling everyone how they used yak meat for money.

He encountered some difficulty with his ecumenical beliefs, however, when interviewing the Archbishop of Canterbury, Dr Robert Runcie, who had explained the importance of their marriage vows to Sarah and Prince Andrew. Paul Handley, who used to work at Lambeth Palace, opined that Wyatt was 'a terribly bad interviewer', adding, 'Lord Runcie laid great stress on the Christian's duty to the poor and social justice. This offset Mr Wyatt's "everybody ought to be happy and I'll start with me" philosophy. Wyatt continued, "God is very real to me" and clenching his fist, he added, "We all need to . . . "before slicing the air in a diagonal karate chop.'

He never enjoyed battles, however, and held back when Doug – backed and encouraged by Oscar – took Robert Sakowitz to court in 1991. Lynn saw her son and brother bitterly pitched against each other in one of America's nastier public feuds. Robert successfully defended the action in which Doug and Oscar alleged that he had been squandering the Sakowitz family inheritance. Fraud, betrayal, cult influence, manip- ulation, envy and greed were all mentioned when the court heard Doug's charges that Robert had taken advantage of his position as head of the family-stores group to enrich himself by $8.5 million. The stores' bankruptcy, making the family's enormous shareholding worthless, was a result, Doug alleged. 'All of our money is gone,' he said, but of her husband's part in the action Lynn declared: 'I tried and begged and pleaded for Oscar not to sue, not because I thought Bob was right and he was wrong but precisely because it broke up the family.'

Robert clearly believed that Oscar was the wicked genius behind Doug's lawsuit, which his brothers eventually joined. He held that Oscar, who was bred in backwoods Navasota in east Texas, had a pathological loathing of inherited wealth. 'Oscar has always despised Robert because he thinks Robert was born with a silver spoon in his mouth while he had to work for everything,' said a Sakowitz employee of forty years.

Robert had taken a degree in history and economics at Harvard, but had to work as a trainee executive at Bloomingdale's and Macy's in New York and the Galleries Lafayette in Paris before becoming a buyer for Sakowitz. His title in Houston's society columns was the Merchant Prince. He was in the international list of best-dressed men almost as often as Lynn graced the women's section. The French Fashion Federa- tion awarded him the Epingle d'Or as a mark of respect.

He was also an active member of the Brotherhood of Knights of Wine and other gastronomic societies. One of the things Doug de- manded was that Robert surrender the contents of his wine cellar to make restitution to him and his brothers. 'I don't know whether this action was filed for sport or spite, the sport of rich men or the spite of little men,' said Robert's lawyer David Berg. Oscar's mother-in-law, Ann Sakowitz, told John Taylor, who covered the case for *New York* magazine, that an irresistible urge to dominate was simply a part of Oscar's nature. But there were other reasons why Oscar loathed his brother-in-law. He once said: 'I don't give him short measure on anything. He's got the testicles of a brass monkey.'

After Robert married Laura, the couple moved into a handsome house on River Oaks Boulevard, and although it was much smaller than the very grand Allington, the purchase infuriated Oscar, according to the neighbours. Another of Doug's demands was that Robert give up his mansion, his furniture and his art collection. Things deteriorated between the two branches of the family to such an extent that Lynn assigned her shares in Sakowitz Inc. to Douglas. When her sons and husband flew out to attend one birthday party at Cap Ferrat, Lynn told Doug: 'I'm not going to sue my brother. You investigate.'

Behind his oversized wire-rimmed glasses, Doug had intense violet-blue eyes which had peered deeply into his own soul. His favourite book was *The Road Less Travelled*, M. Scott Peck's psychological text on love, traditional values and spiritual growth which begins with the words: 'Life is difficult.' Doug, who worked for a Houston law firm specializing in the energy business, was more introverted than his older brother Steve and more unorthodox in his search for truth. He was deeply wounded when *Vanity Fair* reported that he was a member of the Eternal Values cult in language he found offensive. Founder Frederick von Mierers, a social-climbing interior decorator, claimed that he had psychic powers and drew astrological charts to give life readings to his disciples. He peddled jewellery which, he said, was imbued with mystical powers to protect the owner from malevolent forces. Lynn Wyatt bought a ring which cost her $70,000. Doug was quoted as having said: 'Frederick has helped so many people. He saves them from their egos. When you wear your gems, you can't be fooled by people and things that are evil.'

Doug felt that the article had presented a false and malicious picture of Mierers, whom his followers believed was an extra-terrestrial with advanced spiritual powers. Doug had introduced to Mierers one Roger Hall, a Houston businessman who later swore a deposition in which he claimed that, through Doug, he had bought $44,000 worth of jewellery from Eternal Values which he believed was basically worthless. When Doug and Mierers refused to give Hall his money back, he approached Robert to see if David Berg would represent him in a court action as well. Hall claimed that he felt Doug needed to be de-programmed to be freed from the influence of the cult.

'When you meet Doug, he doesn't seem like an eccentric person who has been brainwashed.' said John Taylor. 'He's pleasant, well-dressed and soft-spoken; he's not dumb, he's single and leads a rather conventional life. It's not the profile of a typical cult lunatic, but he was very powerfully influenced by Freddie von Mierers.' Doug's southern drawl on the telephone was calm and well-modulated, and he used phrases like 'I really appreciate and respect what you're doing' even when he was turning down requests for interviews.

Hall claimed that Mierers, a blond Aryan homosexual, 'told me that all women were selfish c***s. He told me that all Jews were evil.' Hall explained that Mierers taught that evil people were punished by being reincarnated as Jews. Hall said that Mierers had told Doug he did not have to worry about the fact that both his real parents were Jewish because even though Doug himself 'was reincarnated as a Jew, he was not a Jew'. Hall testified: 'Doug has been manipulated, brainwashed and totally controlled by Eternal Values. Doug believed that in a former life, his Uncle Robert was an evil gunfighter in the Old West, his adopted father was the sheriff and his grandmother Ann Sakowitz was a saloon owner. These guys hated each other then, and they came back to fight it out in this life.'

Another of Mierers's outlandish prophecies was that the planet would be virtually destroyed in 1999. A time and space traveller himself, he had returned to earth from the planet Arcturus to train a group of young people to run the world in 'the new age' that would arrive after Armageddon. The judge ruled that Hall's deposition was irrelevant unless it could be proved that Eternal Values had helped to persuade Wyatt to sue his uncle.

Quite how Ann Sakowitz felt about being regarded as a former saloon owner – albeit in a previous life – the matriarch never disclosed, but she did take the stand during the trial in Harris County Probate Court to prove that Lynn's prediction of the family being torn apart was correct. Ann, despite her seventy-eight years, valiantly revealed that everything Robert had done had been both legitimate and reported to the board, whose members included Lynn and herself. Lynn, she insisted, was to blame for the quarrel that had torn the family to pieces. 'If there is a betrayal, it is by Lynn', her mother said. 'She is my child and I love her. But she has disappointed me greatly by what she has done or allowed to be done to me and her brother.'

David Berg further savaged Lynn for failing to pay attention during the various efforts her brother had made to explain his business deals. 'It's very difficult to explain something to someone who is always under a hair dryer,' Berg said. Pointing out that Lynn had been the hostess of a gala dinner for Placido Domingo at the Houston Grand Opera the night before the trial began on Monday 30 September 1991, Berg added: 'She is always on her way to a party. She lights the fuse and then steps back into her vast wealth and retreats to a position where she can't hear the explosion when it goes off.'

When Lynn was called to give evidence, she was as cool and fragrant as a fresh magnolia even though her mother, red-eyed from crying, stared at her across the court. She denied that she was 'a manipulative woman orchestrating things from under a hair dryer'. It was a wonderful performance but it did no good. The jury cleared Robert of all charges against him and he returned happily to Laura in their corner of River Oaks Boulevard.

·   ·   ·

Steve Wyatt never cared much for the kind of business wars his stepfather thrived on. Where Oscar bullied, Steve charmed, and a London society hostess said of him: 'He's very hunky, gorgeous, very Richard Gere – an all-American boy, very into his body, aware of his muscles and tan, but not brain-thick either.' Although in London he could occasionally be viewed at Annabel's and Tramp, it was only when escorting a woman who wanted to go to one of those places.

Bryan had joined Wyatt in London in 1987 – the year of the cataclysmic Big Bang – looking for investment chances on the Stock Exchange. He and his father Tony, whose experience as a director included the Chrysler group and Federal Express, bought a high-tech company called Oceonics Group plc in 1988. The company's interests included offshore marine electronics, precision navigation and computer systems for the Ministry of Defence. As Communist states east of the Berlin Wall began to disintegrate, the Bryans expanded into Germany with an offshoot called Oceonics Deutschland, which specialized in putting the finishing touches to the interiors of new office blocks. The move proved that, even if the opportunity were right for such a venture, the operating costs were punitive. Losses for 1990 reached £7.5 million and Oceonics was in trouble. Former British Army supremo General Sir Harry Tuzo, one of the directors at the time, said: 'What basically went wrong was that the company was in too many things, construction and computers particularly. When the time came, John and his father behaved absolutely correctly.' The Bryans bought out the over-stretched German division and resigned from the company.

Bryan went to Annabel's to find an ambience suited to his social aspirations, and it was there that he made several important contacts, one of whom was the young aristocrat Lord (Harry) Dalmeny, son and heir to the Earl of Rosebery. 'He was on first name terms with the waiters, but, they're all like that there,' said one who partied with him at Annabel's. 'He was good fun, though – one of the most exciting people I'd met in a while. I thought he was definitely potential. He's really smart, hyperactive and grandiose.'

Bryan started escorting a succession of upper-class girls including Lord Rothermere's daughter, Geraldine Ogilvy, and Lady Antonia Fraser's daughter Flora. Other friends he made included Lady Liza Campbell, Natasha Grenfell of the banking family and Detmar Blow, a relative of Lord Tollemache, and on whose Gloucestershire estate he rented an eighteenth-century cottage. 'He's a very fast mover – very fast,' said one who attracted Bryan's eye at a dinner party. 'I've done the dating scene for a while now and he's hand-on-the-knee very quickly. He fixes on a girl and says, "I'm absolutely in love with you." It all seemed a bit practised to me.'

Bryan's style attracted the interest of journalist Christa D'Souza, whom he persuaded one night to leave the Fire Ball, a charity function attended by Princess Margaret at the Inter-Continental Hotel in Park Lane, and transfer to Annabel's for a nightcap with two others. 'It wasn't that he necessarily knew everyone there that night but he was doing a brilliant impression of a Very Powerful Person, bouncing around the room like Zebedee, ordering a bottle of Moët before we'd even sat down, peppering the conversation with the name of Fergie and joshing affectionately with a very slightly mystified waiter,' she said. 'Bryan is one of those lucky types who has winged it through life, upping the social ante as he goes along radiating confidence and goodwill. That said, "Promise little, deliver everything" may not necessarily be his family motto.'

One of his dates, who preferred to be called Sally, was the recipient of Bryan's fluctuating generosity. 'He called me up and said, "Let's go to lunch and then we'll go to Browns and buy you something." I said, "Lunch would be great, but you don't have to buy me anything." He said, "No, no, we'll buy you an outfit." I got a call, "Too busy for lunch – but go to Browns anyway, pick something out and I'll meet you there." I went over there, picked something out and said, "My boyfriend is just about to come over." He never was able to make it. This went on and on. I went to his place for drinks and he called the shop and said, "Hold on to it. We'll pick it up tomorrow."

'He picked me up in his rented car to go to his country cottage and we drove up Sloane Street, past the shop and he didn't say anything at all. I said, "I think I'll get the outfit anyway. I'll buy it." He said okay and pulled the car over, parked right on Sloane Street and stayed put. I go huffing and puffing into the shop, wondering what do I do now? I really wanted this outfit, but I went back to the car without anything. He said, "Why didn't you buy it?" I said, "Let's go now." Then he gave me his credit card and said, "Put half of it on mine and half of it on yours." I didn't know what to say because you sound like a pushy girl. I just sat there and gave him his credit card back. The outfit was only about £300 as well. I got out of the car, said, "You're full of shit," and slammed the door. He called up and said, "You need a shrink." I was far too conservative for him. Promise the world to get you in the mood – that's how he is. But he was very sweet on the phone and we parted friends.'

Steve Wyatt was an accomplished dinner-party animal who preferred situations where he could talk and be heard, always spraying his conversational partner with their name in every other sentence. At one dinner party, he had the bad kharma to meet Christa D'Souza, editor-at-large for *Tatler* magazine. 'The conversation veers soulward,' she recounted. 'Everyone was quite drunk or smoking furiously except Steve. One of the men points out how pure Steve is compared with the rest of the table. "I *lahke* a little red wine," he admits, but goes on to say he does not really drink very much and steers clear of dairy products. Someone talks about the inherent duplicity of the human psyche – me, I think. This is right up Steve's alley, the subject of feelings, emotions, getting in touch with oneself: all completely alien territory to your average Englishman, though perhaps slightly less so to your average Englishwoman. "Duplicity?" drawls Steve mellifluously. "That's a good word. Ah've never heard that word before, what does it mean?" '

Steve was as careful with his money as his health. He never threw it around and one man invited by Wyatt to a pre-Christmas lunch with him and Bryan at a South Kensington restaurant recalled: 'When the bill arrived, Steve said, "Okay, fellas, let's have your Gold Cards," and he handed them all to the waiter instructing him to charge an equal amount of the total to each. We all thought it was fair.'

Despite his popularity with women, Steve had not been altogether successful in love and rarely allowed it to show when he reciprocated the feelings a woman was showing him. He was in his thirty-seventh year and still eligible as ever when Lynn informed him that his presence was required at home to meet a special guest. The Duchess of York had accepted her invitation to visit Texas. Sarah was pregnant for the second time, but she was clocking up as many air miles as usual. Before heading for Houston, she flew due south to Uruguay to see Susie and Hector, who were planning an exciting new venture. Backed by Peter Brant's money, Hector was building a polo centre at the resort of Punta des Este across the River Plate from Argentina. Sarah, accompanied by four staff and a doctor, flew in as the guest of Whitbread, the brewers, to start the second leg of the Round the World Yacht Race. She and Susie went for long walks on the beach during which Sarah confided in her mother about the state of her marriage. 'We have an excellent relationship,' said Susie. 'We don't have any secrets. We're more like friends than mother and daughter.'

The trip exhausted Sarah so much that she was forced to drop out of a ship-launching ceremony she was supposed to attend in Aberdeen on her return. Andrew stood in for her somewhat reluctantly, and caused astonishment among the guests when he said: 'Thank you for inviting me to take over from my wife who is resting up at the moment and about to disappear again on another trip, leaving me behind to do all the work.' He was only half-joking and soon events were about to involve the Windsors and the Wyatts in headline news. Before long, Lynn Wyatt was telling her own boisterous offspring Steve: 'Just hold your head high. You've done nothing wrong. The truth will always come out.'

TEN

At a Gentleman's Shooting Party

'Mah woman and I sit together.'

STEVE WYATT

J ust thirty and still slim despite her unplanned pregnancy, the Duchess of York boarded a jumbo jet for the ten-hour flight from Gatwick to a rendezvous in Houston, Texas, that would prove to be a critical turning point in her life. She had celebrated her birthday in her beloved Klosters with Prince Andrew and a group of friends, a happy evening which had been ruined by a hurtful public reprimand from her husband.

As the Yorks were leaving the restaurant, newsmen camped outside in the snow asked the Duchess if she had enjoyed her party. 'Fergie started to answer – until Andrew darted his wife a cold look and said sternly, "Shut up," ' recounted one of the reporters. 'Fergie, looking hurt, asked, "Why?" ' It was reminiscent of a scene during their first trip to the Swiss ski resort when, after a similar outburst from Andrew, the Duchess was overheard to say: 'Why do you have to keep embarrassing me and pointing it out in front of other people when I get things wrong? It's not very charitable. Sometimes you're as bad as your father. If you're going to say something like that then why don't you wait until we're on our own instead of embarrassing me? Unlike some people, I haven't been doing this for twenty-seven years.'

As Sarah crossed the Atlantic, she was far from happy with Andrew and not only because of his bullying attitude. In particular, she was distressed about his friendship with a married woman in whom he was confiding his secrets. Any agony aunt could have read the situation as clearly as the signposts which directed traffic to Houston's main landmarks on Route 45 heading into the big Southern metropolis that Thursday, 2 November 1989. Buckingham Palace described this as an official trip because the Duchess was travelling as a guest to a British festival at the Houston Grand Opera. Her hostess for the five-day stay in Texas was Lynn Wyatt, wife of Oscar and mother of Steve and Doug. As her limousine glided along River Oaks Boulevard, the Duchess saw the Wyatt mansion for the first time.

The architect John F. Staub had designed Allington for another oil mogul, Hugh Roy Cullen of Exxon, as a grand Southern residence in the neo-classical style. Visitors passed beneath Ionic columns into a superb black and white marble entrance hall and gazed in wonder at its central feature – a magnificent staircase enhanced with crested panels of Lalique glass. When Oscar bought Allington for Lynn as a Christmas present, it became known to the locals and other royal guests, such as Princess Margaret, as the Wyatt Regency. Andy Warhol's portrait of Lynn was framed above one of the mantelpieces.

Although Lynn knew the Duchess from London and Palm Beach, her sons had never met her before. Steve had flown home from London at his mother's behest to attend the Lone Star State's tribute to three hundred years of British opera – and to meet the Duchess. 'I introduced Sarah to Steve and to Doug, and at the time she was five months pregnant,' said Lynn when she was called upon to dampen speculation of romance between her son and the Queen's daughter-in-law. 'Steve and Sarah are just good friends. People in London are so protective of their Royalty, and they resent it when foreigners become friendly with them.'

Oscar Wyatt, the uncapped King of Crude, did not find that a problem, not personally. His millions had given him a certain immunity from what he called 'bullshit'. One of his favourite sayings was: 'Bullshit walks and money talks.' 'I think Sarah is a helluva fine young lady,' he said in the gravel voice which was his trademark on the oilfields. 'You know, I'm an easily impressionable guy,' meaning he was exactly the opposite. 'She likes to fly helicopters, she likes to fly airplanes. She might not get along with the Royal Family for all I know. I probably wouldn't either, but I don't judge her for that. She's a fine girl and I like her father – he's a good guy.' Ronald Ferguson had turned up in Texas to play in the Ralph Lauren Royal Invitational at the Houston Polo Club. He and Oscar were soon on 'good buddy' terms.

It was, however, the impact that Sarah made on Steve, and vice versa, that became a talking point among people who met them during the next few days. 'It was obvious that Sarah was enormously attracted to him,' said one other who was present at a dinner during the Duchess's stay. 'It's not just that he was handsome; Steve has a fun personality and she has always been drawn to fun people. They laughed a lot at the table, and she was very comfortable in his company. It's a very Texas thing to put people at their ease, but with Steve it's an art-form. He used her name in every other sentence, and I would say she was smitten from the off. Steve is a quietly confident man who has no hang-ups about his family's wealth. He was attentive, she was receptive. For his part Steve seemed enchanted by this royal lady – although I'd say that that was the Lynn Sakowitz in him coming out. There was clearly a chemistry between them.'

Like most of her foreign trips, Sarah's itinerary was packed. 'When Diana goes anywhere abroad on a job, she goes on her own for that purpose and comes straight back,' observed the well-placed royal watcher. 'When Fergie travels, she always tries to incorporate a holiday and invariably includes family among her party. It's an interesting difference between them.'

The British consulate, aware of criticisms labelling Sarah as a royal slouch, made sure she had a full schedule. She visited the High School of Performing and Visual Arts where students performed part of *Julius Caesar* in her honour; she paid a courtesy call on Kathy Whitmire, the Mayor of Houston; and she saw an anti-drugs programme at work in a school. She wore a bright crimson suit for a tour of NASA's Lyndon B. Johnson Space Center where she delighted the urban spacemen of mission control with her lively banter. Picking up a toilet roll, she asked flight director Wayne Hale: 'What's this for?' 'We're cutting costs,' he explained, 'and that replaces the box of tissues.'

Steve was never far from her side. He drove her to the polo, helped her from the car and saw to it that she was shielded from a downpour with a big beach umbrella. After the match, she trudged across the churned-up playing field in high heels to present trophies to the winning team as the rain pelted down. She was not wearing a coat, she declined the offer of an umbrella and her hair was soaked. 'It was a typical Fergie gesture – it enabled the American photographers to get better pictures. She does her best to please, you know,' added the royal watcher.

The opera festival was the focal point of the trip and Steve squired her to a performance of *The Mikado*, produced by Jonathan Miller and starring Eric Idle as the Lord High Executioner. She wore a revealing Bellville Sassoon gown in yellow as bright as any Texas rose. When someone asked her if she liked Gilbert and Sullivan, she confessed she preferred Dire Straits. Her honesty was sometimes a problem. For the world première of *New Year*, an opera composed by Sir Michael Tippett, she wore a long pink gown, baring her shoulders. 'Her five-month pregnancy wasn't very visible, though she did put two pillows behind her back at one formal dinner,' noted society watcher Jeannie Williams.

In the middle of all this, the Wyatts whisked Sarah two hundred miles south for a barbecue at Tasajillo, their ranch in Duval County close to the Mexican border. The name, she was told, came from a cactus which had the self-destructive habit of exploding on contact. The Duchess took over the controls of the helicopter as it criss-crossed the 16,000-acre spread. One night, she and Lynn popped into Armando's for a late-night snack where she met a fellow ski enthusiast who invited her to join him on the slopes. 'I'll drop by Buckingham Palace and honk to let you know I'm there,' said the Texan.

'I don't know what my mother-in-law would say about that,' said the Duchess, wide-eyed in mock horror.

After her stay, a signed photograph of a smiling Sarah was to take pride of place among souvenirs from other visiting celebrities in the drawing room at Allington. When she bade the Wyatts a grateful farewell, Sarah told Steve that she hoped they would meet again. They did – but only after Sarah flew back to New York to promote her *Budgie* books, which had just gone on sale in the US, one reviewer describing them as 'perfectly ghastly'.

She stayed in the same rooms Princess Diana had occupied at the Hotel Plaza Athenée on East 64th Street between Madison and Park Avenues near Central Park. Mort Janklow, her agent, held a dinner party in her honour where she was seated next to Tom Wolfe, author of *The Bonfire of the Vanities*, and opposite Norman Mailer, the ageing *enfant terrible* of American literature. What passed across the table between Sarah and Mailer swiftly moved straight into legend. Sarah politely asked the author to recommend one of his books for her to read as, she admitted, she was unfamiliar with his work.

'*Tough Guys Don't Dance,*' said Mailer.

'What's it about?' asked Sarah.

'C***s,' said Mailer.

There was an audible intake of breath from Wolfe and the other guests. Sarah was not fazed. 'You know, Mr Mailer,' she said, savouring the pause, 'the most interesting thing for me at this moment is watching everyone's face at this table.'

The nicely executed put-down brought her enormous kudos when the story zipped around New York as fast as Bell Telephone could manage. 'Everyone present was impressed with the way she handled a very tough situation so gracefully,' said a highly placed publishing source. Simon & Schuster held a cocktail party for her at the Rainbow Room on the sixty-fifth floor of the old RCA building at the Rockefeller Center. She also attended a reading class at the Children's Museum of Manhattan. Somewhere in between, she found time to do her Christmas shopping in the emporiums on Fifth Avenue.

When she returned to London, the baggage handlers at Heathrow could scarcely believe the number of suitcases, trunks, parcels and packages bearing her name which came tumbling out on to the carousel. They counted fifty-three items, fifty-one of which were classed as excess luggage. 'Not even Joan Collins has this much,' one complained.

．　　．　　．

Whatever Sarah's problems with Andrew, they seemed minor compared with the marital difficulties of Jane and Alex Makim. After a trial separation, which Sarah had discussed with Alex at the Sheraton Hotel during her Australian visit, the couple had been reunited on St Valentine's Day four months later. But the reconciliation was falling apart, and Jane needed the comfort and support of her famous little sister of whom she said: 'As kids there were only the two of us and we did everything together. As sisters we couldn't be closer.' The two young women and their children spent ten days on holiday together at Lizard Island on the Great Barrier Reef where Jane told Sarah that the reunion with Alex had failed. She wanted her freedom. Soon after Sarah and Beatrice had flown back to London, the briefest of statements from Alex's lawyer said: 'Alex Makim wishes to announce that his marriage to Jane Makim is over.' Only those closest to the rough-hewn Australian knew the intensity of the emotional pain he was suffering.

With her sister's new life firmly on her mind, the Duchess, now six months pregnant, headed north to Yorkshire on Friday, 8 December. As patron of Opera North, she attended the gala première of the musical *Show Boat* at the Grand Theatre in Leeds. Fog made it impossible for her to return to London in the plane which was waiting on the runway. Her hosts offered her overnight accommodation in the city, but she declined. With Carolyn Cotterell, her lady-in-waiting, Sarah drove to Constable Burton Hall, Charles and Maggie Wyvill's 3000-acre sporting estate near Leyburn, North Yorkshire. Sarah had not been there before, but had heard about the house. The oldest section dated back to 1500 and had been 'modernized' in 1768. It was now, in the words of Maggie Wyvill, 'a very beautiful Georgian house'.

Maggie had served dinner to her guests, who included the Queen's cousin, Patrick (the Earl of) Lichfield, the Royal Ballet star Wayne Eagling, Brian Alexander, brother of Earl Alexander of Tunis, banker Nicky Villiers, and actor Nigel Havers, with his wife Polly, and an unaccompanied Steve Wyatt. Also there with his fourth bride-to-be Dawn Dunlap (a Texas-born theatrical agent who found work in America for Havers) was Frank Lowe, the advertising genius who partnered Tim Bell in the agency which they had taken to enormous success. It cannot have escaped Sarah's attention that another guest was her husband's close friend and confidant, Charlie Young.

'Maggie Wyvill seemed a little surprised by the arrival of the Duchess in her long black evening dress, but she excused herself and went to supervise the preparation of a double room next to her own for Sarah and for Carolyn, who was also pregnant with Harry's first child,' said Diana's tennis friend. 'Brandies were served and as the night wore on, the conversation grew more ribald. Sarah seemed to know even cruder jokes than most of the men and, one by one, most of the ladies at the table slipped away to their beds. Sarah and Steve were among the last to retire.'

'It was a bit of a surprise when she arrived,' said Maggie Wyvill, the mother of four young children. 'She was stuck at Leeds and she just thought it was rather fun to stay here. Steve Wyatt and another member of the shooting party had to share a room because we were all pushed. I actually had to move him out and bung him into another room with another man. The Duchess shared a room with her lady-in-waiting. So two men shared a room and two ladies shared a room. The whole thing was tremendously innocent. It was the first time anybody knew that they were seeing each other. But at that stage she was very much pregnant, and at that point there was nothing going on between them.'

At breakfast that Saturday morning, Sarah was still wearing the long black evening dress she had paraded at the show in Leeds. Before the eight guns set off for the day's shooting, she joined the all-male group for photographs posed on the balustraded steps of the Palladian-fronted Constable Burton Hall. Maggie herself took several pictures of the group in which Sarah sat at Wyatt's feet and one photograph of the assembly was to be proudly displayed in the hall until controversy about Sarah's friendship with the Texan became public and the picture, along with Mrs Wyvill's others, were placed under lock and key for safe keeping. Patrick Lichfield, who earns his living as a photographer, said that the back of his camera flew open and ruined the film he had shot.

This was a pity, because the friends had made an annual event of the trip to Constable Burton and liked to keep a photographic record of the occasion. 'It's always that weekend,' explained Maggie. 'You get into a slot, you see, and a lot of people want it. It's a very good slot – excellent shooting. They've got it and they come back year after year.'

Before the group set off to shoot pheasants, Sarah told them she and Carolyn were setting off for Leeds Airport to join Prince Andrew, who was shooting with the Royal Family at Sandringham that weekend. They were surprised on their return later that afternoon, therefore, to discover that the Duchess and Carolyn were still there. Their plane had been unable to take off, and they planned to stay a second night. Maggie Wyvill's feelings were somewhat mixed. 'It was exciting for my staff,' she said. 'It was very nice having the Duchess of York staying, but it was not exciting for me or for the rest of my guests. She was an excellent guest – great fun, very lovely, enormous fun, actually.' At the end of her stay, Frank Lowe picked up the bill for Steve Wyatt, who was already his guest, and for the Duchess.

Sarah returned south on the morning of Sunday, 10 December, but not until a second late night, which she illuminated with more blue humour, had elapsed. She later told a friend that she had asked Frank Lowe to help her with her public image: 'She said that she told him she was really upset about the bashing she was taking in the newspapers. She implored Frank to take her under his professional wing,' said Diana's tennis-friend. 'According to her, he declined. Whatever it was he had said to her, she wasn't very pleased. She had become quite used to people doing whatever she asked.'

A thoughtful man, Lowe – who was credited with the idea for the campaign based on the claim that Heineken lager reached the parts other beers cannot – said: 'I've always had a passionate belief that advertising should be a force for good and that it should enrich the environment, not impoverish it.'

Even he would have been powerless over the media which delighted in publishing a photograph of the Duchess sprawled on a Mayfair pavement a few weeks later. Sarah was leaving Harry's Bar with Prince Andrew when she tripped and fell. One who witnessed the incident said that Andrew seemed disinterested in the accident to his seven months pregnant wife, but a Palace source insisted that by continuing to walk to his car he was doing exactly what his security training had instilled in him. Two days later, Andrew set sail in HMS *Campbeltown* for several weeks of naval exercises off Gibraltar. Sarah, still bruised from her fall, waved him goodbye from Portland. Before he boarded his helicopter to fly out to his ship, Andrew acknowledged that frequent separations were affecting his private life. 'The three Services are a fantastic job for a single man,' he said. 'But it is getting less and less so for a married man.'

Sarah headed straight for the mountains of Klosters with Beatrice, then made an overnight trip to Megève in the French Alps. The next day she refused to allow her pregnancy to deter her from making a seven-hour trip to New York, her third flight in forty-eight hours without a doctor, after receiving an emergency call from Susie. Hector had been flown to the United States in Peter Brant's private plane for treatment at the Memorial Sloan-Kettering Cancer Center after an operation in Buenos Aires revealed that he was suffering from cancer of the lymph gland. The only concession Sarah would make in her haste was that she flew a Virgin Atlantic 747 from Gatwick to Newark, instead of Concorde from Heathrow to JFK, because it was a quieter route and she had more room on the jumbo jet. At Newark, a helicopter whisked her to the clinic in Manhattan where she and Susie spent an hour at Hector's bedside. The next day she took him champagne, back numbers of *Horse and Hound* magazine and family photographs. She also visited patients in nearby rooms to apologize for the presence of her British detective and a large detail of State Department bodyguards.

'You're so trim,' a woman visiting the ward told Sarah.

'Well, after I blimped out when Beatrice was born, I promised I wouldn't with this baby,' she replied. She left a comforting note for a little girl she had chatted to the day before who was receiving treatment during her second visit.

Hector faced an anxious wait of several weeks before specialists could ascertain whether the disease had been arrested by chemotherapy. He bravely dismissed his illness as 'the first great inconvenience I've ever encountered'. Less sanguinely, he said: 'I'm not afraid of dying. Having a clear conscience makes you face death in another way. I do know I have to get some personal things in order. It is now time to consolidate what we have. In the end, we die and one dollar here or there won't change our lives.' Sarah kept Andrew informed of Hector's condition. Another who was always on the end of a telephone when she needed to share her distress was Steve Wyatt. She telephoned him at his Delaney Petroleum office in St James's by day and at his Chelsea flat by night.

In London, Sarah's car and ever-patient detective were sometimes to be seen parked outside the entrance to No. 34 Cadogan Square and on other occasions outside an address in Shepherd's Bush where Wayne Eagling threw dinner parties. The assembly once transferred to 'a ghastly restaurant' in Shepherd's Bush where the Duchess was on top form, although at least one other diner did not appreciate her colourful vocabulary.

She also attended a dinner party at the elegant apartment Wyatt was renting. 'Be nice to the Duchess, remember who she is,' Wyatt cautioned his guests. One was Pricilla Phillips, an American actress who was living nearby in Pont Street. The two women started to chat. Pricilla told the royal guest that as well as studying t'ai chi, a mixture of martial arts and yoga, she shared with Steve an interesting New Age philosophy. To her delight Sarah discovered that the actress was naturally irreverent and publicly unfazed by celebrity. Pricilla's brazen sense of humour appealed to the girl from Dummer Down Farm and Sarah saw her as an exceedingly trustworthy, down-to-earth buddy. Just the kind of girl to take on a hush-hush holiday.

Pricilla was appearing in a production of *Breakfast, Lunch and Dinner* with Julie Anne Rhodes, the American wife of Duranduran keyboard player Nick Rhodes, in a small theatre above the Man in the Moon pub in Chelsea. She invited Sarah to attend. Sarah liked the play about an eternal triangle involving two sisters in love with the same man so much that she went to see it again.

More theatrical outings were on the agenda when Wyatt escorted her to a performance of Keith Waterhouse's comedy *Jeffrey Bernard is*

Unwell, starring Peter O'Toole, at the Apollo Theatre in Shaftesbury Avenue. As the curtain came down, Sarah's detective whispered to her that a photographer was waiting outside the theatre's main entrance. Taking evasive action, Wyatt lingered behind in the wings while Sarah, heavily pregnant and dressed in a low-cut evening gown, slipped out through the stage door and drove away in her chauffeured car. Minutes later, a crestfallen Wyatt emerged through the same door and, head bowed against the midnight drizzle, sauntered down the street with his hands buried deep in his pockets as though he had happened to be there by pure chance. The charade fooled nobody. He and Sarah met up at a nearby nightspot a short time later.

.   .   .

The Duchess was rushed from Buckingham Palace to the Portland Hospital after going into labour just before teatime on 23 March 1990. Andrew drove the 218 miles from his naval base at Devonport to the hospital non-stop in his Jaguar to be present when Eugenie Victoria Helena was born by Caesarean delivery at 7.58 p.m. A Palace spokesman said that surgery was necessary because the baby, who weighed 7 lb 1½ oz, 'was the wrong way round'. Eugenie – pronounced, the Yorks insisted, U–Jany – was named after the grand-daughter of Queen Victoria and daughter of Princess Beatrice. Eugenie made her first public appearance when she left the clinic eight days later, cradled in the arms of her mother's bright pink Yves Saint Laurent outfit.

But Sarah's joy over the new baby was mixed with some unfortunate news from Susie. Hector's benefactor Peter Brant had pleaded guilty to evading tax payments of £625,000. He admitted that personal and family expenses, including the purchase of antiques, jewellery and clothing, were loaded on to the company books. He was freed on bail to await sentence.

Six weeks after Eugenie was born, Andrew remained at Castlewood House, the home King Hussein of Jordan had loaned the Yorks rent-free, while Sarah, with Beatrice and nanny Alison, joined Wyatt aboard a private jet. They flew south to Agadir on the Moroccan coast on 2 May and then drove fifty miles to La Gazelle d'Or, the hotel resort outside the ochre-coloured earthen walls of Taroudent. With them was Pricilla Phillips, who had holidayed there before, and two detectives from the Royal Protection Branch. For five idyllic days, Sarah enjoyed the sunshine and the freedom that Wyatt's excursion offered. Each of the thirty cottages in the hotel complex had its own private terrace where guests taking breakfast were treated to the sight of the snow-capped Atlas Mountains in the distance. Lunch was invariably eaten beside a swimming pool near the central clubhouse and dinner was served in a tented dining room surrounded by luxuriant gardens. There was a beauty salon and hammam, or Turkish bath.

No one gave it a second thought whenever a member of the group produced a camera and captured what for Sarah were obviously blissful moments. Nothing was more natural than to take photographs of Steve and Sarah as they rode two of the hotel's Arab horses through the olive groves and palm trees which bordered the Sahara Desert or cavorted beside the heated pool. Wyatt clutching Beatrice as the photographer attracted the child's attention seemed an innocent-enough action. Lounging together on a swing chair, their arms apparently around each other's backs, Steve and Sarah smiled at the camera oblivious to any danger. In another, Sarah posed with a dagger she had bought on a visit to the bazaar. The pictures reflected the relaxed way they were feeling. Without a second thought, the rolls of film were packed for processing back in London. Yet, even as the baggage stickers were being put on for their return journey, an informant moved to a public telephone at El Vino's in Fleet Street where he had been drinking with a special contact. He dialled 828 2150, the direct line to the Confidential diary desk of the *Today* newspaper.

'You might like to know that the Duchess of York is having a secret holiday abroad with someone very interesting.'

'Where is she?'

'Try Morocco.'

'What's so interesting about the other person?'

'He's Texan and very rich.'

A member of the Confidential team called a news agency in Tangier and initiated enquiries. The answers came back within twenty-four hours. The Duchess of York, Princess Beatrice, two member of the Royal Protection Branch and the nanny Alison Wardley had all been registered at La Gazelle d'Or for the past few days. So had Mr Steven Wyatt, who had settled the bill for the party. A phone call to the hotel established that Pricilla Phillips had also been with them. At the Man in the Moon pub, the theatre manager directed a reporter's questions about Miss Phillips to press agent Connie Philapello, who faxed a page of detail which the actress had supplied on notepaper headed with her Pont Street address. The actress, it showed, had spent a year at the Strasberg Institute, had played a bit part in the Francis Ford Coppola film *The Cotton Club* and had another small role in Paul Mazursky's film *Moscow on the Hudson*, which starred Robin Williams. She had also been in a handful of commercials, including one for American Express, one for the New York store Bloomingdale's and a third for Harvey's Bristol Cream Sherry. Nowhere in Pricilla's cv did it mention that she had been married to a German called Nito and was at the time she met the Duchess, friendly with Wayne Eagling. He had met Pricilla when she had spent a Swiss holiday with him and his friend, Baroness Francesca 'Chessie' Thyssen, whose father Heini owned the world's finest art collection.

Further enquiries by the Confidential team uncovered Sarah's first meeting with Pricilla at Wyatt's dinner party in Cadogan Square and the sudden friendship that had sprung up between them. One who saw the two women on several occasions at La Gazelle d'Or remarked: 'The Duchess struck me as being quite an insecure person and vulnerable to anyone out to score points, but Miss Phillips was not the sort to take advantage of a weakness like that.' No such credentials were immediately available about their holiday host, and the reporter telephoned contacts in Houston to elicit more about the intriguing Texan bachelor. The paper's editor was David Montgomery, who had volunteered to leave the mass-selling *News of the World* for the then struggling daily when Rupert Murdoch bought it in July 1987. Montgomery published the scoop in which Wyatt's name not only appeared in print in Britain for the first time, but was linked to the Queen's daughter-in-law.

Her Moroccan tan shining like burnished armour, Sarah steeled herself for an encounter that had been on her mind for five years – her first meeting with Koo Stark. The occasion was a Swinging Sixties party thrown at the Kensington home of Michael Pearson to mark the thirtieth birthday of his wife Marina. Sarah wore a black and white mini-dress and Prince Andrew donned a gold Beatle jacket. Viscount Linley, who was only nine when the sixties ended, commemorated the seventies instead by wearing a punk wig. Patrick Lichfield was decked out in an embroidered jacket and other guests, who all wore wigs, flared trousers, psychedelic shirts, headbands and John Lennon glasses, included the racing driver James Hunt, Duranduran musician John Taylor and his girlfriend Amanda de Cadenet . . . and Koo Stark.

'If I say so myself my outfit was rather good,' boasted Dai Llewellyn. 'My ex-wife Vanessa looked sensational and she won the best-dressed girl prize. Prince Andrew looked such a dreadful plonker that he was clearly out in front for the worst-dressed man. But as Fergie was presenting the prizes, they could not do that to her. So Pearson said to me, "Look, you're a good sport. Can we award it to you?" So I won this wooden spoon and there was Fergie pretending to beat me with it when she presented it to me.'

There was no confrontation between Sarah and Koo, who looked stunning in a black lace, off-the-shoulder mini-dress. She arrived alone and left the same way at 2 a.m., twenty minutes before Andrew and Sarah called it a night. Koo had great style.

.　　.　　.

As Hector's condition continued to deteriorate, Sarah became 'very upset and concerned' about his gaunt appearance when she visited him while he recuperated at Peter Brant's White Birch Farm. Chemotherapy had withered away El Gordo's bulk, and some of his hair had fallen out. Andrew had stayed behind to attend King Constantine's fiftieth birthday party at Spencer House – the London home of Princess Diana's family until her father sold it to the Rothschilds. He joined her for the one official engagement they had agreed to undertake, the opening of Jaguar's new North American headquarters in New Jersey. They also visited Barney's, a Seventh Avenue store which sold British-made men's clothes. He told a rapt audience about 'the pucker factor' which happens when a plane suddenly loses height. 'I'm not sure if I can explain this in front of women,' he said. 'Things shrivel when you go down fast.'

He did not join Sarah when she attended a private dinner party at the Fifth Avenue apartment of socialites Jeanette and Bobby Fomon, the son of her Palm Beach host Robert Fomon. 'She was in high spirits to say the least,' observed one who was unaccustomed to the Duchess in full flow. 'She showed several guests how to dance like a Duchess.' Then she picked up a knife, tapped the Fomons' pet dog on either side of his ears, and said: 'Arise, Sir Rutherford.' When the harmless prank was reported back to SW1, her mother-in-law shared the astonishment of a guest who said: 'It kinda surprised us when she knighted the dog.' The Queen might have been even more surprised if she had ever caught Sarah doing one of her impressions of Her Majesty to amuse her friends.

Just two days after the Yorks' visit to his estate, Brant was sentenced at a court in Bridgeport, Connecticut, to a one-year jail term, to be suspended after ninety days (in fact, he served eighty-four days in a federal prison camp), five years probation and five hundred hours of community service. In addition, he was fined £65,000. Brant had been a good friend to Susie and Hector, and Sarah's loyalty towards him did not waver. The favour she was about to bestow on Steve Wyatt, however, was another matter entirely and it turned into the biggest *faux pas* she had ever made.

Just before the Iraqi invasion of Kuwait at the beginning of August, Sarah arranged a small dinner party at Buckingham Palace for Steve and Dr Ramzi Salman, the head of Iraqi state oil marketing. Iraq had become the pariah of the international community after Saddam Hussein's regime had unleashed a reign of terror against its opponents. Innocent people, many of them Jews, had been executed in public 'to teach them a lesson'.

After the meal, Sarah said that she had agreed to put in an appearance at a soirée given by the Conservative Party Treasurer Lord McAlpine and his wife Romilly at Le Gavroche in Upper Brook Street, Mayfair. She astonished the McAlpines and their guests by arriving around 11 p.m. with Wyatt and his Iraqi friend in tow. Romilly offered Sarah her own place next to Lord McAlpine and was about to show the men to another table when Wyatt grabbed the Duchess's hand and jested: 'Mah woman and I sit together.'

The dinner that Sarah had hosted for Wyatt and Dr Salman created an international incident when news of it leaked out. Members of the Royal Family and the Palace secretariat were appalled that Sarah could have been so indiscreet as to entertain an Iraqi, particularly as the Kuwaiti Royal Family were on excellent terms with the House of Windsor. Most of them, including the Emir of Kuwait, were living in Kensington in exile as the Middle East reached flashpoint.

What made the offence even more grievous was that Oscar Wyatt was not only buying 250,000 barrels of crude oil a day from the Iraqi government, he was also in the process of negotiating a deal which could give Saddam Hussein a share in his East Coast American refineries. Sarah, trying only to repay some of the Wyatts' hospitality, could not have stumbled into a more explosive political issue if she had tried. Oscar Wyatt had known Saddam Hussein for twenty years and Salman, one of the Saddam's closest confidants, was also his friend. The matter did not go unnoticed at the headquarters of British Intelligence in Curzon Street, Mayfair – or among their American cousins at the CIA in Langley, Virginia. It was not long before something happened.

When the fuss over the Moroccan holiday had all but died down another informant – this time an American – telephoned the Confidential team about Sarah's next excursion in a jet provided by Steve Wyatt. The Duchess would be leaving from an airport in the North of England after an engagement with the Duke at the Yorkshire Show in Harrogate at midday. Andrew would return home to Castlewood to be with Beatrice and Eugenie. Sarah, the source correctly predicted, would not be at her husband's side when he presented trophies at the Royal County of Berkshire Polo Club the following day.

The informant suggested that, this time, she was bound for Greece. In fact, he meant Nice and the mishearing cost the paper valuable time in following up the lead. While journalists made calls trying to locate the Wyatt plane at airports and islands in the Ionian and Aegean Seas, Steve and Sarah had touched down in the South of France and headed for Cap Ferrat. As they followed the Corniche towards Monte Carlo, mountains rose up to their left and to their right were rocky shores and dazzling white beaches washed by the azure blue Mediterranean. The car bore them along Somerset Maugham Boulevard to a point where she caught her first sight of the white house positioned above the legendary Hôtel du Cap. This was the house to which Prince Rainier had brought his children, pointing out the fine blue and white Chinese porcelain in the drawing room; which Niarchos had visited from his yacht, and at which David Niven had swum in the pool while Oscar Wyatt pulled Henry Ford off to a less crowded part of the lawn to talk serious business. When money had become a bit tight, Oscar had sold La Mauresque and rented another villa nearby.

To Sarah, who lived in palaces, this was a magical new playground where money made the rules. No stuffed-shirt courtiers raised genteel eyebrows and coughed pointedly behind gloved hands here. This was the preserve of very rich people with all-over tans and the best teeth implant surgery could provide. On one occasion, workaholic Oscar pronounced: 'I don't know what I'm doing here year after year. I have to show up here for Lynn. What a waste of time.' Just then, his beautiful wife, whom time seemed to have passed by, appeared before him in a creation Karl Lagerfeld had fashioned for her, and Oscar's resentment over the 'wasted days' slipped away. Now preparations were well-advanced for the most elaborate of all Lynn Wyatt's parties: a celebration for her sixtieth birthday. That night, under a canopy of stars, Sarah could see the yachts moored along the cape and listen to the cow-bell tinkle of the rigging against aluminium masts. Nestling down on the shore not far away at St Jean Cap Ferrat was Chabanne, the home of her favourite composer, Andrew Lloyd Webber.

'Sarah looked as though she belonged to the South of France rather than some dreary stately home in the United Kingdom,' noted a retired

Englishman who lived nearby. 'She seemed terribly free and although he was only supposed to be her escort, I didn't see Steve give one other woman a moment's attention.' By the time the Confidential team had located Sarah, Steve Wyatt's plane had safely returned her to England in time for Sarah to open the Dorset Children's Centre at Dorchester the following afternoon.

Sitting in the Coastal Tower, his Houston office block, Oscar Wyatt was reluctant to talk about the time Sarah spent at Cap Ferrat. 'She was in the South of France part of that summer, but she wasn't at our villa for the birthday party,' he said, choosing every word with great care. 'She was never at one of my wife's birthday parties. No, sir. Why should I lie to you? The security would have been outta sight,' He confirmed that none of Coastal's planes had been used for either that flight or the one to Morocco in May, 'not that I wouldn't have been perfectly delighted for her to ride in one of our airplanes,' he chuckled.

Sarah's friendship with Wyatt was further cemented that summer when Wyatt accompanied her on a flight across the Atlantic to visit her now rapidly failing stepfather in New York. By way of thanking him, she took Steve to dine at Windsor Castle on their return and arranged for him to sit next to the Queen. As Wyatt had become a friend of Prince Andrew as well, and the Prince was more often than not away on naval duties, he was accepted by Her Majesty. Lynn's son had carved out a privileged position among the highest born family in the kingdom.

Nor was Wyatt the only citizen of the United States to benefit from the Yorks' largesse. Their unconventional attitude toward so many things was crystallized in a venture which they planned with another American friend, Gene Nocon. They accepted an approach from the Marquesa de Varela, a friend of Hector and Susie Barrantes, to co-operate in an exclusive, and unheard-of, publishing deal with *Hello!*, a new showcase for the lifestyles of the rich and famous. *Hello!*, in common with virtually every other woman's magazine in the Western world, wanted to photograph the Yorks at home with Beatrice and Eugenie as a family unit. The pictures would illustrate a question-and-answer interview conducted by the Marquesa at Castlewood House. It was agreed that Gene Nocon would be credited as the photographer, but in fact Prince Andrew took the pictures. He used a delayed shutter device to snap those pictures in which he was seen frolicking with his daughters.

Such a coup was fraught with danger. Spanish-owned but edited chiefly in London, *Hello!* was an interloper in the highly competitive

British magazine market where its reverential treatment of the rich had opened doors other editors could not breach. Envy alone would guarantee hostile headlines in the daily newspapers. Andrew and Sarah went ahead with the enterprise and the Yorks' day was recorded amidst scenes of domestic bliss; bathtime and nappy-changing with Eugenie, four months old; feeding time for Beatrice, almost two; and both little girls splashing in the pool with Daddy. The extremely rare interview provided some excellent quotes. Asked 'what quality of the Duke impressed you most?' the Duchess replied: 'The most important thing that I felt – and now, looking back, I know this definitely – is his amazing ability to make one feel like a lady, like a woman. He has no macho side to him, he's a gentleman through and through, and he doesn't make any effort to do it. He's beautifully mannered. And I think it's so refreshing to find a man who could easily be spoilt be so unspoilt at such a young age. At twenty-five or twenty-six. I just couldn't get over how in my life outside, as I call it, there were so many men strutting around thinking that they were so smart while they were being so foul to women.'

For his part, the Duke repeated something he had said before: marrying Sarah was undoubtedly the best decision he had made in his life. Contributors to the theory that the Yorks' marriage was shaky had to review the evidence once *Hello!* hit the news-stands.

The magazine's UK editor Maggie Goodman knew a scoop when she saw one and splashed seventy of the pictures across forty-eight pages of the magazine. She was more inhibited when it came to discussing the financial arrangements *Hello!* had made with the Yorks – unknown, it was believed, to Buckingham Palace. Asked about rumours of a deal in the region of £250,000, she astonished everyone by saying that the Yorks had received no fee. Commenting on the deal Barbara Cartland, Princess Diana's step-grandmother, prophesied darkly: 'If the Royal Family lose their mystique, they will go altogether. The younger ones don't seem to understand this. It's all very well them wanting to be liked, but this is taking the common touch too far.'

Gene Nocon saw it differently: 'There's a peculiarity about the English – it's like their attitude towards children, "You can have them but don't bring them into my restaurant." Likewise, "Our Royal Family can be seen with sceptre and crown and pomp and circumstance, but never at a very personal level at which they too have feelings." That was basically the idea behind the *Hello!* spread, to show that there was a very personal life to this family.'

The phone call Sarah had been dreading came through from Argentina while *Hello!* was still processing its world exclusive at the end of July and as Andrew was preparing to join HMS *Cambeltown*. Hector Barrantes was dying and had returned home to El Pucara to spend his last days on the ranch that had become his and Susie's life-work. He made one last request of the woman he held as dear as any daughter. Before he died, he wanted to see Sarah and Beatrice one last time – and, if it were possible, he wanted to hold baby Eugenie in his arms. With tears in her eyes, Sarah willingly agreed. Nanny Alison packed their bags and travelled with Sarah and the little princesses to Buenos Aires, where a light plane ferried them to a makeshift grass runway at the ranch.

Even so near the end, Hector did not lose his indestructible love of life. Eugenie brought happiness to the dying man, and he insisted that the visitors should enjoy themselves. He watched from a car as Sarah took Beatrice for her first horse-riding lesson. They trotted past the strapping young trees which Sarah had helped to plant ten years earlier to the polo field Hector had carved out on the pampas. With Susie at his side, he died the day after Sarah and the girls flew home from Argentina. He was buried at Peace Garden cemetery in Buenos Aires. El Gordo was only fifty-one.

Sarah gave vent to her feelings for Hector at a party in aid of a cancer charity given by the Pakistani cricket captain Imran Khan at the Natural History Museum in South Kensington. 'The pain and suffering is beyond understanding,' she said. 'The lonely fight of a sufferer from a normal, healthy life to, within six months, the total inability to walk, even talk, knowing the treatment – if you're lucky enough to have it – makes you almost unrecognizable.' She said a tearful farewell to Hector at a memorial service arranged by Lord Vestey at a church near Hector's home pitch, Stowell Park in Gloucestershire. Her voice shook with emotion as she began her memorial reading: 'Death is nothing at all, I have only slipped away into the next room.' She comforted Susie as they mourned the man whose sudden intervention in their lives had enriched them as much as he had changed them.

That evening, Sarah and Andrew hosted a black tie house-warming party at their new home, Sunninghill Park House. Changed from her mourning clothes into a stunning emerald-green dress, a matching bow in her hair, Sarah greeted guests who included Michael Caine and his wife Shakira, and Lady Helen Windsor and her art-dealer fiancé Tim

Taylor. Steve Wyatt was also there and he brought with him his old friend from schooldays, Johnny Bryan.

'This was the first meeting between Sarah and Johnny, and in Steve's presence he was relatively subdued – a bit overawed, I'd say,' commented a friend who observed his behaviour. 'That night saw the start of a change in him. For one thing he started to cultivate more English ways and asked us to call him John instead of Johnny.'

Whatever their tastes in architecture, no one could have failed to have been impressed by the magnificence of Sunninghill once they had crossed the threshold and stood on the natural stone floor of the vast white entrance hall crowned by a glass-domed ceiling. A medieval minstrel's gallery attested to bygone times in Olde Windsor, but the kitchen was modern in the American ranch-house style. Sunninghill would never rate as one of the great stately homes, but its refreshing combination of old and new made it as special as everything else with the A&S brand on it.

'We built Sunninghill because we were walking at Windsor one day by the lake, and we came across a ruined nursery garden where the Queen and Prince Philip once had a house which was burned down,' Sarah told *Tatler*. 'We decided to build a house, and we realized we were going to take an awful lot of criticism. I'd have been delighted to live anywhere feasible. I'm many things, but I'm not materialistic. That's why Andrew did most of Sunninghill; it's mostly his hard work. A lot of people think that I'm very strong, but when it comes to the Duke of York, his decision goes. I did it the day I married – I said I would obey him in my wedding vows. So I wasn't pushing for anything. I was just happy. It's the first house I've ever had. I rented a room in Clapham until we were engaged.'

The English designer Nina Campbell had replaced Sister Parish after pointed suggestions were made to Sarah that her American tastes were hardly *de rigueur* in a house of such sentimental value to the Queen. Sister Parish decorated one guest suite, but the overall décor of the rooms under Ms Campbell's jurisdiction reflected a 'tidied-up version' of an English country house – chintz, tartans and wall-length drapes. 'Nina was given *carte blanche* to rummage around in the cellars of Buckingham Palace and Windsor Castle to select pictures and furniture,' said a well-informed royal observer. Viscount Linley, who liked to refer to himself as Joe the Carpenter, designed the huge walk-in wardrobes. There were personal touches, too. Andrew's framed photographs adorned the walls and Sarah's oversized teddy bears added a cuddly feeling to the big comfortable sofas. Her peach-coloured boudoir contained a marble bath so big that the builders christened it HMS *Fergie*.

For the house-warming, a marquee had been erected in the garden of the five-acre estate, and Elton John provided the night's entertainment, singing and playing a selection of his hit songs. As he ended with 'Your Song', Sarah and Andrew gazed tenderly at each other while their guests applauded. Elton's romantic music underlined that whatever people might think, there was no disharmony here. Steve Wyatt and Johnny Bryan joined in the chorus.

When he returned to his Chelsea flat, Bryan phoned New York to score some points. 'He said he had just been to this fabulous party at the Duke and Duchess of York's house,' reported Whitney Tower. 'He said Elton John had played the piano and they stayed up very late. He said the Duchess was very nice and he had a good time.'

A fortnight later, Sarah flew yet again to New York to attend a fundraising dinner and dance in aid of the Royal Academy. She stayed at the British-owned Plaza Athenée. She was joined by Lynn Wyatt who took an adjacent suite which, like her own, was decorated with French period furnishings and, like Sunninghill, had a large marble bath. From Houston, Lynn brought with her a belated present for the Duchess's thirty-first birthday the previous week. It was a travel bag hand-painted with portraits of Sarah, Andrew and their daughters by the Texan artist Clayton Lefevre. Inside were shoes for Beatrice and Eugenie which Lefevre had also decorated. Lynn's spending did not end there; before the trip was over she accompanied Sarah on an extravagant shopping expedition. Late one night, the Duchess took her group for drinks at Au Bar on East 58th Street, the nightspot Johnny Bryan had enthused about at her party. He had made a favourable impression on her on their first meeting and, before long, he would become a close friend.

· · ·

It was during the first week in December that the mysterious Mr G contacted the Confidential desk at *Today*. He wanted £30,000 for information about the next meeting between the Duchess and Steve Wyatt, and he demanded a contract to guarantee payment. An agreement using the aliases 'Lady Smith and Steve Texas' was drawn up and read to the informant at 11.45 a.m. on 5 December. When reporter James Steen kept his appointment in the car park at Streatham railway station, he had the contract in his pocket. Mr G got out of his car and shook hands with the reporter.

Five thousand miles away in Baghdad, there were handshakes all around after three men completed an hour-long meeting in Saddam Hussein's private chambers at the Presidential Palace. Unknown to Steen, or anyone else in the world's media, Oscar Wyatt had flown secretly to Iraq in the Coastal 707 that same day and had just negotiated the release of American hostages with the country's military dictator. Along with fifteen tons of medical supplies, Oscar had taken his friend (and employee), the former Texas Governor John B. Connally, into the Iraqi capital. Saddam, in full military uniform, had listened impassively as Connally, silver-tongued veteran of political persuasion that he was, presented their case. Saddam's response was to unbuckle his gunbelt, wrap it around his gun and place it on the table. Then the two Americans went back to their hotel to wait.

'Mr G said, "Hello, James" in an educated English accent,' said Steen. 'He was very formal and very tall – about 6 ft 2 in. It struck me from his manner that he might be connected with the police or the security forces, though I thought he must be mad if he was. After he provided proof that he wasn't a phoney [Andrew's private phone number and the fact that a picture of Sarah clutching the Moroccan dagger was beside Wyatt's bed], he signed the contract, which he kept, and a copy that I had to return to the office.

'Remember, nothing had been printed about the first visit to Constable Burton the previous December. I'd never even heard of the place. Mr G then told me that Fergie and Steve would be spending the next weekend there. Fergie, he said, would be travelling up first class on a certain train. He named the other guests who would be joining the shooting party as Frank Lowe, Wayne Eagling, and Nigel Havers with his wife Polly.

'The blonde sitting in the car knew exactly what Mr G was doing. I wondered if she might be the real source and he was acting as middle man. It occurred to me that she might be someone's jilted girlfriend. I tried to catch her eye, but she wouldn't make eye contact. Whatever the source, if Mr G's information turned out to be true, it would provide a story which would definitely embarrass the Duchess and the Royal Family.'

In Baghdad, Oscar Wyatt had waited five long hours at the Al-Rashid Hotel before being told that his jet could take off with twenty-two American hostages. Saddam had been preparing to use them as a human shield in the looming Gulf conflict. Oscar's humanitarian efforts received no gratitude from the US Government. The Bush Administration, the oilman believed, had been using the hostages as political pawns. 'We got no co-operation from the [American] Government – none!' he said. 'It is my opinion that the State Department wanted to use the hostages to affect public opinion.'

Sarah Hay, a young Australian reporter who had come up with the breakthrough on La Gazelle d'Or, caught the train north to Darlington with photographer Jim Bennett to follow the trail Mr G had marked out. There was no sign of the Duchess on the train, but the reporter saw Frank Lowe and Dawn Dunlap. 'We checked into a bed and breakfast place near the gates of the Constable Burton estate,' she said. 'The landlord of the local pub said that the Duchess often turned up at Constable Burton Hall and had dropped in for a drink on a previous visit. The next morning we followed the shoot, but we couldn't get close enough to recognize anyone for sure. However, we did establish that Steve Wyatt was definitely there by phoning the big house on Jim's portable. We were told Steve couldn't come to the phone as he was out shooting.'

A heavy overnight snowfall made roads impassable and, although the journalists kept watch as best they could in the conditions, the Duchess was not sighted and the stake-out was called off. The episode proved, however, that someone with access to highly sensitive information was trying to give the press an inside track on the story. Mr G was traced to an address in Epsom, Surrey, where the trail went cold. He was never heard from again, which was not surprising once the motive behind his actions started to become apparent.

Through the Duke and Duchess of York, Steve Wyatt was getting much too close to Buckingham Palace for the liking of people involved in the sensitive area of foreign relations. The Kuwait Royal Family, personal friends of the Queen, had already lost face in the Middle East over Sarah's dinner for Steve and the Iraq oil minister at the Palace. Now, as Allied forces prepared for the liberation of Kuwait and the invasion of Iraq, Oscar Wyatt – the maverick with enemies in Washington as well as Houston – had pulled off a coup which had humiliated the White House.

President Bush, a former director of the CIA, was livid that Wyatt had almost single-handedly taken the initiative away from the State Department and made US diplomacy a laughing stock throughout the Arab world. 'There are various ways that things can happen, various favours that can be done through inter-departmental outlets revolving around security and the Palace secretariat,' said a well-informed royal source. 'There are seven or eight operative departments within Buckingham Palace that are interconnected one way or another, and through those links all sorts of things can happen.'

.   .   .

The most important date circled in deepest blue on the royal calendar that year was a ball on Tuesday, 12 December, to mark milestones in the lives of four generations of the House of Windsor: the Queen Mother, who had turned ninety, Princess Margaret, sixty, Princess Anne, forty, and Prince Andrew, thirty. The Queen Mother, in fact, was older than the House, which came into being in 1917 after George V changed the family name from the Germanic Saxe-Coburg Gotha to the very English Windsor during the Great War with his cousin the Kaiser.

If anyone doubted that Steve Wyatt had arrived on the royal scene, the invitation to this gathering of the *crème de la crème* was absolute clinching proof. Under the gilded ceilings of the Palace Picture Gallery, hung with blue drapes and lit by a constellation of white starlight, nearly eight hundred guests were greeted by the sophisticated musical strains of the Grahamophones. As the evening progressed, they gave way to the livelier beat of Chance, a six-piece band which had played at Andrew's twenty-first birthday party. As well as Wyatt, the Yorks brought Ronald and Sue, with whom they had dined at the Turf Club following a reception at the Argentine Embassy in Belgrave Square which, diplomatically, was not shown in their list of public engagements. It meant that, as far as Prince Andrew was concerned, hostilities had ceased in the South Atlantic.

The Waleses chatted to Charles's chum Lady 'Kanga' Tryon and her husband Anthony, Jane Roxburghe and Lady Jane Fellowes. Prince and Princess Michael, Mark and Diane Thatcher, the singer Cleo Laine and her musician husband Johnny Dankworth, jockeys Willie Carson and Richard Dunwoody and racing driver Jackie Stewart were others selected from a fairly representative cross-section of British society.

If Wyatt felt at ease with those around him, the feeling was not necessarily mutual. A senior courtier said that he winced as Wyatt approached him, offering his hand and announcing: 'Hi, I'm Steve, Sarah's friend and guest.' The word was already being passed around a tight-knit circle that Steve Wyatt was about to become *persona non grata* at the Palace. Oscar had learned the hard way not to try to please all of the people all of the time, and Steve seemed to have picked up the trait. He did not give a damn what people thought about his father or his friendship with the Duchess of York. Three nights after the Buckingham Palace ball, he held a bizarre fantasy party at a semi-derelict house in South London, and this time Sarah and Andrew were his guests. 'A report was filed to Scotland Yard and passed on to Buckingham Palace,' revealed a former royal minder. 'It always happens like that on such occasions – anything to do with personal matters goes through a channel for sensitive information. The protection of lives and property, which is a more practical concern, goes through another.'

Even as they partied, the Wyatt Problem was being discussed over a dinner table a short walk from the Palace. Steve Wyatt's influence over Sarah had not only furrowed the brows of the establishment; it continued to arouse the interest of British Intelligence. Now that Andrew, fourth in line to the throne, was clearly becoming just as big a buddy of the Texan as his wife, the repercussions of any scandal would reach right to the heart of the Royal Family. From that night on, eyes were to be kept on Steve Wyatt.

On New Year's Eve a less official ear was listening in to a highly personal conversation between the Princess of Wales and her special friend, James Gilbey. Gilbey, it transpired, was speaking from the mobile phone in his car, which was parked in a layby near Oxford. The dialogue between them revealed just how precarious Sarah's position had become. Speaking from the very mansion, Sandringham House, where her sister-in-law was also lodged, Diana heard her confidant say that Sarah was 'desperate to get back in'. The redhead, as Diana referred to Sarah, was being called 'a lame duck' among the royals gathered downstairs.

ELEVEN

The Other Elizabeth

'He seemed to look upon Liz as a sort of mother figure, rather like Camilla Parker Bowles was to his elder brother.'

Until Sarah arrived in his life as the One, no woman was closer to Prince Andrew's innermost thoughts than Elizabeth Nocon, the wife of his photographic guru. Hers was the shoulder on which he had cried about Koo Stark and several other girls who had slipped in and out of his royal world. He had been a regular visitor to the Nocons' house at Beaconsfield, and Liz frequently called on him in his rooms at Buckingham Palace for an intimate chat over coffee. 'There was never anything going on between Andrew and Liz. They were never lovers or anything like that, but she was enormously fond of him and he was of her,' confirmed a girlfriend who dined at the home of Liz and Gene Nocon when their royal guest was also present.

Gene's wife established a rapport with the Prince that amazed others around him. 'Liz was the ultimate confidante,' continued her friend. 'She was someone he could tell everything to and did. I mean, Liz was always there for Andrew. He could talk to her about the romances that were going wrong and those that seemed to be going right. He felt that she understood him and his problems. Although she was not a great deal older than him, he seemed to look upon Liz as a sort of mother figure, rather like Camilla Parker Bowles was to his elder brother. I always supposed that men in their position needed such a woman, because the Queen was almost fully occupied in her role as Mother to the Nation.

'In any event, even if Liz had been a free woman and not the wife of his close chum, she was never Andrew's type. She is a large lady, very tall and she gives the impression of being very domineering, although in reality she's a sweetie.'

Their friends believed, however, that Sarah saw Liz as a challenge to her position. She was certainly aware that Andrew had discussed her suitability with Liz Nocon, not only as a girlfriend, but on the delicate subject of whether she might be a potential princess. This gave Liz great power, something that Sarah found particularly unacceptable. 'It is very intriguing in many ways, because Liz and I had obviously been used to seeing Fergie as a very bouncy sort of girl,' said the friend. 'She was great fun, but she changed a lot after she and Andrew were married. This is not, after all, unusual: a woman in her position especially would want to make sure that she was right in there with her husband and she wouldn't want any competition.

'It seemed to some of us that Sarah set about getting rid of a lot of Andrew's friends in an unmerciful way. And she played a lot of double games. She got really close to Liz, then she pulled back – only to rush over to her with an extravagant present. She couldn't get rid of Liz even if she wanted to because, of course, Gene was really important to Andrew's passion for photography. But when Liz was very close to Andrew, she had always been popping in and out of the Palace – and that stopped. She and Andrew had been in almost daily contact and I know they shared a lot of secrets. At one stage, he was almost a lodger in the Nocons' home. It was a nice upper-middle class home, nothing ostentatious, but the Prince was obviously very comfortable in it and he was there a lot.

'Of course, all that had to change when he got married; it would have been quite wrong for it not to change. But in setting out to establish her position, Sarah definitely kept Andrew away from Liz as much as possible. Sarah was in this difficult position of not being able to put her foot down totally, so we had what I called "Operation Wedge". Sarah would have Liz over to tea and give her all these guilt presents – track suits, that sort of thing.'

Asked about his wife being closer to Andrew than any other woman up to the point of Sarah's arrival and Sarah making an effort to end that friendship, Gene Nocon responded: 'I suppose there is truth in that, but I suppose it's only a matter of how people observe it from the outside.'

On the subject of Liz having access to Andrew's rooms at the Palace until Sarah came on the scene, Gene said: 'I don't know if one has access to the Palace in that regard. We certainly were very, very friendly with Prince Andrew – still are. It goes both ways, he would come and see us, he was very much a part of the family. We enjoyed his company; he's just a nice man period. He was, of course, who he was but he's a nice guy. He had no pretences, which is kinda nice to see.'

Sarah's fear was that Liz Nocon knew too much about her husband from the secrets he had imparted to her. It was very much a one-to-one relationship and she, like Gene, was excluded from it. 'I always maintain a sort of distance with those kind of activities between my wife and Prince Andrew or whoever, I just don't want to know,' continued Gene. 'If that was the case, then Sarah must have felt that. But I've never queried my wife about any discussion she has had with Prince Andrew and, likewise, it's not meant for me to be a party to that.'

'Liz was originally a La Fontaine,' said Liz's friend. 'She came from Jersey, but her mother moved to Canada when Liz's father died. There is money in her family but like me, she has always been a free spender!' It was over the controversial At Home feature in *Hello!* magazine that Liz's friend believed the Yorks and the Nocons finally fell out. The Nocons were hoping to obtain some payment in recognition of their services, but this did not transpire. Gene Nocon played a crucial part in the picture session. The Nocons moved to California shortly after Andrew and Sarah had helped to stage a surprise farewell dinner party for them. Gene had returned specially to help with Andrew's photography and to process the valuable film. Andrew, who had used a time-release exposure for shots in which he figured, knew that Buckingham Palace would never sanction such a project. Apparently Liz wrote to Andrew, but the letter didn't reach him. Liz followed it up and the matter was discussed by Sarah and Andrew, but Liz heard nothing further.

Asked about the financial arrangements, Gene Nocon said: 'I'm not familiar with that side of it.' He insisted that there had been no falling out with the Yorks. His decision to move back to America had been based on several factors, including the recession. 'At the same time Prince Andrew and Sarah's marriage seemed to be on the go and go, and they were quite independent, they were on their own now,' he said. 'It was almost like there was no need for us to be around any more, not that we felt there was a real need for us to be around in Prince Andrew's role as his adviser in any way, shape or form.' Gene conceded that his and Liz's relationship with the Yorks had cooled, though: 'After the marriage, it sort of tapered off. I felt there was no need for me to be around in that capacity any more . . . the closeness of his bachelor days was over and we just felt it was time to move on. But there was no falling out, it was just another phase of life going on between two groups of people.' Pressed to declare whether he had expected to receive some money from the *Hello!* project, Nocon – of whom the Queen grew very fond once she learned how her son depended upon him and his wife – responded firmly: 'That I won't discuss.'

Gene was adamant that presents he and his wife had received were not 'guilt gifts' but rather items sent to them on such occasions as birthdays and at Christmas. 'It's the way the Royal Family works,' said Gene. 'They have day-to-day lists of people's birthdays and special events, like wedding anniversaries. It seems to be an everyday activity; the first thing they do is sort out whose birthday is coming up and attend to it – they're very good about that, so I don't call that guilt gifts.'

.   .   .

Matters financial were just one of the problem areas Sarah encountered in her efforts to match up to the Windsors. But like the famous East Front façade of Buckingham Palace, which was little more than a veneer masking the original 1847 stonework, she discovered that illusion counted for more than truth in so many facets of royal life. Her attempts to live up to Palace doctrine meant that she was forced to revert to similar tactics to disguise her real self.

The resulting masquerade ensured that Sarah remained an infuriating enigma to many people outside her immediate circle, even after four years in the royal spotlight. Those who met her on one of her informal walkabouts in city centres came away with the impression that they knew her really well – and they may have been right. Ordinary people accepted her on face value, and they liked what they saw. She was spontaneous, refreshing, unpatronizing – and it was impossible for her to be boring. Princess Diana would never have dared, as Sarah did, to walk up to a crowd in the North of England and say: 'I like coming here because people are so friendly – better than down South.' Such unscripted remarks were instantly seized upon and presented as 'Fergie's latest gaffe'. The Doctrine clearly stated that one should be diplomatic and solicitous, not controversial. These trivialities taught Sarah a lot about her priorities in life. 'I never worry about a headache or trivial ailments now because I meet so many dying people who don't think they are the slightest bit brave,' she said. 'It teaches me to grab life for every minute of every day.'

Her apparent unselfishness won over many people who came in contact with her through charity work. By April 1990, she was patron of twelve organizations, including the Chemical Dependency Centre, the Tate Gallery Foundation and the Sick Children's Trust, and president of four others. 'She puts in so much of her own free time for us,' said Peter Cardy, director of the Motor Neurone Disease Association. 'Sending us hand-written notes when she is supposed to be on holiday, dashing off to gory medical briefings when she is meant to be off duty awaiting the birth of her second baby – that tells you about her commitment. And when our research physiotherapist demonstrated a new technique for us, it was on the Duchess's own back.'

Away from the spotlight, the Duchess made several private visits which were not listed in the Court Circular to the Trinity Hospice, a refuge for people with terminal illnesses just around the corner from her previous home in Lavender Gardens. The hospice was not one of her 'official' charities, but she helped its fund-raising activities and made surprise visits to cheer up its patients. 'She always has a long chat with me,' said Mrs Eileen Cashier, a 65-year-old patient. 'She takes a real interest – it is not just a questions of doing her duty.' She learned the rudiments of sign language to enable her to communicate with deaf people whom she met at charity functions or on her walkabouts. Much to the delight of young deaf children, she learned to spell out 'Father Christmas'.

It was precisely because of this self-sacrificing quality that Sarah's apparent desire to enrich herself while doing her royal rounds puzzled so many people. 'It's a funny thing, her greatest character defect is also tied in with one of her greatest virtues,' said the royal insider. 'She is intrinsically a fairly kind and decent person, but she genuinely does not understand the effect her behaviour can have on less well-intentioned people. She is quite non-judgmental herself: her philosophy is Live and Let Live. If you're not harming anyone, do it. Enjoy yourself! She doesn't appreciate to what extent behaviour that she regards as perfectly innocent, because it is not malicious, can be condemned by others around her. More than anything else, that has got her into deep trouble.'

On paper, the Yorks were comfortably off. Andrew's allowance from the Civil List had more than doubled from £20,000 to £50,000 a year as soon as he married and stood at £250,000 a year in 1992. But 70 per cent of this went towards the salaries of their Private Secretaries, Equerry, lady-in-waiting, nanny, personal dresser, chauffeur and butler. Andrew's service pay as a lieutenant was £26,000. If the Yorks wanted anything within reason, they had only to ask: the item would be ordered from the appropriate store and the accounts section would deal with the bills. Whenever they travelled abroad on royal tours, they returned laden with expensive gifts. Their 2000 wedding presents alone were worth a fortune, perhaps £1 million in 1986 and some, such as six pairs of silver pheasants with gold inlay worth up to £14,000 a pair, would have appreciated in value. The Aladdin's Cave at Sunninghill Park House was packed to overflowing with six hundred dinner plates in eight different patterns, twenty-four antique-silver serving dishes at £1500 to £8000 each, thirty-six silver and glass condiment sets at £10 to £200, one thousand crystal glasses from £10 each and some three hundred German, French and Swedish vases costing up to £600 each. The bride had also received heirloom jewellery valued at £250,000, the centrepiece of which was a diamond tiara from the Queen, a gift worth £90,000.

Anyone who thought that this was surely enough did not understand Sarah very well. As she saw it, she had earned none of it on her own merits. If anything, her priorities matched the aspirations of her show-business friends rather than the more limiting horizons of other royals. She had never had any real money when she was growing up at Dummer Down Farm nor when she was mixing with the free-spending Verbier Set. 'I am not well off,' she said. 'I do not have any money of my own at all.' To prove the point, she often asked top designers if she could wear their clothes in exchange for the prestige it would bring them.

This was the biggest difficulty people faced in trying to understand Sarah's move into commercial ventures. Readers who drew their impressions from the public prints were shown a distorted picture of her and, in the absence of anything to balance it, more or less accepted what they were told. Once the Killer Bimbos of Fleet Street had decided that she was a disaster, they took deliberate aim. Her so-called greed was only one area of attack. Piles of transparencies from her public engagements were sifted through on light-boxes and then projected on to screens in search of the most suitable shot to illustrate some unflattering feature: her woeful dress sense, her latest hairstyle, her fluctuating weight. Sarah rarely let them down. 'She simply does not know how to get out of a car without showing her thighs or her underwear,' sighed a leading Killer Bimbo. 'She must have seen the results, but she does it time and again. Okay, she's got great legs.'

The true self that Sarah desperately wanted people to admire remained hidden except to friends and the minority associated with her charity work and her household. To everyone else, she was an unknown quantity. For one thing, comparatively few people had actually heard her speak. This was also true of her two rivals for the limelight, Diana and Anne. Considering the amount of time and space the media devoted to the Royal Family, they were all extraordinarily mute. Viewers of *Spitting Image*, the satirical puppet show, were more accustomed to actors lampooning their accents than hearing the real thing. The Queen's Christmas Broadcast was one of the rare occasions when the nation could tune in and be sure of hearing their monarch addressing them in person. Not that the Queen did not speak. She was always chatting to people at State receptions, private audiences in Buckingham Palace and away-day visits on the Royal Train.

Prince Charles, who actively courted television to propagate his beliefs on architecture or the environment, was the exception. His voice and views were probably better known to the masses than those of any other royal. Sarah's televised utterances were few and far between. To meet her in person in the surroundings of her *pied-à-terre* at the Palace was even rarer still. Georgina Howell was granted that opportunity for *Tatler* – and made the most of it. 'To be honest, I went to the interview not expecting to like her, but I did like her. I went expecting a big, bouncy personality like a labrador, but she was much paler and less obstreperous than she was painted. She was quietly spoken and interested in the arts; not the sort of person I had expected at all. The big surprise is her voice. It is warmly inflected and has a mesmerizing musical quality.'

Like Diana, Sarah visited many half-way houses for recovering drug addicts, hostels for the homeless and hospices for AIDS and cancer victims, but the headlines were more than likely to cherish her latest holiday freebie. Dubbed the Duchess of Do-Little, she increased her workload to 190 engagements in the first six months of 1989. Her image worried her so much that she talked to Andrew about calling in a public-relations consultant. When she did appear on television in her own right, it was usually to promote her books and that only reinforced the notion that she was self-seeking. She chose her friend and dinner-party guest David Frost on TV-am, the commercial breakfast channel, to plug publication of *The Palace of Westminster* rather than the more popular Terry Wogan, who went out at primetime on the state-funded BBC. For her children's books about Budgie the helicopter, she chose Sue Lawley, whom she had encountered during her days with Durden-Smith Communications.

The motive for writing the Budgie books – a series of ten was originally planned – was to make her financially independent, she told friends. Some of the earnings would go to charity. 'She cannot live on air,' said Ronald Ferguson. 'Everyone thinks that because you are married to a member of the Royal Family, you were rich beforehand.' Sarah discussed ideas for the books with Mort Janklow, her American attorney-cum-literary agent, the day she received her helicopter licence in December 1987. Janklow was intrigued. He happened to know the right people at Simon & Schuster, and the US conglomerate acquired world rights to *Budgie* for its highly competitive children's books division.

Simon & Schuster paid a reported advance of $500,000 to buy the series, although the terms of the contract remain confidential. Once the publishers had recouped their investment through their cut of serial rights and royalties on sales, Sarah would receive the rest, minus her agent's fee. 'I'm giving a percentage to charity,' she said. "I don't understand where the criticism comes from, but they are going to find fault because, at the moment, I'm flavour of the month.'

The Budgie Experience would long remain engraved on the memories of those who dealt with Sarah and, more particularly, Buckingham Palace during the months before the projected worldwide publication date for the first two books in October 1989. She actually started writing the books at Castlewood when she was pregnant with Beatrice. She would scribble on notepaper with a pencil during the week and read out the results to Andrew at weekends.

'I met the Duchess in person the summer before publication in her office at Buckingham Palace,' said John Sargent, president of Simon & Schuster's children's books division in New York. 'The manuscripts were already written and my purpose was to discuss plans for promotion in the States. I've always liked her very much. She's very down to earth, she's personable and we've always had a very good relationship.' Others found the going more difficult, proving there were different strokes for different folks. 'Sarah was flown in by helicopter for a Simon & Schuster conference,' said one who was present. 'She looked very smart in a business suit, but it was a rather stiff, formal kind of thing where she was asked questions about the books. I thought she was very cagey in her answers. I got the impression that her lips were sealed and she really ought to go back to the Palace and get it checked out. The Queen knew about the deal, but Sarah seemed terrified of saying the wrong thing.'

Denise Johnstone-Burt, an experienced editor of children's books, was put in charge of the manuscripts. *Budgie the Little Helicopter* told the story of how the helicopter saved a girl called Rose Wright from a gang of kidnappers. *Budgie at Bendicks Point* saw him rescuing two little boys from a clifftop. It was noted that Budgie was the name of her training helicopter, Bendicks was her pet Jack Russell, Rose was wearing a Daneshill uniform, and Wright was her mother's maiden name. Lots of identification there.

'Sarah had to be handled with kid gloves all the time, and there was a lot of interference from the Buckingham Palace Press Office,' confirmed the Simon & Schuster source. Everything had to be checked with them. Any change in the text, any bit of publicity we wanted her to do. Everything. As her hands were tied, it took ages although things had to work quickly for an autumn publication. It was a question of day and night. You couldn't just go home at 5.30 and leave it until the next morning. There were lots of evening phone calls.'

The Simon & Schuster team, in common with every other big publishing house, had its own way of dealing with the dozens of titles that passed along the conveyor belt to the printers and, ultimately, the bookshops. Sarah, however, had ideas of her own. 'She thought she knew a lot about book production and this is where a lot of hold-ups happened. This was large-scale commercial publishing, very different from the sort of thing she had done with, for instance, *The Palace of Westminster*. We had a red-hot production director, but Sarah wanted people she already knew to do the books. That wasn't possible because we had promised it to our people. She tended to muddy the waters an awful lot.'

The publishers held an auction for serial rights to the first two Budgie books with the added incentive of a rare and exclusive interview with the Duchess of York going to the highest bidder. Rupert Murdoch's *Today* emerged victorious from the auction, but there was an unexpected intervention from Buckingham Palace. They strongly disapproved of the serial being published in *Today*, said the Simon & Schuster source. 'We had to tell the editor, David Montgomery, and the literary editor, Maggie Pringle, "We're sorry, but Buckingham Palace says you can't have Budgie." Montgomery wrote a letter to Sarah, via us, saying, "Please reconsider. We'll do a very good job." It didn't make any difference and the books went to the second-highest bidder, the *Daily Express*, for £126,000.'

The *Express* proprietor, Lord Stevens of Ludgate, chortled over *Today*'s apparent loss and its editor, Nick Lloyd, briefed writer Philippa Kennedy about the questions she should ask the Duchess. One of them was whether she was pregnant, and the answer was No. The *Express* planned to include the denial in its serialization. Sarah then pre-empted the newspaper by giving a television interview to Sue Lawley on the BBC. This also failed to mention that she was pregnant. The Palace announced the news the very day on which the *Express* published its denial. Lloyd was livid. 'She broke her contract with us,' he argued. The *Express* withheld a substantial amount of the agreed fee and the row rumbled on for months.

Elsewhere, Budgie was a big earner. Janklow secured £80,000 from *Redbook* magazine for the US rights and the first two stories sold well over 100,000 copies each, more than enough to justify the publication of two more Budgie books, *Budgie Goes to Sea* and *Budgie and the Blizzard,* in October 1991. Sarah split £30,000 from the profits among ten charities in the Prince Andrew Charitable Trust, but not before Lt.-Col. O'Dwyer resigned as her Private Secretary. Royal protocol decreed that all income from books by close members of the Royal Family should go to charity. 'The parting is purely by mutual agreement,' said Ronald, who had recommended O'Dwyer for the job. 'There is nothing acrimonious about his decision.' The words 'Her Royal Highness' were printed on the cover of each Budgie title although at Sarah's insistence, they were missing when all four titles were reprinted in one edition in October 1992. The special package included a compact disc of Sarah reading her own stories against a background of music and sound effects.

Asked how the Duchess had been consulted about the new package deal, Sargent replied: 'We have on-going discussions about various aspects of the Budgie property, and John Bryan handles a lot of that. She said she wanted me to deal with him on this matter. I don't know what his specific role is; I keep things on a straight business relationship. At various times, she has had various advisers I have dealt with.'

When Mort Janklow discussed the Duchess's next literary project with her, Sarah suggested using diaries and letters stored in the Royal Archives at Windsor Castle for a book about Queen Victoria. The book, *Victoria and Albert: Life at Osborne House,* which Sarah co-wrote with

Irish-born author Benita Stoney, told the story of the mansion Prince Albert built for his wife and children on the Isle of Wight, where they could escape 'corridor-creaking, lots of staff and prying eyes'.

Sarah became an expert on Victoriana and found, she said, a large number of similarities between herself and the monarch. Victoria's diaries had been expurgated by Princess Beatrice who felt some of her mother's reminiscences about her nights of passion with Prince Albert were unsuited to the sanctity of her memory. To ensure there was no comeback over the final resting place of royalties earned by this handsome volume, every penny of Sarah's share was pledged to the Prince Andrew Charitable Trust.

·   ·   ·

One area of the Yorks' value in material terms, which escaped neither Sarah nor her husband even before the *Hello!* saga, was the price put on their heads by the picture editors of newspapers and magazines. This was impressed on no one more rigorously than Gene Nocon, who printed all of their pictures and was responsible for the safe-keeping of their vast store of negatives. He had been Andrew's assistant when the Prince conducted Princess Beatrice's first photographic session shortly after her birth. Some time later, the Royal Family gathered at Balmoral for their late summer holiday where Prince Philip photographed Sarah holding baby Beatrice and flanked by the Queen and Queen Mother. The film was sent to Nocon to process at his Photographer's Workshop in Covent Garden. He returned a selection of prints to the Royal Family at the Scottish castle, aware that the Queen had a special use in mind for the one she liked best. 'The print was coming back to me from Balmoral,' Nocon explained. 'I never received it. I waited three days and I rang Balmoral and said, "It's still not here." There was a postal strike, so I waited a week – and the next thing I knew it was published in a newspaper. Andrew called me up to ask what was happening and I told him, "I did what was required on my part, Sir" and he said, "Thank you very much." '

The Queen had intended to use the now famous Four Generations portrait on her Christmas card that year. Its publication all over the front page of the *Sun* under the headline THE QUEEN BEA spoiled the plan. The newspaper apologized graciously to Her Majesty and paid £100,000 to four charities of which she was patron. A seventeen-year-old printer's assistant lost her job after she admitted selling the snapshot to the newspaper for £1000. The teenager explained that she had been working overtime at a publishing firm to help sort out a backlog of mail. 'Suddenly on top of my pile there was this big white envelope with Balmoral stamped all over it and when I opened it, this picture of the royals fell out,' she said. With it was a letter from the Queen's secretary saying that Her Majesty wanted the picture to be used on her Christmas card. Caught up in the chaos of the postal strike, it had been delivered to the wrong firm. The girl phoned the *Sun* who offered her what sounded like an enormous sum – almost a quarter of her year's salary. So seriously did the police regard the offence that even after she had owned up to Scotland Yard that she was the culprit, the head of the Serious Crime Squad, Commander Roy Penrose, was sent to interview her.

The importance of safeguarding the royal material in his care was not wasted on Nocon, who said he had seen every photograph Prince Andrew had ever taken, including the most private pictures in his portfolio. 'One day I should write a book. There are some very interesting things that have happened of an historical nature.' One item of particular historical interest was a picture of the royal couple which appeared on a stamp to commemorate their wedding.

'Terence Donovan took the engagement pictures and Albert Watson took the wedding pictures,' said Nocon. 'One photograph was to be chosen and made into a stamp, but in every one of the photographs their heads were too far apart. I'd taken this kind of snapshot of the two of them together when I was helping Prince Andrew to take pictures of Sarah alone for the wedding souvenir brochure. Prince Andrew was just wearing a T-shirt and sweater and she was wearing her nice outfit. I said, "Just stand there and let me put a roll of film through." The Royal Mail enquired directly to the Palace if there was a picture of their heads a bit closer together than in the ones submitted and Prince Andrew suggested the one I took, so yours truly got in on the act by default.' Nocon took the utmost care to protect the negatives he held for the royal couple. 'The negatives were theirs. I kept them on file, but it was their file.'

The Photographer's Workshop, however, became an early victim of the recession and more than one investor lost money. After the Nocons returned to the West Coast of America, Gene sent all of the negatives on file back to the Yorks. There was dismay at Buckingham Palace, therefore, when photographs which Nocon had taken behind the scenes at the Yorks' wedding were published in the *Sunday Express*. 'On the balcony I captured a unique picture,' Nocon said. 'As Prince Andrew and Sarah waved to the crowds, I dropped on my hands and knees and crawled out there with them. They turned to go in. They saw me seemingly kneeling in obeisance on the balcony's Wilton carpet and laughed. I hit the button.'

From his privileged position, Nocon took other pictures which showed the couple arriving at the Palace on their return from Westminster Abbey and walking through the State Rooms with Sarah's bridesmaids. They showed not only a female guest adjusting Sarah's train, but Prince Andrew lifting and carrying great bundles of it in his arms after the bridesmaids abandoned it in their excitement. Asked at the time what he intended to do with the pictures, Nocon said that they would form part of an album which he hoped to give to Andrew as a belated wedding present. The pictures saw the light of day, however, just as the furore over the Yorks' separation had reached its height, and publication of such private and sentimental snaps only made things worse. An executive at Express Newspapers admitted that the company had paid Nocon £20,000 for his candid photographs. But Nocon insisted: 'They were my pictures. I never said I wouldn't do anything with them, I just tucked them away – then, when the split happened, I had the world and its mother on to me about buying my pictures and I made a nice deal with the *Sunday Express*.'

When the Duchess of York visited California in 1991, she spent a day in San Diego, where the Nocons were living. She did not contact them. 'I was kinda surprised, but I just guessed she had too much on,' said the printer. Asked if he and the Yorks were still friends, Nocon replied: 'I'd like to think we are. I've done everything I can to be discreet about them.' Prince Andrew's friend Liz Nocon would certainly testify to that.

TWELVE

More Kamikaze than Camelot

'Steve likes me in tight black denim.'

SARAH, DUCHESS OF YORK

As the Duchess, the Texan Dude and their party-going friends became a fixture on the Chelsea scene during the start of the New Age nineties, Sarah carried on as she did before marriage, but on a much grander scale. 'She tried to recreate the good times in Verbier, with herself in the central role,' said a Chelsea socialite. 'She was a thirtysomething who wanted some fun outside her royal responsibilities. The Americans told her, "Get real – join the real world." It was a challenge, and she took it up.'

So it was that Sarah's Court, more kamikaze than Camelot, came into being. She told anyone who would listen that she more or less had to socialize without Prince Andrew because he was away from home so frequently. She had spent no more than forty-two nights with him in 1990, she complained, and they had been together for less than six months in one three-year period of their marriage. Anyone who saw the Duchess holding court could have been forgiven for believing that she was actually enjoying her status as a single married woman.

On one notable occasion in early February 1991, she swanned into Toto's, the Italian restaurant in Knightsbridge, with Wyatt and ten other New Ageists bringing up the rear. The group had arrived crammed into a van for a pasta and wine bash during which Sarah, in a black and white check suit, pursued her new freedom in accustomed style. The decibel level rose correspondingly and the wine flowed, according to other diners, one of whom felt so miffed that he telephoned the *Sun* to complain. Sarah drank wine and smoked several of the cigarettes she had decided to give up for her husband, but which she found helpful as an appetite suppressant. This was only one of many similar nights on the town and, naturally, it attracted attention.

Steve Wyatt and Pricilla Phillips, the two main participants, were described as 'part of a socially visible group of young Americans who have relentlessly partied, charmed, networked and spent their way into upmarket London.' The group consisted of 'hangers-on, career socialites and wannabes who have flocked to Fergie, all hoping in equal measure to pick up some royal cachet as she trips in and out of their salons.' This view failed to appreciate the very salient point that these were precisely the people in whose company she felt comfortable and secure. It was no accident that some of them happened to be Americans. Nor was it coincidental that Johnny Bryan was starting to shine in Sarah's presence. He was wittier and easier to be with than his deep-thinking pal. Happiness, the Duchess was beginning to believe, might be on the other side of the Atlantic with the 'Get Real' People.

Prince Andrew, a Lieutenant Commander in charge of the two Lynx anti-submarine helicopters on board HMS *Cambeltown*, was not due back at Sunninghill Park until May. The Gulf War, however, was still raging, and Sarah had already stoked up criticism by taking Beatrice on a skiing trip to Klosters just before the Allied liberation began. She dashed home once the fighting started. 'It's my own decision,' she said. 'I have not been called back. I think it's the right thing to do.' In an editorial attacking members of the Royal Family over their lifestyles, the *Sunday Times* – proprietor: Rupert Murdoch – criticized the duchess for 'playing with her gang, very publicly, at a high-spirited dinner in a London restaurant'. After that reprimand, Sarah joined the war effort with gusto, making trips to HMS *Osprey* in Dorset, the Aldershot garrison in Hampshire and RAF Honington in Suffolk. She chatted to the wives of naval personnel over lunch and visited hospitals.

One of the voices raised loudest against her came from a quarter which had begun to have misgivings about Sarah's judgment. 'Fergie's antics have become an embarrassment to the Windsors. Her skirts are too short and the list of her indiscretions too long,' noted *People* magazine. 'Steve and Fergie have palled around so much that British Intelligence, which monitors royal activity, is said to have confidentially alerted the Prime Minister's office that the pair could create a major royal scandal.'

Some of the 'palling around' took place a ten-minute drive from Sarah's home at Sunninghill in the healthy surroundings of the Royal Berkshire Racquets Club, a new sports complex near Bracknell which she had been invited to open in October 1990. Steve looked on from the spectators' benches while the Duchess improved her tennis. 'He often came with Sarah and sat and watched her play – but he would never dare to criticize her game,' commented Gary Drake, Sarah's personal tennis coach. 'He is a great bloke and fun to be with, just like Sarah. They are very good friends and enjoy each other's company. They share the same sense of humour and laugh a lot. I've never seen them play together; he is of a much better standard. He sometimes arrived with her and left with her after her lessons. I remember one Saturday morning when they were both here. Steve was playing against me and Sarah was watching. She thought he was a very good player – and kept telling me. They like it here because the atmosphere is very friendly and nobody bothers them. Nobody takes any notice of them.'

It was obvious to Sarah's friends that Steve was fulfilling a necessary role in Sarah's life. 'Andrew has neither the ability nor the interest in the sort of sparky conversation that Sarah liked before the marriage, and I think that probably drove her up the wall,' said one who knew her in Verbier. 'Sarah longed for someone to spark off – just as she did in the old days. She had always made goofs of the "Whoops, silly me, I've done it again!" variety, but now she had turned into a more sophisticated Sloane prankster and she wanted a playmate. Steve Wyatt was a master of that game and knew exactly how to take her best shots. You hit each other very fast and in a way that goes over the heads of everyone else at the table. It's sometimes tiresome, of course, because it excludes others. But she had been used to that in Verbier, and I think she missed it so much she was prepared to risk her reputation for a bit of fun. It was very unfair to blame her for everything.'

'Fun' cropped up in Sloanespeak so often that it required a definition. 'Fun?' considered Dai Llewellyn. 'It's doing something yummy. If you're having fun, you're smiling. It shows in the laughter lines on your face. It means not taking yourself or life too seriously. It's a survival technique in a wicked old world.'

'Fun is doing everything except the things you would be ashamed to tell your sister over breakfast the morning after,' said a young Chelsea socialite who encountered some of Sarah's set on the scene.

If fun were synonymous with happiness, then Sarah was happy. 'My face and my eyes tell a story,' she said. 'You can always tell the way I'm feeling by looking at me.' Sarah started to practise a technique to improve her self-esteem based on the principle: Let others love you until you can love yourself. Every morning, she looked in a mirror and asked herself the question: 'Who loves you, baby?' In reply, she recited the names of her family, including Andrew, Beatrice and Eugenie, out loud. She then asked two more questions: 'What are you most proud of?' and 'What are you glad about today?' 'By the time I have answered, I feel much happier,' she said. 'It sets me up for the day.' Sarah described the ritual during a visit to a rehabilitation centre for drug addicts at Lewisham in South London. 'People tend to be very judgmental about drug users,' she said. 'But I see drug addicts as my equals. I know what it feels like to be judged because I am always in the limelight myself.' Recovering addicts attending counselling sessions at another centre on the other side of town drew strength from pictures of the Duchess pinned to a wall.

Her appearance began to brighten up and she took greater care with her make-up. Three times a week, she worked out at the Bodyfit routine of Josh Salzmann, an American from Massachusetts who now lived in Windsor. Among his other clients were actor John Cleese, David Frost and *Death Wish* film director Michael Winner. She changed hairdressers, and her new stylist, Nicky Clarke, brushed out her curls to give her long, straight tresses which suited her new svelte shape. She asked those who advised her on fashion and sometimes shopped on her behalf at Browns, Harvey Nichols and Harrods to buy her a particular style of skirt. 'Steve likes me in tight black denim,' she told one.

'The fact is that this young lady owes her status in life to that one memorable day [when she married Prince Andrew] and that's all that's changed her from being any other girl on the streets of London to the person she is,' said Gene Nocon. 'Now title does not make for anything, title is just something bestowed upon you by virtue of marriage. The reality is the character behind it and that character I've seen change. I've seen it change and not for the better. You know she was such a nice person when we first met her, we are beginning to wonder if that niceness was all just an interesting ploy. It's not because of any vindictiveness on my part, it's just recognizing characters as they come and go. I've been around a number of characters in my profession and in my personal capacity and the real person is Prince Andrew. That's the real person. He's the person I met and still love very much. They don't come any better.'

.   .   .

By the spring of 1991, gossip reaching the Queen about the intensity of the friendship between Sarah and Steve had reached such a pitch that a Royal Family conference was held to discuss the matter. Sarah was ordered to 'chill out Steve Wyatt', her mother Susie was quoted as saying to a friend. She was also told to sever her connections with other members of the set. It would be best, senior courtiers suggested firmly, if the Duchess ceased to associate with Wyatt or his friends in public. The Texan only discovered the existence of this edict when Sarah sent her regrets to a small dinner party he was expecting her to attend. 'It's very embarrassing,' said Lynn Wyatt. 'Prince Andrew even called Steve to tell him how sorry he was about it all.'

After Sarah had introduced them, she had discovered that Steve was a man with whom the Prince could share confidences, and this made the rift doubly hurtful. Wyatt shrugged and, working on the principle of 'win some, lose some', gave notice on Apartment F in Cadogan Square and prepared to return to the US. Sarah told friends that she felt the episode was just one more example of the Palace interfering in her private life. She felt cut-off and her mood of helplessness returned. Her hair had started falling out after the birth of Eugenie, and Nicky Clarke advised her to wear it short until the problem cleared up. She emerged with a twenties bob cut which was widely misinterpreted. 'It cost £72 and Andrew hated it,' she said. 'But what could I do? My hair had started to drop out.' People who believed that she did it to upset Andrew were completely wrong.

Something had to give. The carousel was still spinning on its royal axis, but the Duchess of York no longer felt like humming in tune to the music. Confused and filled with self-doubt, she sounded decidedly off-key whenever the subject of her relations with the Palace was raised. Expressed as a stark choice, Sarah seemed to feel that she had only two options: escape or surrender. It had come down to the same alternatives her sister Jane had faced as they sat on a tropical Queensland beach and discussed whether Jane should return to the Outback and accept the responsibilities of married life, or whether she should follow her mother's lead, listen to her heart and make a fresh start somewhere else. Jane had walked. The paradox was that the older woman had been seeking precisely the kind of glamorous lifestyle that her younger sister was now contemplating giving up.

When the Makims' marriage had first run into trouble, Jane had flown to Sydney where she was able to stay with Sarah at Admiralty House, the Governor-General's grand mansion. She flew to London to attend Princess Beatrice's christening in the Chapel Royal at St James's Palace and, along with Lynn Wyatt, enjoyed regal hospitality once more. Then, in August 1989, Jane had come to London in the middle of her reconciliation with Alex and stayed with the Yorks at Castlewood. Sarah had given a party in her honour, and the sisters went to see Dustin Hoffman playing Shylock in *The Merchant of Venice*. After drinks back stage, the superstar actor joined them for dinner at Harry's Bar. None of this could have made it any easier for Jane to settle down again with Alex at Wilga Warrina near North Star with its population of 120 and lifestyle to match.

The first signals outside Sarah's immediate circle that she had made a decision to sacrifice just about all of this came from her own lips in the summer of 1991. 'It is only now, as I think over her words and sad demeanour, that I realize she was giving the first indication of the trouble that was to come,' said Georgina Howell, the writer to whom Sarah gave her last interview before the separation. 'I got the impression that she had been trying very hard and hadn't got the credit due for her efforts. I thought she was very crushed.' Reading between the lines, it was apparent that Sarah was desperately unhappy with her life as it stood, despite all the advantages of wealth and prestige.

'It is very difficult to get any privacy. In fact I don't have any,' she told the writer as they sat in her cluttered office at the Palace. Beatrice kept running in, demanding attention. A typist was working away on some correspondence. Prince Andrew was in the next room. 'Oh, there are times when I don't have anybody in the house [at Sunninghill] and we can just be a family together. I sometimes give everyone the night off and go into the kitchen and make a cheese sandwich. But you have staff, you have security, you always have to be aware. You're always on show, twenty-four hours a day; you've just got to accept that.'

Acceptance, it was obvious, was the one virtue that Sarah was having trouble finding in sufficient quantity. Somehow, it amounted to surrender. 'I just wanted to get away,' she said. 'To get away from the

System and people saying, "No, you can't, No, you can't" – that's what the System is.' The coded messages had been coming through softly but persistently since the winter of 1989, and they appeared to be saying that her life was in disarray. Marriage to Prince Andrew had tied her to the Royal Family which automatically bound her to the strictures of the Palace. Unhappy as she was with the status quo, she could not realistically cut loose from the Palace without first severing her links with the other two. It boiled down to one question: Did she love Andrew enough to sacrifice her own will? She knew from Jane's experience that trial separations, such as the one she had recommended to Alex Makim, had very little chance of succeeding. It had become an all-or-nothing situation.

Ronald was only too well aware of Sarah's feelings. People who knew him said that his attitude towards Prince Andrew seemed to undergo a marked change. He never criticized his son-in-law, but he stopped making the usual complimentary remarks that had been an integral part of his conversation ever since the engagement. 'He always used to mention Andrew,' said one who met Ronald at polo. 'Suddenly that stopped.'

Jane and Susie shared Sarah's anxieties as they came tumbling out whenever they spoke on the telephone, and she was not short of real friends to meet for a heart-to-heart chat. One she confided in was Vanessa Calthorpe, the friend she had met in Verbier and with whom she had enjoyed so many good times. Vanessa had married a baronet's younger son, John Anstruther-Gough-Calthorpe, known for the sake of brevity as Joe, after her divorce from Dai Llewellyn. Sarah drove down to Vanessa and Joe's estate at Martyr Worthy in Hampshire and talked long into the night. The two women were so close that the Duchess allowed Vanessa's daughter Arabella to hold her birthday party inside Buckingham Palace.

Andrew's home life had settled into a pattern. He liked to play golf at Swinley Forest, a course not far from Sunninghill, 'to refresh the mind and escape from the madding crowd'. He had been taking lessons from the club's professional, Doug McClelland, since 1990, and found it provided 'a test of patience, application, perseverance and character'. He watched videos, some of them showing Sarah larking about with her friends, or splashed about in the pool with his daughters. As the rift between him and his wife deepened, he had few other outlets through which to express his feelings. Amenable as he could be in male company, an active life in the Royal Navy had taught him to be self-sufficient and

211

that, coupled with his royal upbringing, had made him more cautious about explaining his emotional needs.

'He is easily the most boorish man I have ever met,' said a titled lady of his generation. 'He is self-opinionated, self-indulgent and totally self-seeking. What's more, he is a bully. On one occasion, I was at Windsor Castle for dinner and he asked this girl who was only about eighteen what she did for a living. He asked her in the snootiest way and when she replied that she was a secretary, he looked at everybody around the table and said, "How terribly uninteresting. It that the best you can find to do?" The trouble is that he's the Queen's favourite child, he's always got his own way and the result is a thoroughly spoiled man. He can do no wrong in his mother's eyes, but he's the last person in the world I would want to be stranded on a desert island with.'

Andrew did, however, have one friend whose support was no longer as available to his wife as it had been: the Princess of Wales. The girlish shopping binges, followed by coffee in Harvey Nick's cafeteria, had long been a thing of the past. Andrew had known Diana all her life and she was more than willing to listen to his side of the story whenever he visited Kensington Palace. It must have hurt Sarah that her own one-time BF (Best Friend) had replaced Liz Nocon as the woman to whom her husband took his problems.

One thing which Sarah's closest allies found hardest to tolerate was Andrew's abrupt, service-style behaviour towards his wife. Those who had observed the Yorks in non-public situations declared that this was often appalling. On some occasions, he bullied her mercilessly. His patience could wear incredibly thin with Sarah's inclination to enjoy herself in whatever company she happened to find herself. Charlie Young understood this darker side. When black moods overtook the Prince, Young would warn him that he believed he was heading for trouble. Geoffrey Crawford, his Australian-born Press Secretary, also had genuine feelings for Andrew's well-being, but protocol forbade a real friendship between them. When difficult decisions had to be made, though, Andrew could usually be heard saying: 'I'll get Geoffrey's advice on that one.'

He missed the counsel of his friend Norman Parkinson, the royal photographer, who died in 1990. In a similar manner to that in which Dickie Mountbatten advised Prince Charles, Andrew found in 'Parks' an older man to whom he could turn for pearls of wisdom. Parks once confided that he felt Andrew was a young man who believed that he owed it to his family to be seen to be winning – even when he was wrong. 'I have told him that he brings pressure on himself which is entirely unnecessary. It is no sin to be wrong from time to time, but it festers like an open sore if, once you realize it, you don't admit it.'

Few of Andrew's pals had been so prepared to point out to him the error of his ways. One who did put him in his place was the Earl of Caernarvon's married daughter Carolyn Herbert, a Princess Diana lookalike. She treated Andrew like a brother and had acted as a decoy in some of his romantic liaisons before his marriage. When Carolyn had married bloodstock agent John Warren in July 1985, Andrew escorted Diana to the wedding, Prince Charles having had a more pressing engagement playing polo. This friendship had continued, and Sarah began to feel excluded from it.

Once again, she turned to outsiders for help. During a trip to California in September, she met Sylvester Stallone and developed a rapport with him which was to sustain her in the difficult times ahead. Stallone, the actor famed for his staccato speech and Ramboesque exploits on the screen, found it easy to open up to Sarah about his own marital disasters with his first wife Sasha and then actress Brigitte Nielson. The actor said that he and the Duchess became friends during a dinner party in her honour at the home of studio mogul Marvin Davis in Beverly Hills. Asked about the party Davis, a twenty-one-stone Denver oil billionaire who sold 20th Century Fox to Rupert Murdoch, said: 'We don't give any information.'

Sylvester Stallone was more forthcoming. 'As we sat at the dinner table, Fergie became fascinated with a large gold ring I was wearing,' he said. 'She asked if she could take a closer look so I handed it to her and she put it on her finger. Then as she was taking the ring off, it slipped and landed in her soup. I fished it out with a spoon and Fergie let loose with an outrageous roar of laughter. I'd expected her to be snobbish, but she was warm and friendly.'

The next night, Sarah, Stallone and the actor's girlfriend Jennifer Flavin, went to Granita's restaurant in Malibu with Billy Connolly and Pamela Stephenson, at whose home Sarah and Beatrice were staying. *Batman* star Michael Keaton and Sidney Poitier were among the eight other guests. 'We had such a good time that we made a date for the following evening,' said Stallone. 'She loves laughing and telling jokes – but she also loves to talk about art and the theatre and sports. We both love polo and we shared our riding experiences.'

Stallone's publicity image as a tough guy from the Hell's Kitchen slums west of Times Square belied his middle-class origins. His mother

Jacqueline had once said that her son was only fit to associate with royalty. 'The only woman she is kinda partial to is Princess Diana,' said Stallone. 'She is very taken by status – that is why she wants me to end up with someone like her.' Anyone who had met the muscle-bound star knew that he was far more self-effacing than Rambo and much more sensitive than his other celluloid stereotype, the two-fisted Rocky. He assured Sarah that it was all right to contact him if ever she needed a shoulder to cry on. She had made another ally who was guaranteed to send the Ladies of the Bedchamber at Buckingham Palace reaching for the smelling salts.

During Sarah's four-day idyll in California, Prince Andrew was sweltering in the jungles of Papua New Guinea on the other side of the Pacific. Tribesmen decorated him with strings of beads and shells, made him a chieftain – and elevated him from a prince to a god in a ceremony which marked their great respect for the Queen during his official tour. They gave him a grass skirt to take home to his duchess.

Sarah did so much last-minute shopping of her own in Los Angeles that she almost missed her flight home when her limousine was held up in traffic on the way to the airport. Passengers on the London-bound British Airways 747 were told that 'routeing problems' were to blame for the ninety-minute delay on the tarmac. When Sarah finally turned up, she was flustered and apologetic, and Beatrice was close to tears. 'The hold-up was all down to the royal party,' said an airline official. 'We would have preferred not to wait. We don't like lying to passengers.'

.   .   .

This piece of bad public relations was a mere trifle compared with the main event which was about to be staged in Houston. The Palace's exercise in damage limitation over Sarah's image was already being fully tested in the case of Wyatt v. Sakowitz, which had been previewing to rapt audiences all through the North American summer. Although this real-life soap opera did not reach its courtroom finale until October, the reason for Sarah's need to distance herself from the Wyatts as early as April now became apparent. Her name was inevitably linked with that of Steve Wyatt, one of the plaintiffs in the action, in the television and newspaper reports which set the scene for the legal showdown.

Allegations about Doug Wyatt's connections with the Eternal Values sect were part of the public court record long before the case began. Roger Hall, the Houston real-estate broker, claimed in his deposition that the group's leader preached anti-Semitism, misogyny and the superiority of male homosexuals. Doug Wyatt strongly denied that any of this was true, but the House of Windsor were not taking any chances. Removing Sarah from the ring had seemed the best line of defence. Doug understood. 'Sarah is a friend of the family and a nice person,' he said afterwards. He was, he confessed, 'just amazed' at the press treatment of the friendship between his brother and the Duchess.

The *New York Times,* which usually sanctified Lynn Wyatt's activities in its social columns, reported on 8 October:

> *The lesser foibles, the big financial dealings and the most intimate family quarrels of one of Houston's most celebrated families are being put on display in a little courtroom with linoleum floors; in a city where dynastic battles and business rivalries are followed like major league sports, the case of Wyatt v. Sakowitz is a championship match. It is a courtroom conflict between people who used to be known for their glittering appearances at charity galas. With the bitterness that can only be generated by a feud among kin, they publicly baited each other in a trial that began last week.*

Lynn Wyatt, the *New York Times* said, 'has combined down-home charm and *haute couture* to become an international socialite whose guest lists have included the likes of Mick Jagger, the Duchess of York and the Aga Khan'.

Sarah may have had the case on her mind when she told David Frost on TV-am two days earlier that she was horrified when she picked up a newspaper to discover that journalists knew when she got up and what she did. 'I think it is better there are little facts that are unknown,' she said. Her fear of intrusion had become so intense that she had given up keeping a diary, she said, and any personal letters she received, including Andrew's love letters, ended up in a shredder. 'Andrew used to write me wonderful letters from ship. When he goes to sea for six months he writes good letters, but I haven't kept them. I did for a bit, in the bank, but then I thought the bank would be robbed.'

Referring to her diaries, she said: 'I got too frightened that some of my entries might end up in rather the wrong places, so I decided to forget them.' The programme was intended to promote her book *Victoria and Albert: Life at Osborne House,* but it provided several clues to her real state of mind. 'We have the same pressures as Victoria and Albert had,' she said. 'I know how important it is to come home and just relax by myself. Just to be able to feel happy and relax, to take the make-up off and to let the hair down, as they say, is a real treat.'

She was letting down her hair in other ways too. Defying the

Queen's wishes she met Steve Wyatt, who was making one of his flying visits to London, at the Royal Berkshire Racquets Club. 'Steve comes here a lot when he is in the country,' said Gary Drake. 'He is very keen and often phones me up to ask for a knock-about. He doesn't really need coaching. He is about the best player we have got here and I am more of a partner. The last time Steve was here was in October. Sarah was here as well.'

Whenever he was in London, Wyatt also checked in with his friend Johnny Bryan, who was living with his father Tony in a Chelsea apartment. His sister Baby – real name Pamela – had married a Belgian aristocrat, Count Guy de Sallier. The couple lived in London and were able to introduce Johnny to some well-connected people. Invitations to dinner parties and country weekends soon started to drop through his letterbox in Cheyne Place, a short walk from the white canopied entrance of Foxtrot Oscar.

'London is a challenge to Americans like Johnny Bryan,' said the young Chelsea socialite. 'If you can win London after New York, you've really done something. Johnny has dated lots of society girls who like to go to the country for the weekend. *He's really got it down.* But girls are getting pretty smart these days. My girlfriends in New York are only interested in money – they're quite blatant about it. They're all trying to marry as rich a guy as possible and they know the good-looking ones haven't got the money. All the guys have to do is name-drop and drive a car that indicates wealth. The New Age is really "Who's got money left after the eighties? Let's have fun before we die or lose it all." I've seen these people in action. The rich are different. I've monkeyed around with the yachties and I swear to God they are different. When it comes to the sex game, no rules apply. The richer you are the more you get away with.'

Johnny showed little inclination to modify the street smarts he had picked up in New York. His style jarred with people in polite London society. 'He told me he knew Fergie within the first ten minutes of sitting next to me,' said one who met him at dinner. 'Fairly aggressive name-dropping, I'd call it. In fact, he dined with Fergie only the other day. He said he, Steve Wyatt and the Duchess sometimes formed a threesome. It might be all right to say something like that among the preppies in the Surf Club or the Au Bar in New York where he told me he liked to go, but I thought it sounded a bit brash. He was just too fast for me. I'm a Mini and he was a Ferrari.'

In fact, Bryan was still driving a rented Vauxhall.

Experience, though, had taught Bryan to make his own luck, and he made use of a written mandate from Howard Stein authorizing him to open a European branch of Au Bar in either London or Paris. The Florida end of the operation had unexpectedly become known around the world as the venue where William Kennedy Smith had met the alleged victim of the 'date rape' charges of which he stood accused. The nephew of Senator Edward Kennedy had met the thirty-year-old woman at the bar in Palm Beach on Good Friday and, the prosecution alleged, committed the offence on the lawn of the Kennedy mansion. There was no better place for Johnny to start looking for potential business partners than on his own doorstep at Foxtrot Oscar, the local wine bar.

'A very nice man called Johnny Bryan was introduced to me because of my background in nightclubs,' said Dai Llewellyn. 'He had approached Michael Proudlock, who owns Foxtrot Oscar, about the Au Bar project. The Kennedy Case was going on in Florida at the time and the name Au Bar was so topical that it looked like a good idea, even though we were in the middle of a recession. We had two lunches with Johnny at Foxtrot Oscar to discuss the idea. I was going to do the décor and organize the membership, and Michael was going to run the restaurant and wine systems. We drew up a business plan and I went looking for backers. Even though Kennedy Smith was acquitted, it proved impossible to raise the money. I approached some Islamic financiers who said, "We will not invest in a place that is notorious – not famous, notorious." They were very prudish about it, so I stopped trying.'

Bryan was not too bothered about the rejection; his friendship with the Duke and Duchess of York had opened up an exciting new prospect. The Yorks had found that Bryan was a man who could find his way around a balance sheet without reverting to the dry, impenetrable jargon of accountancy. He made it sound so easy, it was almost fun. They asked him to advise them about their financial affairs, particularly those of Sarah whose literary efforts had brought a vast amount of cash, but whose spending had resulted in a hefty overdraft. This was the basis of Bryan's relationship with the Yorks, and it would become far more personal and important. Sarah was invited to his flat to discuss a business opportunity. 'He said he had a film company and Sarah had introduced him to some chap who was going to buy it,' said the Chelsea socialite. 'He said she was coming over to his flat to talk about it. He talked about Fergie a lot. They were like brother and sister, good friends and good for a laugh.'

'He's the sort of guy who just loves women, and he gets on with them better than men,' said one of Bryan's ex-girlfriends. 'To get to his flat, I went through a red door opposite the Chelsea Physic Garden and up the stairs. The flat, which doubles as an office, looks like a rental – adequate but a bit tight. In the living room, there are two big red sofas, a glass-topped coffee table and, above the fireplace, a sixties-style canvas painted all in red. There is also a grand piano which he likes to play. When I went to the ladies room, I saw all these boxes of medical supplies out in the hall. Through the window facing on to Cheyne Place, I had a clear view of the pagoda on the other side of the Thames.'

.   .   .

Across the King's Road in Belgravia, window cleaner Maurice Maple opened the oak door of Apartment F at 34 Cadogan Square with the caretaker's pass-key to spruce up the place before a new tenant moved in to Steve Wyatt's old service flat. He was cleaning the windows of the guest bedroom when he saw some dusty packets on top of a 9-foot-high fitted shelving unit. 'You couldn't see what was on the top from ground level, but from the top of ladder I could see plastic packets,' he said. 'My first reaction was that they had been hidden there by someone. I thought they may have been sex magazines – it's the sort of place people hide such stuff. I took my ladder to the bookcase and retrieved the packets. I had a quick look at the contents – dozens of colour snaps of people on holiday in the sun.'

Maple recognized the Duchess of York, but was only able to put a name to the man in many of the 120 pictures when 'a friend' to whom he showed them recognized Steve Wyatt from his appearances in gossip columns. Maple admitted that his first thought was that he might 'make a few bob' by selling the pictures to a newspaper. He discussed the idea with 'a titled lady', who approached the *Daily Mail* on his behalf during November and offered the whole collection for sale. Probed later on whether everything reported at the time about the discovery was accurate, Maple replied: 'Of course not.' Asked if it had occurred to him to leave the pictures where they were and alert the managing agents of the block, he responded: 'I did what I did.' What he did not realize was the possibility that he was being used to recover the holiday snaps in such a way that public attention would be brought to them for the same reason that Mr G – on someone's authority – sought to focus a spotlight on the Duchess's friendship with Wyatt. Should anything be seen to be going wrong in the Yorks' marriage, the party at fault would be deemed to be Sarah. Andrew had been safely established as the victim.

Neither Sarah nor Steve Wyatt knew that the pictures had been found, but it was apparent that, without any outside assistance, the Yorks were going through another period of self-imposed estrangement. After an engagement in Canada, Sarah stayed behind to weekend at the Vancouver home of millionaire Galen Weston, leaving Andrew to join the Royal Family for the annual commemoration of Britain's war dead at the Cenotaph in Whitehall on 11 November. The following week she flew to New York, returning home only briefly to Sunninghill Park to pack her bags before setting off on a shopping trip to Paris while her husband remained at Sandringham with the Queen.

There was no immediate reason to doubt that Wyatt had simply left the pictures behind when he packed his bags and moved out of Cadogan Square. Some, however, became less convinced as the pieces started to fall into place. 'All aspects of security are involved in the Queen's protection,' said the well informed royal source. 'It was known that the Duchess had visited Steve Wyatt in that apartment. Closed doors can be opened. People can have a look around to see what's involved. Many people, not just the Palace secretariat and the courtiers, wanted the relationship ended once and for all. It isn't the first time something like this has happened. How did Princess Anne's letters from Commander Timothy Laurence get out of her briefcase and into the *Sun?* The only person who had access to that briefcase apart from Princess Anne were her security people or her maid at the time, and she has insisted absolutely and categorically that it wasn't her. In the case of the Moroccan pictures, the motive existed for planting them and there was ample opportunity. The powers-that-be knew from security reports that Sarah was still in touch with Wyatt and had seen him as recently as October despite the clearest advice to steer clear of him. There is nothing a single member of the Royal Family can do without it being logged and monitored at the time. Only the security service know where that information is channelled to eventually, but once the reports are in, all sorts of things can be made to happen.'

If the pictures were planted, whoever did it must have been astonished that nothing happened for two months after Maurice Maple found them. The Yorks continued to lead separate lives, unaware of the timebomb that was ticking away. Andrew was nowhere in sight when Jane Makim, her children and companion Reiner Leudeke, visiting from Australia, accompanied Sarah to the Children of Courage awards at Westminster Abbey. Six days before Christmas the Prince went alone to a dinner at the American Embassy in Grosvenor Square.

When the Yorks were reunited, the rift between them was highlighted in a bizarre fashion during what was intended as a bit of Christmas fun at Buckingham Palace. They organized a party-time version of the popular television lonely-hearts game *Blind Date*, in which contestants choose their ideal partner by questioning candidates of the opposite sex, who are screened from view, about their attitudes to love and marriage. The Yorks joined in the game along with friends and some Palace employees, and answered *risqué* questions to choose their companion for the remainder of the festive night's activities. A television personality accepted the Yorks' invitation to act as host 'to give the event some professionalism'. By all accounts, *Blind Date* Palace-style could never have been shown on British television, certainly not in the family-viewing slot filled by the game which singer Cilla Black compèred so cheekily.

. . .

As 1991 drew to a close under the grey skies of Norfolk, the royal New Year at Sandringham was a suitably dismal affair. To break the tedium of doing jigsaw puzzles or following the shooting parties around the estate, Sarah and Princess Diana took William, Harry and Beatrice – third, fourth and fifth in line to the throne – to the Knight's Hill Health and Leisure Club at King's Lynn. The sisters-in-law worked out with weights, swam in the pool – and plunged into a jacuzzi with their children. It was just like the old days and, for the first time in many months, they talked about the problems in their marriages face to face. The sharing brought them closer together, so close that one source suggested they made a pact to leave their husbands at the same time. But Diana had no intention of leaving Charles; she had worked out a plan of action which would aid her recovery from bulimia nervosa – the illness that had plagued her for nearly ten years – and still leave her with room to manoeuvre inside her marriage. It was Sarah who talked about making a clean break.

Not without some irritation, the Queen spoke to Charles and Andrew about the marital minefield through which they were treading so clumsily. To Her Majesty, the dangers not only to themselves but to the future of the monarchy were all too evident. The two brothers, twelve years apart in age and dissimilar in every way, could not have reacted more in character. Charles made it crystal clear that he had absolutely no intention of altering his attitude towards his wife or changing his ways to suit anybody. He was a stubborn man, some would say intransigent. He would continue to live mainly at Highgrove and Diana at Kensington Palace with William and Harry.

Andrew recommitted himself to a career in the navy and said that, while he loved Sarah, he expected her to carry out her duties as his wife and mother to their children. He could not bring himself to accept that his marriage was so severely damaged that he could not retrieve the situation. For the first time the marital difficulties of the Waleses on the one hand and the Yorks on the other had been very openly exposed within the Royal Family. Diana returned to Kensington Palace with William and Harry while Charles remained at Sandringham. Shaken by the gravity of the situation, Diana rang Penny Thornton and it was then, in the course of seeking some guidance from the stars, she confided that the Yorks were in a state of severe marital disarray.

Even now the existence of the Morocco pictures remained a closely kept secret. Maurice Maple's contact at the *Daily Mail* was Peter Burden, the newspaper's highly experienced chief crime reporter. 'We met at a restaurant in Sloane Square where we examined the pictures,' said Burden. 'This convinced me that they should be passed to the police.' Maple, accompanied by Burden, finally went to New Scotland Yard in Victoria on 7 January 1992 after Burden had contacted Assistant Commissioner William Taylor to make an appointment. The pictures were examined by Deputy Assistant Commissioner Charles Rideout, head of the Royalty and Diplomatic Protection Squad. They were then handed over to Captain Alexander Buchanan-Baillie-Hamilton, an equerry of the Royal Household, and returned to their rightful owners. Scotland Yard said that no investigation had been held and none was planned at that stage. Everything, it appeared, had been taken on face value.

Oscar Wyatt was philosophical after the *Daily Mail* broke the story of the Moroccan pictures and published the fact that the lawyers had been called to Sunninghill to discuss a separation with the Yorks. 'Steve is working in Washington and, let me tell you, he couldn't care less [about any dirty tricks]. He's a friend of Andrew as well as Sarah. I haven't talked to Sarah for months, but let's say that she spent the weekend with Andrew and the children – okay, fine – so maybe a week from now, two weeks from now the same thing might occur again and they might get together.' Oscar Wyatt liked to describe himself as 'meaner than a junkyard dog'. Sometimes, it was easy to see why Lynn Wyatt loved him so much.

THIRTEEN

The Golden Chains of Freedom

'There is no romance – John is just sorting out my problems.'

SARAH, DUCHESS OF YORK

When she arrived at Nicky Clarke's salon in Berkeley Square, the Duchess of York looked even happier than she did in the smiling portrait of herself which greeted every customer, and the explanation was simple: she had, she said, everything she wanted. Johnny Bryan had just secured a contract with the independent television producer, Sleepy Kids, to turn her *Budgie* books into a cartoon series for television, perhaps even a feature film. With merchandising rights for *Budgie* toys and games, she expected to make at least £2 million from the deal and possibly as much as £5 million. For the first time in a very long while, she would be free of the heavy burden of debt which her spending binges had resulted in. 'I love John – but not literally,' she confided. 'There is no romance, he's just sorting out my problems in a way that I had begun to think no one ever could. He's wonderful with money.'

All the privileges previously afforded to her at Buckingham Palace, but withdrawn soon after the separation, had been restored, including her private office and staff to sort out her correspondence. Captain Neil Blair, RN, answered letters on her behalf, and Jane Ambler acted as Personal Assistant in dealing with unwelcome enquiries from the media. Even better, Sir William Heseltine was helping the Queen settle what she knew they regarded as the Fergie Problem, a sure sign that she was winning her battle against Sir Robert Fellowes, the Palace secretariat and the courtiers. The House of York might be divided, but Sarah's fortunes had improved beyond her wildest dreams.

She and her daughters were comfortable in their new home, she said, and, above all, she loved the new freedom she had risked everything to find. Her bold move in forcing the separation was paying off, and she had not had to dilute her demands to gain this measure of independence. Most revealing of all that afternoon on Tuesday, 23 June 1992, was her view on Prince Andrew. She still loved him, but she had no plans to go back. While she was enjoying the life of a single woman, she knew he was living in hope that she would call off the separation and return to the marital home. He was prepared to wait as long as it took to win back the woman he refused to accept that he had lost.

As usual, Sarah sat at a dressing table facing a circular gilt mirror in the long, narrow private room downstairs where VIP clients were given de luxe treatment. She could relax and chat behind the brass-studded door while Nicky, a slender man in black leather trousers and cowboy boots, tended to her hair as other members of his staff slipped quietly in and out. Clarke, who called his most famous customer the Duchess, had designed the £100-an-hour room for elegance and comfort. A friend could sit in a burgundy leather Louis XV chair to chat over a glass of chilled Krug champagne or mineral water. There was a selection of videos, including *Shampoo*, coffee-table books to leaf through, a sound system to play Sarah's favourite CDs and a menu from which she could choose snacks. When staff had commented on her fashionable new dress sense, Sarah replied: 'How does that mean I looked before?' She thought about that for a moment, and added: 'I'll take it as a compliment.' Knowing she was among friends, Sarah talked quite openly about her life and, according to one, she was 'more relaxed in herself since all that happened'. Sarah explained that she wanted her hair to look extra special for a dinner party that evening at Harry's Bar, where Billy Connolly was hosting a table for twelve.

'Now they will all see that my hair is looking as good as I feel,' she declared as she gazed at her tresses in one of the mirrors before she left the salon. Sarah headed back to Buckingham Palace to change and meet up with Prince Andrew. Connolly was not a member of the club, so another guest had made the arrangements to hire an exclusive back room off the main dining area. Prince Andrew and her mother Susie would be there, as would Elton John, David Frost, his wife Lady Carina, Michael and Shakira Caine, Jimmy Connors and his wife Patti, and Connolly's own wife, Pamela Stephenson. Oh, and Johnny Bryan.

The champagne which Connolly had ordered in advance was already chilling nicely in ice buckets on the flower-decked table when the Yorks and their friends stepped through the Georgian double doors to acknowledge bartender Giovanni's welcoming smile. The staff were agreed that they were seeing a very different Prince Andrew from the withdrawn man who had joined owner Mark Birley's party eleven weeks earlier on the eve of his wife and daughters' departure for their long trek around the Far East. Sporting Nicky Clarke's splendid work on her hair and resplendent in a leopard-print jacket by Versace over a revealing black mini-dress, Sarah passed beneath the Venetian chandeliers and made her way past the tables favoured by the club's illustrious members: the kings of Spain, Greece and Jordan, and Andrew's own brother, Prince Charles.

Princess Diana's step-mother Raine, the Dowager Countess Spencer, was among the diners that night, and it could not have escaped her attention that this was an exceptional occasion for the Duchess. Gone was the unkempt look of the woman whose tribulations had been so publicly aired since the year began, and in her place was a chic young lady brimming with self-confidence.

Another patron recalled hearing 'a lot of laughter which usually followed the sound of Billy Connolly's voice' coming from the enclosure. 'It certainly did not sound as if the guests of honour had recently gone their separate ways,' he noted. To all intents and purposes, the party had the ambience suited to a reconciliation of the estranged Yorks, but it was nothing of the sort. It was, in fact, a declaration to those who rated most highly in Sarah's circle that this was a new beginning in her extraordinary life, and Andrew's presence merely indicated that it had his consent if not his approval. Tired-out after his professional exertions at Wimbledon, Jimmy Connors had been told that none of the group was to raise the matter of the separation unless either Sarah or Andrew chose to do so, and neither did. Instead, one of the few family matters to come up in conversation was Beatrice's sports day at Upton House School the following day.

The bill presented to Connolly was for well in excess of £2000, a testament to the fact that in addition to the finest offerings from *sommelier* Valentino's wine list, the dozen happy eaters had selected from the very best of Harry's fare: the splendid Risotto Milanese at £16 per portion, Fegato di Vitello, Linguine al Picatta at £14 a portion. The bill included a large gratuity equivalent to fifteen per cent of the total and an obligatory donation of £2 to the St Thomas's Hospital Baby Fund.

If any of the other members of Harry's Bar – subscription £800, plus a £500 signing-on fee – thought it incongruous that a glowing Sarah marched between them with Johnny Bryan, the man who had recently escorted her across the Atlantic, at her side and her husband following in their wake, no one mentioned it, at least not within earshot. Sarah, against all the odds, had joined that select group of women like Ivana Trump, another star of Harry's Bar, who had discovered there was more than just life after marriage.

.   .   .

Her return to Sunninghill Park from her month-long Asian holiday with Beatrice and Eugenie had been a very different homecoming from that in January when she arrived back from Florida in a highly disturbed state. She had started the year deeply embarrassed by the much-publicized discovery of the Moroccan pictures and full of fear about the prospect of separating from her husband – a move she knew she had to make if either of them were to find lasting happiness.

Johnny Bryan's continuing presence was not only a mark of the gratitude she owed him, but a sign that she was as close to him now as she had been to Steve Wyatt. 'He just denies flatly that there is any kind of romance going on,' said Whitney Tower. 'He went to the Far East with her because he had certain connections there, and he was a go-between to convey her wishes to her husband. He called me a couple of times for public-relations advice when the reporters were camped outside his house and it was really hitting the fan. I just said, "Be honest with them. The more you say, the more they're going to trip you up. I suggest coming out with something that's not going to offend anybody."' Bryan told the Press whenever they buttonholed him that he and the Duchess were just good friends. He told others a different story.

'Fergie and Johnny are actually getting a kick out of playing to the public,' said the young Chelsea socialite. 'It's a game and they're really enjoying it. They're having a bloody good time while everyone else is going, "Oooh, Aaah, Golly, Gee Whizz!" and trying to work out what's happening.'

Bryan's role as honest broker had resulted in the Queen agreeing to make life considerably easier for her daughter-in-law. No large sums of cash were to change hands at that stage, but Sarah would have no reason to fear that the banks would press her for settlement of overdrafts totalling more than £300,000; those debts were, in effect, royally secured. Nor would any attempt be made to take away her daughters, even though the Queen had been made aware of Sarah's expressed wish to set up a home in the United States. In return, the Duchess had agreed to do everything in her power to make the agreed separation period of up to two years as amicable as possible, as had a very willing Andrew. For her part, that meant saying a firm and definite no to a multi-million pound deal she had been offered to sell her personal account of life inside the Royal Family to an American publisher. More than any other single factor, that prospect had chilled courtiers when it was first uttered after Sarah had found her Buckingham Palace office closed, a discourtesy she considered one of several hostile acts which followed the separation. 'She went to the Palace one day and found the door locked and her staff dispersed,' said Bryan Morrison.

On a more immediate and practical level, the Queen had agreed to finance a home for Sarah for as long as it took her to make her long-term plans. A house called Romenda Lodge had been found close to Sunninghill Park and convenient for Beatrice's school in Windsor. It had been tracked down by Expat Home Minders of Ascot and duly rented at £4000 a month from its owner, a Nigerian businessman known as Chief Williams. The mock Tudor residence had stood empty since Chief Williams had left it two years before, asking estate agents to find a buyer willing to pay £1.5 million. Situated between the fifteenth hole of the Wentworth Golf Course and a stretch of the A30 Sunningdale to Egham road, it was hardly a mansion compared with her own home or those in which she was used to residing in Florida, Houston and Beverly Hills. But after an early-morning visit, she expressed herself satisfied with the six-bedroomed, thirties dwelling on Sherborne Drive subject to certain improvements. A team of painters, decorators and carpenters was immediately drafted in and telephone engineers set about installing six extra lines.

To the amusement of neighbours – who included the comedians Russ Abbot and Bruce Forsyth, the golfer Sandy Lyle and the film-maker Bryan Forbes – two vanloads of hired mock-antique furniture, paintings and ornaments were delivered by Roomservice Designs of Chelsea for Nina Campbell to make the décor as tastefully comfortable as she could in a matter of days.

Up to that point, Sarah had been unable to convey her thanks personally to her mother-in-law for what she saw as a turn for the better in her fortunes. The opportunity arrived when she took Beatrice and Eugenie to one of her favourite events, the Royal Windsor Horse Show. The girls, neatly decked out in matching pink floral dresses, were heading for the funfair in a distant corner of the field when Sarah spotted the Queen seated in the back of a Vauxhall estate car waiting to watch Prince Philip take part in a carriage event. Her Majesty invited the trio to join her, and for twelve minutes they sat together, smiling and giggling as the Duchess expressed her gratitude for the Monarch's personal rescue plan. Before they parted company, the Queen invited her granddaughters to bring their mother to tea at Windsor Castle that same afternoon, and Sarah marched them off to the amusements with a newly acquired spring in her step.

Mother and daughters returned for the second day of the show – with Prince Andrew as well. He drove his family to the event in a Range Rover to be greeted by his bowler-hatted father-in-law, Major Ronald. Looking summery in a bright baggy silk shirt and long blue skirt, Sarah was in sharp contrast to her husband, who looked stiff and uncomfortable in a suit. He was also wearing a bowler hat as the occasion demanded, and not once was he seen to take the hand of either of his children or his wife. He was keenly aware that even as they appeared in happy family style, removal men were at Sunninghill Park House loading up his wife's possessions and the children's toys into two unmarked vans. Sarah broke up her last hours at her old home with a visit to Romenda Lodge to show her daughters where they would be living. In the evening, Andrew took her out for supper at the Cottage Inn at Winkfield. While they dined on liver and bacon in a dark corner of the country pub, locals overheard Andrew repeatedly declaring: 'You can keep it, you can keep it.' As the casually dressed couple left, Sarah remarked by way of unlikely explanation: 'We are celebrating.'

The next morning Johnny Bryan made sure that Sarah settled down among the comedians without any last-minute hitches. He brought in modernist designer Tchaik Chassay, the 'society architect' responsible for the decor of Groucho's Club in Soho, the now defunct Zanzibar in Covent Garden and other avant-garde establishments, to add more lasting touches to Nina Campbell's hurried furnishings. 'The intention is to make it a pleasant surrounding for the Duchess and the children so the move is not unnecessarily upsetting,' he said. He had a royal connection of his own which Sarah would have appreciated: his Russian grandmother designed banknotes for the last Tsar. Emphasizing the haste in which the work had been accomplished, Chassay explained: 'Sunday we measured up, did the drawings on Monday and were finished by Friday.'

Although she appreciated the superhuman efforts which had gone into her move, the day itself was clearly not a happy one for Sarah. She snapped at Beatrice as she delivered the child to school, and then burst into tears when she discovered that a well-meaning soul had left her a 'welcome pack' containing food, milk and a bottle of wine in the kitchen at Romenda Lodge. If nothing else, it reminded her that she was on her own: the servants remained at Sunninghill leaving her to manage with just Alison Wardley and a maid on loan from the Queen's personal rota. Workmen were busy both inside the house and in the garden, where emergency fencing was being constructed to shield her from the 30,000 people attending the PGA championships on the Wentworth course.

After her first night under the new roof, Sarah told the workmen that she was going to get out of their way and dashed off along the tarmac pathway in bright blue cycling shorts, a sloppy T-shirt and red headband to work out at Josh Salzmann's gym attached to the Colonial-style Wentworth tennis club. She had put on weight since the separation, a sign that happily reassured her husband that she had, as promised, forsaken the slimming pills which had caused such unpredictable changes in her behaviour.

Sarah's sudden presence, and its attendant media circus, caused some consternation among the neighbours. Author Ian Sayer, who lived next door, said: 'I drove home in a Range Rover and was jumped on by dozens of photographers who thought I was someone entirely different.' 'A lot of celebrities live here and they like to be quiet,' said another. 'I'm afraid Fergie's arrival means our privacy is going to be battered.' Another woman complained that Sarah took Eugenie to her morning work-out sessions. 'A number of us do an exercise class in the bar area two mornings a week,' she said. 'Fergie is behind the partition in Josh's gym, howling with laughter, and the child is left out here with her nanny and detective. We feel it is fine to come, but Eugenie is so uncontrolled. She runs around between our legs and it is very distracting. Can you believe that Fergie calls that poor little girl "Euge"? I thought she was saying "Huge" at first. I hope the princess doesn't grow up thinking the same.'

The change of scenery, however, improved Sarah's mood. Johnny Bryan was able to relate to one of his aristocratic chums in Cambridge that he had received an amusing present from her. Having learned that his rented Vauxhall had been clamped outside his Chelsea flat, Sarah sent him a car of his own – albeit a second-hand 850cc Reliant Robin. She had paid £1850 for the plastic three-wheeler. It was an expensive joke, but one she thought she was now well able to afford.

Sarah's prospects appeared so rosy that she set about planning what to do with the fortune she expected to receive in the near future. With the confidence of an heiress, she joined other commuters aboard an early-morning British Airways shuttle to Edinburgh to call on the city's highly respected stockbrokers, Baillie Gifford. Although she was travelling without a bodyguard, Sarah was met at Edinburgh Airport by two Special Branch detectives who drove her to the investment house and waited on her until she was ready to return to London later in the day. Clearly enjoying a cat-and-mouse game with the media, she had the policemen drive her first to the Caledonian Hotel where she sipped coffee while journalists gathered outside. Then she had her temporary minders lead a chase through the city's streets to her real destination. She wanted the world to know that she was now a woman of means, no longer dependent on her Duke or his family for her well-being.

She had, however, given an undertaking that she would be available to Andrew whenever he required her and she did not hesitate to agree when he suggested a return to Scotland a few days later so that they could spend the weekend together with Beatrice and Eugenie at Craigowan Lodge on the edge of the Grampian mountains in the heart of the 50,000-acre Balmoral Estates. Despite what he called its 'pretty unwelcoming interior', Prince Charles had used this house in his courting days and Sir Robert Fellowes and his wife Jane used it for summer holidays to be within reach of the Queen.

In much the same way as Sarah had made her movements in Edinburgh known, Andrew had allowed a Palace source to leak plans of their trip to Craigowan Lodge in advance. It was as if he wanted to counter her solo PR exercise of the previous week by letting the world know that they were playing happy families, taking walks with the children and videoing their games. But Sarah was itching to get back to Surrey where she had very independent things to organize. Within days she would be setting off again, this time to Buenos Aires to see her mother. She had persuaded Johnny to go with her to look over Hector's will. But first there was a party to host: a house-warming to show off the dolled-up house at Wentworth to her friends. Eighty of them assembled at Romenda Lodge to bear witness to her new beginning. She apologized for the absence of 'proper food' due to the shortage of a cook and took ten of those closest to her on to the Jade Fountain in Sunninghill where, surrounded by screens, they dined on Chinese food in relative privacy. One of the visitors to Romenda Lodge was Alison Lobel, the old school friend who had stayed with Sarah at Tim Rice's manor before the separation. She was delighted to see Sarah so happy.

Although Sarah no longer officially rated police protection, a detective accompanied the Duchess and Bryan when they set off for Argentina. They stayed two days at a hotel with Mrs Barrantes, the first time she had seen her daughter since her decision to separate from her husband and the Royal Family. Business complete, Sarah extracted a promise from her mother to visit her at the lodge within a fortnight.

As they flew on to New York a new storm was breaking over the Royal Family's head in England following the *Sunday Times* publication of extracts from *Diana: Her True Story,* Andrew Morton's book which claimed that Princess Diana's marriage was so unhappy she had made several half-hearted attempts to take her own life as a cry for help. If this new burden on the Queen troubled Sarah in any way, she did not show it as a three-car motorcade carrying five armed secret-service agents accompanied her to a shop on Fifth Avenue where she selected a £50 pair of men's flowered Ralph Lauren boxer shorts. They might have been planning to take away her policeman in London, but in the United States she was still being treated like the Queen.

Bryan had been so anxious to protect Sarah's privacy that he had failed to tell his mother, Mrs Lyda Redmond, that he was even in the country. 'He called her in Long Island and asked her to come in and meet the Duchess for lunch that Monday,' said Whitney Tower. 'This was twelve o'clock and the lunch was going to take place in an hour, which his mother couldn't possibly make.' Sirens wailed and other traffic was pulled over to the side as the Duchess hopped from the Plaza Athenée Hotel to lunch at Mortimer's and dine at the Four Seasons. Bryan could not help but be impressed by the importance with which his countrymen regarded his client. The Queen was touring France to a tumultuous reception and Diana's woes filled the headlines in London, but Sarah had taken Manhattan and she clearly relished it.

Concorde brought her home and, as if to show her that most privileges remained intact, a car was driven up to the plane as it landed to whisk her and her financial adviser away without the formalities required of non-royal passengers.

.   .   .

As the pressure on the Prince and Princess of Wales mounted, Diana called at the west London home of Carolyn Bartholemew, a former flatmate, who had admitted to revealing some of her secrets to author Morton. But still there was no telephone call to Romenda Lodge from Kensington Palace. There was, however, a call from Sarah's Hollywood friend, Sylvester Stallone, who was making his latest movie, *Cliffhanger*, in Italy. He contacted the Duchess during a four-day break he took in London to sympathize with her over the separation. He was staying at the Halkin, a new hotel in tree-lined Halkin Street, which ran from the back garden wall of Buckingham Palace down to Belgrave Square. The Household Cavalry, swords unsheathed and breastplates gleaming in the brilliant sunshine, clattered past the top of the street on their way to Trooping the Colour. Sarah had not been invited to this most regal of ceremonial pageants, and Andrew stayed away as a mark of solidarity. They watched it on television. 'The Duchess of York is one helluva lady,' said Stallone. 'She is everything a man could want. She is a very beautiful, intelligent, warm, generous, sexy lady.'

'They've been talking on the phone,' said his mother Jacqueline, 'and they've been writing to each other.'

Sarah did her best to avoid the fray and took Eugenie to enrol at the Montessori School in Winkfield, a progressive kindergarten which liked to boast that it believed in freedom. Although the theme certainly met with her mother's approval, the two-year-old princess was not so sure and burst into tears despite being reassured that she would only be going for mornings during that summer term.

Prince Andrew telephoned his wife with the news that during her absence his appointment had been confirmed as commander of the minehunter HMS *Cottesmore*. The ship was based at Portsmouth and fulfilled his request to be given a command as close to his family as possible, although he was made aware that success in the post would inevitably lead to promotion with all the attendant disadvantages of months away at sea again.

Sarah's well-meant return to Salzmann's care had been offset by her latest round of travelling and celebrating and, half a stone heavier than when she had last visited him, she returned to the gym displaying every extra pound in her tight cycling shorts and a T-shirt emblazoned with the message Pump It Up. A period of serious exercise was clearly called for.

She was facing up to life as an ex-royal and getting used to travelling without the minder who had shadowed her since her engagement. As if to emphasize that she had joined the rank and file of Her Majesty's subjects, Sarah took her two daughters to picnic by the roadside at Ascot and watch the Queen's procession make its way to the racecourse for the most royal of sporting occasions. Onlookers were bemused at the sight of the Duchess pointing out the Queen in her carriage to Her Majesty's own grand-daughters. Even the Queen appeared totally surprised at the spectacle. The previous year Sarah had ridden in the procession herself, sharing a carriage with the Queen Mother. Now she was seemingly an outcast dressed in bomber jacket and no make-up handing out handkerchiefs for her seemingly confused children to wave at their grandmother.

Diana, fighting back the misery of her own wretched situation, smiled briefly at the irony and, according to one who dined with her that evening, wondered whether Sarah's 'mad break', as she termed it, might not have been the better course to take. The following day Sarah and the children were back at the same spot to watch the procession go by again and lest anyone think that his wife had mounted a stunt to win sympathy, Prince Andrew was at her side, hoisting Princess Eugenie on to his shoulder to ensure that she got a good view of his family . . . and that they could see her too. After the picnic, Andrew returned to Sunninghill where he was living alone knowing that he would have to make do without servants for the weekend. As a thank-you to those who had tended to her needs, Sarah had promised them a trip to Paris for a day's outing at the EuroDisney theme park.

The Yorks' behaviour earned them the title of the Odd Couple. 'Obviously, there's a hidden agenda here that isn't for public consumption,' said one who knows the Royal Family. 'That's why she has picnics on the grass at Windsor. Who would do that in their right mind? You would only do it if you were making a point. It was like looking at some incredible surrealist painting in which Sarah was making an outrageous statement about the change in her status. But I think there are things within the marriage to Andrew that aren't quite okay and I think that would inevitably have driven a wedge between them whether there was Steve Wyatt or whoever.'

The Duchess and Bryan went on ahead to Paris for meetings at the Banque IndoSuez where the bankers laid out the red carpet, a privilege extended to any client considering investing well over £1 million. The meeting was an exhausting one as attractive proposition followed attractive proposition – a new experience for one more used to explaining to her bank manager why her overdraft had increased when she had promised faithfully that it was going to shrink. That evening they dressed up and made for the Paris Ritz Club, part of the five-star Ritz Hotel on the Rue Chambon. Shown to a dimly lit alcove, they ordered champagne with their dinner and congratulated themselves on a good day's business. Dinner over, they joined other couples on the dance floor and danced cheek to cheek to records which included Sarah and Andrew's courting song, 'Lady in Red' by Chris de Burgh. 'Fergie looked very, very happy as she was dancing,' said another patron, hairdresser Jean-Marie Lefranc. 'They were sort of wiggling in quite an exhibitionist way. At one stage, they were alone on the dance floor, as if there was no one else in the world.'

Elton John was staying at the Ritz for his concerts in Paris with Eric Clapton. When the strains of someone Sarah knew so well singing 'Sacrifice' filled the club, it sounded an especially poignant note for the pair. Later, Bryan was indignant to be asked if his interest in the Duchess were entirely professional. 'My role is as financial adviser to Her Royal Highness,' he replied. 'After a meeting in Paris we had dinner then danced at the Ritz. Then we met one of Her Royal Highness's old school friends. I am now in the final analysis of portfolios for the management of her money. It is ridiculous to suggest we are having a romance – I know the Duke very well.'

The visit to EuroDisney did not pass without incident. Minders employed to protect Sarah and her former employees annoyed other tourists who complained that they were barged out of the way and had their camera lenses blocked to prevent them taking any pictures of the Duchess. With a minder running beside her as she dashed Princess Eugenie along in a buggy, Sarah darted an angry look at a woman who called out: 'Is this another freebie then, Fergie?' But it was. No bill was presented to the party for their day at the magic kingdom although an irate Disney official wailed that the protection squad's ban on photographing their royal charge had spoiled £10,000 worth of free publicity for the fledgling theme park. There was also no charge for the Duchess's accommodation in the park's New York Hotel where the British embassy had booked her accommodation in the name of Clark – tellingly, a new pseudonym.

Sarah was not, however, going to allow any aspect of the Paris jaunt to blot her newly squeaky-clean copy book. She returned to London that night unabashed and prepared for the arrival of her mother, determined that she was going to appear at Billy Connolly's dinner party at Harry's Bar looking as much a winner on the outside as she was feeling on the inside.

.   .   .

Growing more grateful to Johnny by the day, she whisked him back to Paris to celebrate his thirty-seventh birthday on 30 June. She wore an especially eye-catching, knee-length black dress for their dinner date with friends. Then, by advance arrangement, she took him to dance at the Castel nightclub which did not bear a nameplate and where only recognized patrons were admitted. Many of the customers were students, younger than Sarah and Johnny and she seemed pleased when one of their number persuaded her to put down her glass of champagne and dance with him. It was another exhilarating night and, ever the dutiful mother, she was back the next day in time to collect Beatrice from school.

The partying season was far from over, however, and she ended that week by gracing an Independence Day dinner thrown by Billy Connolly in Marvin Davis's honour. The event was staged at Mosimann's in Belgravia and there was a feeling of discomfort in the private room when Sarah arrived on the arm of Eric Buterbaugh, the flamboyant manager of Versace's UK operation, wearing one of the designer's prettiest frocks. Johnny Bryan turned up separately. Other guests included members of the usual Connolly-Stephenson set such as Michael and Shakira Caine, but there were some interesting newcomers: Jeremy Irons and his wife Sinead Cusack, Bob Geldof and Paula Yates, the actress Angharad Rees, Gay Exton and the retired American baseball star, Keith Hernandez. Sarah sat between Davis and Irons, and Bryan chatted with his growing circle of celebrity friends.

There seemed to be a new emphasis on keeping the outgoing royal's presence a secret: the paparazzi had been deliberately lured to San Lorenzo, and even so Sarah was taken in through a back entrance. As Anton Mosimann served his twenty-six diners grilled and marinated summer vegetables followed by his famous risotto al funghi, then baby chicken baked Hoisin style and finally summer pudding in a private room of his most exclusive members-only restaurant, an unusual atmosphere pervaded. According to one of the diners the special problem that evening was that nobody knew how to address her. The waiters still called her 'Ma'am', but word had gone round prior to her arrival that in one of her darker moments she had said, 'The Queen will not go on having me addressed as Your Royal Highness.'

'Just call her Sarah,' suggested one of the actors, so they did. But Sarah, who had arrived in sparkling form, seemed taken aback by the informality. She had greeted Davis – her latest billionaire buddy and the man who introduced her to Sylvester Stallone – with a Hollywood-style hug, but she did not like being treated by the showbusiness fraternity as one of them. She was still, legally, a member of the Royal Family and the way in which she conducted herself for the remainder of the evening left no one in any doubt about that.

To the perceptive, Sarah was clearly having a problem adjusting to the loss of formality that inevitably went with the shedding of her royal duties. It was an occasion, she was to say later, on which she suddenly felt a great need to have Prince Andrew at her side.

Despite her new life, Sarah still dashed off letters to her friends on crested notepaper embossed with the A&S symbol of her marriage. If the Duchess of York was still confused about her sense of identity, she had only to remember her words of a few months 'before all that happened': 'I'm just part of this day and age. I'm just me. I don't profess to be anything else.' No longer a slave to her royal past, the question mark that hung over her titian bob was how long could Sarah continue to live as a hostage to her precarious celebrity?

FOURTEEN

Photo Finish at St Tropez

'We all knew what Johnny Bryan was up to ages ago.'

TAKI

A s Lynn Wyatt had told Steve, the truth will always come out. If ever there were a message he ought to have passed on to his pal Johnny Bryan, that was surely the one. Even after he returned to London with Sarah from a week's holiday at a secluded villa in the heavily wooded hills above St Tropez early in August 1992, Bryan insisted on telling the newspapermen he trusted to print his side of the story: there was nothing going on between him and the Duchess of York. He blamed 'a Buckingham Palace smear campaign' for those who thought otherwise and even went so far as to say that he had dropped Sarah off in the south of France in a private plane that he had hired to take himself to Italy.

The camera told a much different story. Eighty photographs, some of them taken through the pine trees between a hill-top vineyard and the pink-painted villa Le Mas de Pignerolle, showed Sarah cavorting with the man who had always insisted he was merely her financial advisor, a close and trusted friend of her husband's and a man who was acting on her behalf with the blessing of Her Majesty the Queen.

In many of the photographs the Duchess wore only a skimpy bikini bottom; in at least one she was rubbing sun oil into Bryan's balding pate; in others he was kissing her, stretched out on top of her, or positioned at

236

her feet sucking her toes. There were pictures of them with her young daughters in the background, their nanny soaking up the sun while one of the children's two detectives read a book as he sunbathed.

The man named as the photographer was Daniel Angeli, known in his paparazzi trade as 'the hitman's hitman', but a confidential police report into the matter concluded that the pictures were almost certainly the work of two men. Clearly many of them were taken on the same level as the sun loungers beside the villa's scalloped-edged pool and not – as Angeli's associates were to claim – from the wooded slopes above. Furthermore, although Le Mas de Pignerolle (its name means house of the little pines) was surrounded by thickly planted trees, none of them obscured the view of the camera lens.

When Bryan heard about the photographs, he immediately called in lawyers to try to prevent their publication in Great Britain and France. In London, a High Court judge refused his application for an injunction restraining the *Daily Mirror*, who had bought the British rights, from publishing the pictures, and in Paris he failed to convince a French court that, even if the pictures existed, the cameraman had invaded his privacy. 'A great roar went up that shook the newsroom when we heard he had failed to stop us,' said a *Mirror* executive. Within minutes, commercials publicizing the great picture coup were flashed on to television screens across the country. It heralded 'pictures that will not amuse the Palace, pictures that will amaze the world.'

'Bryan thought he had won and he was gobsmacked when Mr Justice Latham ruled against him,' said one of the paper's lawyers. In fact, Johnny Bryan discovered that the compliant press – indeed, the establishment he had manipulated so skilfully – had suddenly stopped playing his tune.

He said, 'There is no doubt that my privacy and that of the Duchess of York has been grossly infringed by Mr Angeli, when he took the photographs, and by the publication of them in the media. Although the law in many jurisdictions protects the privacy of individuals, no such protection is available in England. This case provides a clear illustration of how distressing the consequences of this gap can be for those individuals whom the press persistently follow without regard to any consideration of legitimate public interest.'

No one gave a damn about such worthy sentiments. The truth had finally come out and the public's interest was undeniable. The *Mirror*, headlining its scoop FERGIE'S STOLEN KISSES, sold out as soon as it hit the news-stands. Among those watching Bryan pontificate outside the court on television was his mother Mrs Lyda Redmond in Glen Cove, Long Island. Clearly devastated, she said: 'I've just seen it on the news. I think everybody is very upset about it – I know I am. It's horrible for my family.'

When the photographs were published worldwide just twenty-four hours after Bryan had assured his friends that 'Sarah has been great with her husband and everything has been going well,' they caused a sensation. Here was the proof that their platonic relationship was a lie. 'We all knew what Johnny Bryan was up to ages ago,' said his friend, the columnist Taki. 'All that "financial adviser" stuff had me laughing my socks off.' The intimacy was there for all to see, especially the entire Royal Family assembled at Balmoral with Sarah in their midst.

In the Breakfast Room of the East Wing overlooking the manicured lawn which skirted Karim Cottage and ran down to the fast-flowing waters of the River Dee, the traditional fare had been laid out: porridge, oat cakes, kidneys, bacon and eggs, and kedgeree. But few of the royals had any appetite that morning.

'Never in the Queen's forty-year reign has there been an atmosphere like the one which prevailed from the moment the newspapers containing those photographs were delivered to the castle,' said one who was there. 'I have been at Balmoral before when one or two members of the family were cross or irritable about something – it happens when so many close relatives are confined in one space. But on this occasion every one of them was downright angry. Every one, that is, except Sarah, who acted in the strangest way. You would have thought that she was the person who had been wronged, as if she had every right to go on holiday with another man, kiss and cuddle him and the only people who had behaved wrongly were the photographer and the editors of the newspapers who had published the pictures.

'I think the Princess Royal came close to throttling her; she certainly told her what she thought of her over one dinner, and there was not one voice raised against Anne. Prince Andrew's anger melted into sadness and he buried himself in the special reports compiled for the Queen, which she did not hesitate to let him read. He concluded that his wife had been "set up" and repeatedly asked her if she had been encouraged to drink more than usual or perhaps even been drugged. He was constantly examining the photographs for some clue to prove that Sarah was being manipulated for the enormous financial gain that was to be had by whoever was responsible for the pictures.'

Andrew's theory may well have had something to do with what was surely the most bizarre plan ever to be hatched at Balmoral. The Queen was asked to consider a suggestion that Sarah should be said to have suffered a nervous breakdown. The abnormalities of her earlier life combined with the stresses of joining the Royal Family had resulted in a severe disturbance, it would be said. Prince Andrew was told of the plan, which would make it clear that, due to illness, his wife had not been responsible for her actions for some considerable time. The plan then was to transfer Sarah to a suitable centre for 'treatment' and after a respectable period of time to restore her to the royal fold. Widespread irritation at her behaviour would thus, it was reasoned, have been replaced by public sympathy for high stress, a recognizable twentieth-century malaise that most families in the land could identify with, while many celebrities would have happily agreed, 'She is one of us.'

But the Queen would have none of it. She had never been able to accept political-style manipulation of her subjects, which is one of the reasons she has always insisted on having her press office manned by straightforward public-relations officers rather than those more adept at putting a beneficial curve on a story. In any event she had been bitterly disappointed by Sarah Ferguson twice within a year not two-thirds over and severely doubted that the errant Duchess would ever be sufficiently stable to shoulder royal responsibilities again.

It was doubtful whether Sarah herself was ever told of the desperate last-ditch plan to restore her to grace. Instead the Queen summoned her to her private suite to explain in a curt three-minute interview that it would be better for everyone if she left the castle and returned to Surrey. It remained unsaid that, if she decided to go abroad, her children should not go with her without the express permission of Sir Robert Fellowes, who would conduct future official dealings with her.

.   .   .

Whisked by car to Aberdeen Airport with Beatrice and Eugenie to catch a scheduled British Airways flight to London, Sarah had to face the reality that the Royal Family no longer considered her a member. Even the gates of Romenda Lodge were locked against her when she arrived home. Her embarrassment was prolonged for four interminable minutes while someone found the key. A single detective struggled in vain to block photographers who recorded Sarah's defiant though downcast appearance.

Furthermore, the Duchess now had to stand on her own two feet financially. A woman who had always spent more than she could afford, she had assumed since marrying into the Royal Family that money would never be a problem. Although she was overdrawn when she married, her previously undisclosed wedding present to Prince Andrew was a solid silver helicopter, thirty inches long. Fashioned by England's finest craftsmen in the precious metal, the fabulously expensive keepsake opened up to reveal an Aladdin's Cave of valuable miniatures including a silver teddy bear. It was her love toy to her husband. 'Goodness knows how I will ever pay for it,' she told a celebrity pal at the time.

From the very early days of her marriage, her father was a grateful recipient of her largesse. When she went home to dine at Dummer Down Farm, she took with her food and expensive wine. On other occasions she sent him parcels of goodies and, whenever he travelled with her, she insisted on paying every penny of their expenses. This financial aid was most welcome: Major Ferguson's finances, never rosy at the best of times, were in decline and visitors to the farm reported that 'there was definitely no money about'.

At Sunninghill, Sarah's refrigerator had always been overstocked with such extravagant items as caviare, out-of-season strawberries and every conceivable flavour of exotic ice-cream. When Buckingham Palace sent her warnings about overspending, she would retort that she bought so much because she was not able to predict what Her Majesty's son would most enjoy on his weekends at home.

Cost-conscious Andrew would try to compensate by turning off radiators even in chilly weather to reduce their power bills. Sarah's weekend parties had become so contentious that Palace accountants pondering over the champagne bills sometimes wondered whether the Court of St James had been transferred to Berkshire. The only time a member of her staff could remember Sarah panicking about money was the day a tax demand arrived from the Inland Revenue requiring her to pay £70,000 on her *Budgie* earnings. After another domestic dispute, her husband reluctantly arranged for it to be dealt with.

There was no evidence that Sarah's free-spending ever did much to improve Prince Andrew's often dour spirits, whether they were entertaining at home or enjoying the best of everything in the company of one or other her *nouveaux riches* friends. Once, when dining at the Hertfordshire home of Elton John's manager, John Reid, the host's mother Betty, on finding herself seated next to the Prince, asked him, 'Are you not drinking?' He said he was not, so she went on to ask him if he minded if she smoked. 'No, but it's not considered social to smoke these days,' he opined. Glaswegian Betty retorted: 'Well, it's not very social not to have a drink, either.'

Andrew's company often had that effect on people, and his attitude had frequently been the subject of heated rows between him and Sarah. Nevertheless he had always been supportive of her – and so had his mother's infinitely creditworthy name. Now that the bills were coming in again Sarah did not like to ask the Queen if Her Majesty's earlier promise guaranteeing her overdraft still held good. After St Tropez, she probably knew the answer.

The French excursion had added more than £20,000 to her indebtedness. It had cost £8000 for the round trip in a privately chartered Kingair 200 Turbo-prop eight-seat airliner, which had secretly taken her, the princesses, a nanny and Scotland Yard bodyguard John Hodgkinson from Blackbushe airfield to La Mole airstrip near St Tropez. Two Mercedes limousines were hired at a cost of £3000 for the week, the same amount as businessman Charles Smallbone charged for his five-bedroom villa at the height of the summer season.

But the cost in personal terms was incalculable. Johnny Bryan had managed to achieve something that Steve Wyatt had tried hard to avoid: being caught out by the press. An American oilman, who knew Wyatt well both in Texas and in London, said: 'He was no rocket scientist, but he had enough brains never to let it come to this. When Steve started to tell me about his friendship with the Duchess of York, and then I saw the stuff in the newspapers, I thought they were making a mountain out of a molehill. It was only during a later conversation he said some things that left me in no doubt: their relationship was closer than was realized. But he did the decent thing in the end and backed out when it began to cause trouble for Sarah and the Royal Family. He could never have foreseen what was to come from introducing her to Johnny. Somehow I don't think he can be very happy about it.'

. . .

Neither Wyatt nor Bryan had the benefit of knowing what Princess Diana had long thought of her one-time friend, Sarah Ferguson. When she flew home from Balmoral, a week after Sarah's exit-in-disgrace, Princess Diana privately expressed the belief to one of the authors' sources that 'perhaps Andrew was only a stepping stone for Sarah.' The Windsor boys, she inferred, were never exciting enough for Sarah in themselves, they just had exciting status. But by then Diana was herself at the centre of a crisis which illustrated that her words applied just as much to herself as to her sister-in-law.

Even as Sarah was being vilified, the tabloids were revealing the full impact of another royal sensation: the tape recording of an intimate telephone conversation reportedly between Diana and James Gilbey. Coupled with the St Tropez pictures, the Princess's indiscretions on the so-called Squidgy Tape magnified the Queen's distress. She had wept over the near nakedness of one daughter-in-law frolicking with a man whom Prince Andrew had assured her could be trusted, and now Dianagate was to remove any vestige of doubt that the Waleses were as estranged as the Yorks and had been for years. It created more difficulties for Sir William Heseltine, the Queen's former Private Secretary, who had secretly been consulted to prepare a blueprint for restoring public confidence in the monarchy.

'Sir William not only had to plug the hole in the dyke with his finger, he had to work out a way to reclaim the entire realm,' said a royal insider. 'It was his suggestion to Her Majesty that Charles and Andrew should take centre stage regardless of what happened to their marriages. The family should close ranks and present a united front no matter what happened to the Princess of Wales and the Duchess of York. The Windsors would only survive as Britain's ruling family if they rose above the indecorous behaviour of those they married and re-established themselves on the royal pedestal.'

An ex-girlfriend of Johnny Bryan's had put it another way: 'I think Fergie and Di are brilliant. They're just taking the world for all it's got. They read *Cosmopolitan* and firmly believe that you only live once so make the most of it. These girls are getting pretty smart.'

Back at Romenda Lodge, workmen were hurriedly raising the walls from six to eight feet. 'It's not to keep the press out,' quipped one, 'it's to keep the Duchess in.' Following her return in shame from Balmoral, Sarah, who had been less and less available to tried and trusted friends since her trip with Bryan to the Far East, suddenly found that line 5 – her private contact number – now hardly rang. Those who had tried to contact her about her plan to go away with Johnny Bryan but had found that she was incommunicado, no longer called. One who considered herself enough of a friend to Sarah to be direct was among her few visitors in those awful days of near isolation. She told the Duchess: 'The trouble with your marriage is that it was based on your husband being *what* he was, rather than *who* he was'.

If Andrew's title were, primarily, a highly prized trophy in the Sloane Ranger scale of values, then it had been a means to another end.

But Sarah was never as conniving nor as materialistic as many in the Chelsea sisterhood. She had married Andrew for love and found out that this, in itself, was not enough. Experience had shown her that she was always likely to go on searching for happiness in all the wrong places until she made some painful changes in herself.

'Before she married Prince Andrew, Sarah was just a regular old girl,' said Gene Nocon. 'The Princess of Wales is different – she comes from that stock. This whole thing of Sarah running around with Sylvester Stallone and other actors and actresses is just too much. She is like a winner of the football pools, and she didn't grow up with that.'

Right from the start, Sarah's background had told against her time and again. 'They both came from broken homes in which the mother rejected the father,' said a royal source. 'Whereas Diana cold-shouldered her new stepmother Raine, Sarah welcomed Sue into her father's life because she hoped he would settle down again.'

In truth, the father on whom Sarah lavished such unconditional love could do little to help her but much to hinder her. His sexual behaviour would have guaranteed him instant expulsion from the royal circle if Prince Charles had not stood by him. The Prince had been counselled in this matter by his father who was ever grateful to Ronald for keeping a secret from his own lively past. Philip had long ago become attached to someone in the polo set whom Ronald himself held dear. It was a friendship which could have proved damaging if it had ever become public knowledge.

The Major's pride, however, had been known to reach grandiose proportions: one gentleman whose firm had supplied goods to the Guards Polo Club said that he was indignant to hear Ronald address him by his surname. 'So the next time it happened, I called him Ferguson. He turned round and snapped, "Most people address me as Major." "In that case," I said, "you will have to call me Commander."'

The honorary rank Ronald chose to enforce in civilian life was, in itself, a prop to his damaged ego. When his daughter became a duchess, he knew that the social gulf between himself and the Royal Family only accentuated the differences, and he sallied forth in a predictably boorish fashion. Then he would ask: 'I'm not such a bad chap, am I?'

. . .

To the outside world, Sarah Margaret Ferguson had seemed like a Duchess who, if not exactly born to her role, had no shortage of self-confidence or lack of identity. But her unreasonable fear of Liz Nocon as a woman friend who shared many of her husband's secrets bore testament to the fact that, on the inside, she was still the girl from Dummer riding through life in a glass coach terrified of what the world might see: an Empress without any clothes.

Sarah's remedy for the unhappiness she had experienced in childhood had been to seek escape in the solace of the Swiss mountains once she was old enough to travel on her own. But that freedom had brought her into close contact with others of her generation who turned to drugs to fix their emotional pain or to get their sexual kicks. Cocaine usage in Verbier was particularly prevalent when she was there. 'This very damaging drug was used as a currency,' said one of the Verbier Set, 'to get some young girls into bed.' Later, Sarah was to learn that even Buckingham Palace was not immune from the curse of the age when it was revealed that a dealer even operated from the Royal Mews.

Her unhappiness was not assuaged by her marriage. Although Andrew said he liked her well-rounded figure, Sarah's fluctuating weight often seemed a reason for his anger towards her. She grazed between meals on snacks; a particular favourite were Mars Bars. On one occasion, according to a close friend, her craving for sugar and chocolate was so great that she sent her detective out to buy her a Mars Bar while she was trying on expensive clothes in a salon. Sarah had to learn the hard way that there was no substitute for healthy living. 'I've tried everything, believe me,' she declared, 'all the fad diets, the pills, the lot. But all that is very bad for you. Now I just work out every day, and then I just have fruit for breakfast.'

No amount of working out would improve relations between the Yorks. Their separation had become essential after angry rows in the relative privacy of Buckingham Palace and Sunninghill Park House seemed likely to spill over into the public domain. 'The marriage was going badly and the arguments bordered on domestic violence,' said the royal source. The Queen foresaw that danger when she reluctantly agreed at the Sandringham Summit to the couple living separate lives – if that were the only course that would avoid a scandal of even greater magnitude. Sarah's behaviour could be quite wild.

'Sarah is an exhibitionist,' said one in whom Johnny Bryan confided. 'I swear to God he told me that. I think he was trying to shock me, trying to make me feel less serious. He was giving me shock tactics to make me feel, "Well, why not if everybody else is doing it?"

While the courtiers believed that, once outside the marriage, Sarah should still be made to conform, the Queen knew something which they did not, and it was something so alarming that she believed Sarah had to be nurtured rather than alienated.

Even after the Riviera incident, Her Majesty remained a realist, anxious not to push Sarah beyond the point of no return. For her part, Sarah knew that she had finally lost the Queen's friendship and that, in future, the smiles she received from her mother-in-law would be of the variety that the Monarch bestowed upon her subjects as part of her job. As one of the few who had witnessed the Queen's anger, Sarah could be forgiven for not wishing to repeat the experience. Her silence was, she knew, high on the Queen's hidden agenda to protect her son and the future of the monarchy. Sarah herself admitted that she had failed to bridge the gulf between herself and royal mores. 'You have to understand what I am dealing with here,' she once told a friend. 'I'm married to a man who has never been inside a supermarket.'

The more Sarah lost her direction and fell foul of the royal circle, the more she moved towards outsiders who could ease her path through life. 'He's terrific,' she told toastmaster Ivor Spencer when he enquired after her well-being. 'His Royal Highness?' Spencer asked. 'No, silly. Terry – the butler you sent me,' the Duchess replied.

Her friendships inside the Showbiz Set, particularly with Billy Connolly and Pamela Stephenson, became even more important to her. 'Ever since she split up with Paddy McNally she missed the buzz of being with exciting people,' said one who knew the Duchess as well as Connolly and Stephenson. 'She discovered that the royals are really a dull lot. Then she rediscovered Billy and Pamela, and she loves being with them. Billy talks about a world she knew nothing of, growing up, as she did, in rather limited surroundings. He talks about the tenements in the Partick area of Glasgow where he was raised. She never knew such places existed, and she dotes on everything he tells her.'

Sarah had also placed great store in Johnny Bryan's ability to make her rich and successful in her own right by the exploitation of her children's hero, Budgie. But even the gung-ho Mr Bryan would have been first to admit that the public had still to decide whether it wanted Budgie. For every Beatrix Potter, there were 10,000 wannabes. The St Tropez pictures revealing the intimate nature of her lifestyle with Bryan did nothing to enhance her appeal to book-buying mothers of young children.

As the British establishment abruptly turned its back on Sarah, American society welcomed her to its bosom with all the warmth it reserved for someone so chronically misunderstood in her own land. If her destiny were to live in the United States, then it could not be without special problems. A devoted though arguably misguided mother, she was made to realize in the darkest days of 1992 that she could not take Beatrice and Eugenie abroad with her on a permanent basis. 'The princesses', she was told firmly during a stormy meeting at Balmoral, 'belong to England.'

She was left in no doubt about the forces that could be ranged against her. She learned that her own telephones and those of her friends could be tapped, and that her correspondence was not safe from scrutiny. Well aware of both problems, Princess Diana had taken the precaution of asking friends to write to her privately at San Lorenzo, where the owner's wife Mara handed the mail to her personally. Even more importantly, Sarah knew that those sent to guard her daughters could be programmed to turn their sights inward so that they were, in effect, following her at the same time as they were protecting her.

If she entrusted her daughters to an English boarding school under the Royal Family's watchful eye and established the home in Palm Beach that she enquired about shortly before the separation, would her high-powered friends still be there for her – or would she cease to be, in her own words, 'flavour of the month'? Sarah once expressed the view that 'Americans love the Royal Family for what it is.' Would that love still be available to an ex-member who, unlike the Duchess of Windsor before her, was not even one of their own?

For their part, the Americans were taking Sarah's involvement with a US citizen very seriously indeed. Johnny's father Tony was secretly called to a meeting in Washington soon after the St Tropez pictures appeared in print. He had been staying with members of his family at his holiday home on Watch Hill, Rhode Island, to avoid fall-out over the scandal that had exploded around his son. 'The State Department contacted Tony and invited him to come down to Washington for a meeting – and he went,' said a family friend. 'They did not talk about the weather in the South of France.'

President Bush, fighting for his political life in election year, needed to be kept informed about such a sensitive diplomatic matter that could deeply affect relations between the Royal Family and his embattled Administration. Johnny, it was suggested, had been told to 'back off' to prevent an even bigger furore after his former stepmother, Pamela Zauderer Bryan, said that he might marry the Duchess after her divorce. 'I can't believe she said that,' he confided to a friend. 'It's not true.' He played several energetic games of squash at the Bath &

Racquets Club on Monday, 7 September, to work off his pent-up feelings. Emerging at 6.35 p.m., the red tie around his neck still undone, he sprinted up the street in the direction of Claridge's. A chill autumn wind blew his tie off, but he caught it expertly without breaking stride. The only light relief was an enterprising trader, hawking chocolate toes for people to nibble, St Tropez style. 'I love it,' Johnny Bryan told a chum.

Eyebrows rampant, Major Ron met his daughter for a crisis meeting at lunch-time that same day to discuss the latest trauma in her shattered life. 'They talked for well over two hours – Major Ron was absent from his job at the polo club for nearly four hours,' said a polo source. 'The outcome was that Fergie agreed to seek professional help with her problems.'

Explained a friend of the Duchess: 'Sarah has always had a mercurial personality, but what has been going on since the pictures were published has pushed her very close to the edge. She might appear to have shrugged it off, but she was really floored. She was also devastated by the way the Queen treated her on her last day at Balmoral, and she just cried and cried when she returned to Romenda Lodge. She went to Buckingham Palace one day, where she still has an office, but everyone there froze her out. They wouldn't have anything to do with her, and she returned home in a pretty bad state. Finally she agreed to see a doctor, and he recommended she join a self-help group to sort things out.'

Golden-red hair tied hastily in a pony-tail, the Duchess of York dashed up the steps of the Group-Analytic Practice at Paddington in West London to become plain Sarah in therapy sessions with other patients. 'I think the most important thing is always to go forward,' Susie Barrantes told *Hello!*.

In the grim offices at Buckingham Palace, they hoped to do just that – though the courtiers' overriding fear was that Sarah might be induced one day to tell *their* story, 'without, of course, ruining the mystique of royalty,' to borrow a phrase she once laughingly uttered. As the carousel started up again playing a tantalizingly different tune, the only certainty was that the Duchess who defied the Royal House of Windsor would be famous for a lot longer than Andy Warhol's pre-ordained fifteen minutes. One Prince and two Dudes, to name just three, had made sure of that.